The BNC Handbook

EDINBURGH TEXTBOOKS IN EMPIRICAL LINGUISTICS

CORPUS LINGUISTICS
by Tony McEnery and Andrew Wilson

LANGUAGE AND COMPUTERS
A PRACTICAL INTRODUCTION TO THE COMPUTER ANALYSIS OF LANGUAGE
by Geoff Barnbrook

STATISTICS FOR CORPUS LINGUISTICS
by Michael P. Oakes

COMPUTER CORPUS LEXICOGRAPHY
by Vincent B.Y. Ooi

If you would like information on forthcoming titles in this series, please contact
Edinburgh University Press, 22 George Square, Edinburgh EH8 9LF

EDINBURGH TEXTBOOKS IN EMPIRICAL LINGUISTICS

Series Editors: Tony McEnery and Andrew Wilson

The BNC Handbook

Exploring the British National Corpus with SARA

Guy Aston and Lou Burnard

EDINBURGH UNIVERSITY PRESS

EDINBURGH UNIVERSITY PRESS

© Guy Aston and Lou Burnard, 1998

Edinburgh University Press
22 George Street, Edinburgh EH8 9LF

Printed and bound in Great Britain by
the University Press, Cambridge

A CIP record for this book is available from the British Library

ISBN 0 7486 1054 5 (cased)
ISBN 0 7486 1055 3 (paperback)

Contents

Preface

The *British National Corpus* is a collection of over 4000 samples of modern British English, both spoken and written, stored in electronic form and selected so as to reflect the widest possible variety of users and uses of the language. Totalling over 100 million words, the corpus is currently being used by lexicographers to create dictionaries, by computer scientists to make machines 'understand' and produce natural language, by linguists to describe the English language, and by language teachers and students to teach and learn it — to name but a few of its applications.

Institutions all over Europe have purchased the BNC and installed it on computers for use in their research. However it is not necessary to possess a copy of the corpus in order to make use of it: it can also be consulted via the Internet, using either the World Wide Web or the SARA software system, which was developed specially for this purpose.

The *BNC Handbook* provides a comprehensive guide to the SARA software distributed with the corpus and used on the network service. It illustrates some of the ways in which it is possible to find out about contemporary English usage from the BNC, and aims to encourage use of the corpus by a wide and varied public. We have tried as far as possible to avoid jargon and unnecessary technicalities; the book assumes nothing more than an interest in language and linguistic problems on the part of its readers.

The handbook has three major parts. It begins with an introduction to the topic of *corpus linguistics*, intended to bring the substantial amount of corpus-based work already done in a variety of research areas to the non-specialist reader's attention. It also provides an outline description of the BNC itself. The bulk of the book however is concerned with the use of the SARA search program. This part consists of a series of detailed task descriptions which (it is hoped) will serve to teach the reader how to use SARA effectively, and at the same time stimulate his or her interest in using the BNC. There are ten tasks, each of which introduces a new group of features of the software and of the corpus, of roughly increasing complexity. At the end of each task there are suggestions for further related work. The last part of the handbook gives a summary overview of the SARA program's commands and capabilities, intended for reference purposes, details of the main coding schemes used in the corpus, and a select bibliography.

The BNC was created by a consortium led by Oxford University Press, together with major dictionary publishers Longman and Chambers, and research centres at the Universities of Lancaster and Oxford, and at the British Library. Its creation was jointly funded by the Department of Trade and Industry and the Science and Research Council (now EPSRC), under the Joint Framework for Information Technology programme, with substantial investment from the commercial partners in the consortium. Reference information on the BNC and its creation is available in the *BNC Users' Reference Guide* (Burnard 1995), which is distributed with the corpus, and also from the BNC project's web site at http://info.ox.ac.uk/bnc.

This handbook was prepared with the assistance of a major research grant from the British Academy, whose support is gratefully acknowledged. Thanks are also due to Tony Dodd, author of the SARA search software, to Phil Champ, for assistance with the SARA help file, to Jean-Daniel Fekète and Sebastian Rahtz for help in formatting, and to our respective host institutions at the Universities of Oxford and Bologna. Our greatest debt however is to Lilette, for putting up with us during the writing of it.

I: Corpus linguistics and the BNC

Introduction

This part of the *BNC Handbook* attempts to place the British National Corpus (BNC) within the tradition of corpus linguistics by providing a brief overview of the theoretical bases from which that tradition springs, and of its major achievements. We begin by defining the term *corpus* pragmatically, as it is used in linguistics, proceeding to review some uses, both actual and potential, for language corpora in various fields. Our discussion focuses chiefly on the areas of language description (with particular reference to linguistic context and collocation, and to contrastive and comparative studies), of Natural Language Processing, and of foreign language teaching and learning.

We then present an overview of some of the main theoretical and methodological issues in the field, in particular those concerned with the creation, design, encoding, and annotation of large corpora, before assessing the practice of the British National Corpus itself with respect to these issues. We also describe some particular characteristics of the BNC which may mislead the unwary, and finally suggest some possible future directions for corpora of this kind.

corpus ... *pl.* **corpora** ... **1.** The body of a man or animal. (Cf. **corpse**.) *Formerly frequent; now only humorous or grotesque.* 1854 Villikins & his Dinah (in *Mus. Bouquet*, No. 452), He kissed her cold corpus a thousand times o'er. **2.** *Phys.* A structure of a special character or function in the animal body, as corpus callosum, the transverse commissure connecting the cerebral hemispheres; so also corpora quadrigemina, striata, etc. of the brain, corpus spongiosum and corpora cavernosa of the penis, etc.; corpus luteum L. luteus, –um yellow (pl. corpora lutea), a yellowish body developed in the ovary from the ruptured Graafian follicle after discharge of the ovum; it secretes progesterone and other hormones and after a few days degenerates unless fertilization has occurred, when it remains throughout pregnancy. 1869 Huxley *Phys.* xi. 298 The floor of the lateral ventricle is formed by a mass of nervous matter, called the corpus striatum. 1959 *New Biol.* XXX. 79 As in mammals, glandular bodies known as corpora lutea are produced in the ovaries of viviparous (and also of some oviparous) reptiles, in places from which the eggs have been shed at ovulation. **3.** A body or complete collection of writings or the like; the whole body of literature on any subject. 1727-51 Chambers *Cycl.* s.v., Corpus is also used in matters of learning, for several works of the same nature, collected, and bound together.. We have also a corpus of the Greek poets.. The corpus of the civil law is composed of the digest, code, and institutes. 1865 Mozley *Mirac.* i. 16 Bound up inseparably with the whole corpus of Christian tradition. **4.** The body of written or spoken material upon which a linguistic analysis is based. 1956 W. S. Allen in *Trans. Philol. Soc.* 128 The analysis here presented is based on the speech of a single informant.. and in particular upon a corpus of material, of which a large proportion was narrative, derived from approximately 100 hours of listening. 1964 E. Palmer tr. Martinet's *Elem. General Linguistics* ii. 40 The theoretical objection one may make against the 'corpus' method is that two investigators operating on the same language but starting from different 'corpuses', may arrive at different descriptions of the same language. 1983 G. Leech et al. in *Trans. Philol. Soc.* 25 We hope that this will be judged.. as an attempt to explore the possibilities and problems of corpus-based research by reference to first-hand experience, instead of by a general survey. **5.** The body or material substance of anything; principal, as opposed to interest or income. 1884 *Law Rep.* 25 Chanc. Div. 711 If these costs were properly incurred they ought to be paid out of corpus and not out of income. **phr. corpus delicti** (see quot. 1832); also, in lay use, the concrete evidence of a crime, esp. the body of a murdered person. **corpus juris:** a body of law; esp. the body of Roman or civil law (corpus juris civilis). 1891 *Fortn. Rev.* Sept. 338 The translation.. of the Corpus Juris into French. 1922 Joyce *Ulysses* 451 (He extends his portfolio.) We have here damning evidence, the corpus delicti, my lord, a specimen of my maturer work disfigured by the hallmark of the beast. 1964 *Sunday Mail Mag.* (Brisbane) 13 Sept. 3/3 An enthusiastic trooper, one of a party investigating river, dam and hollow log in search of the corpus delicti, found some important evidence in a fallen tree. **corpus vile** Pl. corpora vilia *Orig.* in phr. (see quot. 1822) meaning 'let the experiment be done on a cheap (or worthless) body'. A living or dead body that is of so little value that it can be used for experiment without regard for the outcome; *transf.*, experimental material of any kind, or something which has no value except as the object of experimentation. 1822 De Quincey *Confess. App.* 189 Fiat experimentum in corpore vili is a just rule where there is any reasonable presumption of benefit to arise on a large scale.] 1865 C. M. Yonge *Clever Woman* I. iii. 80 The only difficulty was to find poor people enough who would submit to serve as the corpus vile for their charitable treatment. 1953 *Essays in Criticism* III. i. 4, I am not proposing to include among these initial corpora vilia passages from either Mr Eliot's criticism or Dr Leavis's.

Definitions of corpus from OED 2

1 Corpus linguistics

1.1 What is a corpus?

We shall discuss what a corpus is by looking at how the word is used, in particular by linguists. What kind of an object is a corpus, and what is it likely to be useful for?

We learn the sense of a newly-encountered word in different ways. Young children experimentally combine or mutate words to see which uses meet with approval; older ones do the same in the process of defining peer groups based on a shared exotic vocabulary. In both cases, meaning is exemplified or confirmed by repeated, socially sanctioned, usage. One of the objectives of traditional linguistics was to overcome this requirement of exposure to "language in use" — an impractical option for those wishing to learn a new language in a short time, or to understand a language no longer spoken anywhere — by defining powerful general principles which would enable one to derive the sense of any newly-encountered word simply by applying etymological or morphological rules. Knowles (1996), arguing that linguistic theory is above all a matter of organizing linguistic knowledge in this way, points for example to the success with which such models have been used in training generations of schoolchildren to understand Latin or Greek unseens.

While only experience can tell us what a word "is understood to mean", such analytic methods tell us what a word "ought to mean". A modern dictionary combines the strengths of both methods, by organizing evidence of usage into an analytic framework of senses.

What, then, does the word 'corpus' actually mean? We might do worse than consider the five distinct senses listed in the second edition of the *Oxford English Dictionary* as a starting point (see figure on preceding page). Of these, two particularly refer to language. The first is that of "A body or collection of writings or the like; the whole body of literature on any subject". Thus we may speak of the 'Shakespearean corpus', meaning the entire collection of texts by Shakespeare. The second is that of "the body of written or spoken material upon which a linguistic analysis is based". This is the sense of the word from which the phrase 'corpus linguistics' derives, and in which we use it throughout this book. The two senses can, of course, overlap — as when, for example, the entire collection of a particular author's work is subjected to linguistic analysis. But a key distinction remains. In the words of John Sinclair, the linguist's corpus is "a collection of pieces of language, selected and ordered according to explicit linguistic criteria in order to be used as a sample of the language" (Sinclair 1996). It is an object designed for the purpose of linguistic analysis, rather than an object defined by accidents of authorship or history.

As such, corpora can be contrasted with *archives* or *collections* whose components are unlikely to have been assembled with such goals in mind (see further
Atkins *et al* 1992). Given this emphasis on intended function, the composition
of a corpus will depend on the scope of the investigation. It may be chosen
to characterize a particular historical state or a particular variety of a particular
language, or it may be selected to enable comparison of a number of historical
states, varieties or languages. Varieties may be selected on geographical (for
example, British, American, or Indian English), sociological (for example, by
gender, social class, or age group), or generic bases (for example written vs.
spoken; legal or medical; technical or popular; private or public correspondence). Generally the texts to be included in a corpus are defined according
to criteria which are *external* to the texts themselves, relating to the situation of
their production or reception rather than any intrinsic property they may have.
Discovery of such intrinsic properties (if any) may, indeed, be the purpose of the
exercise.

Corpora stored and processed by computer, once the exception, are now
the norm. It is worth noting however that there is very little in the practice
of corpus linguistics which could not equally well be done in principle by non-
automatic means. However, in general, corpora are understood to be computer-
processable corpora.

The British National Corpus (BNC) consists of a sample collection which
aims to represent the universe of contemporary British English. Insofar as it
attempts to capture the full range of varieties of language use, it is a *balanced*
corpus rather than a *register-specific* or *dialect-specific* one; it is also a *mixed* corpus,
containing both written texts and spoken ones — transcriptions of naturally-
occurring speech.

1.2   What can you get out of a corpus?

A corpus can enable grammarians, lexicographers, and other interested parties
to provide better descriptions of a language by embodying a view of it which
is beyond any one individual's experience. The authoritative *Comprehensive
Grammar of the English Language* (Quirk *et al* 1985) was derived in part from
evidence provided by one of the first modern English corpora, the Survey
of English Usage. Svartvik and Quirk (1980: 9) observe that: "Since native
speakers include lawyers, journalists, gynaecologists, school teachers, engineers,
and a host of other specialists, it follows: (a) that no individual can be expected to
have an adequate command of the whole 'repertoire': who, for example, could
equally well draft a legal statute and broadcast a commentary on a football game?
(b) that no grammarian can describe adequately the grammatical and stylistic

properties of the whole repertoire from his own unsupplemented resources: 'introspection' as the sole guiding star is clearly ruled out."

A corpus which is designed to sample the entire 'repertoire' offers a tool for the description of properties with which even the grammarian may not be personally familiar. Corpus-based descriptions have produced a few surprises, sometimes contradicting the received wisdom. Sampson (1996) describes how he became a corpus linguist as a result of his experience with theories of recursive 'central embedding' in sentences such as 'the mouse the cat the dog chased caught squeaked', where component clauses nest within each other like Russian dolls. Most discussions of this phenomenon had used linguistic intuition to analyze entirely imaginary sentences, claiming that such constructions were in some sense 'unnatural', though syntactically feasible. However, when Sampson turned to look at corpus data, he found that such centrally embedded structures were actually far from rare, and used in ways which appeared entirely 'natural'. While it does not eliminate linguistic intuition in classifying and evaluating instances, the use of corpora can remove much of the need to invent imaginary data, and can provide relatively objective evidence of frequency.

The utility of a corpus to the lexicographer is even more striking: careful study of a very large quantity and wide range of texts is required to capture and exemplify anything like all the half-million or more words used in contemporary British English. It is no coincidence that dictionary publishers have played major roles in setting up the two largest current corpora of British English: the Bank of English (HarperCollins) and the BNC (Oxford University Press, Longman, Chambers); or that, in the increasingly competitive market for English language learners' dictionaries, four new editions published in 1995 (the *Collins Cobuild Dictionary*, the *Cambridge Dictionary of International English*, the *Longman Dictionary of Contemporary English*, the *Oxford Advanced Learner's Dictionary*) should all have made the fact of their being 'corpus-based' a selling point.

Linguists have always made use of collections of textual data to produce grammars and dictionaries, but these have traditionally been analyzed in a relatively ad hoc manner, on the basis of individual salience, with a consequent tendency to privilege rare and striking phenomena at the expense of mundane or very high frequency items. Corpora, in particular computer-processable corpora, have instead allowed linguists to adopt a principle of 'total accountability', retrieving all the occurrences of a particular word or structure in the corpus for inspection, or (where this would be infeasible) randomly selected samples. This generally involves the use of specialized software to search for occurrences (or co-occurrences) of specified strings or patterns within the corpus. Other software may be used to calculate frequencies, or statistics derived from them, for example to produce word lists ordered by frequency of occurrence or to identify co-occurrences which are significantly more (or less) frequent than chance.

Concordances are listings of the occurrences of a particular feature or combination of features in a corpus. Each occurrence found, or *hit*, is displayed with a certain amount of *context* — the text immediately preceding and following it. The most commonly used concordance type (known as *KWIC* for 'Key Word In Context') shows one hit per line of the screen or printout, with the principal search feature, or *focus*, highlighted in the centre. Concordances also generally give a reference for each hit, showing which source text in the corpus it is taken from and the line or sentence number. It is then up to the user to inspect and interpret the output. The amount of text visible in a KWIC display is generally enough to make some sense of the hit, though for some purposes, such as the interpretation of pronominal reference, a larger context may have to be specified. Most concordancing software allows hits to be formatted, sorted, edited, saved and printed in a variety of manners.

Frequency counts are implicit in concordancing, since finding all the occurrences of a particular feature in the corpus makes counting the hits a trivial task. Software will generally allow numbers to be calculated without actually displaying the relevant concordance — an important feature where thousands or even millions of occurrences are involved. Frequency counts can be elaborated statistically, in many cases automatically by the concordancing software, but should be interpreted with care (see further 2.2.4 on page 40).

Concordances and frequency counts can provide a wide variety of linguistic information. We list some of the kinds of questions which may be asked, relating to lexis, morphosyntax, and semantics or pragmatics.

A corpus can be analyzed to provide the following kinds of lexical information:

- How often does a particular word-form, or group of forms (such as the various forms of the verb 'start': 'start', 'starts', 'starting', 'started') appear in the corpus? Is 'start' more or less common than 'begin'? The relative frequency of any word-form can be expressed as a *z-score*, that is, as the number of standard deviations from the mean frequency of word-forms in the corpus. The number of occurrences of a word-form in the entire BNC ranges from over 6 million for the most frequent word, 'the', to 1 for 'aaarrrrrrrrggggggggghhhhhh' or 'about-to-be-murdered'. The mean frequency is approximately 150, but the standard deviation of the mean is very high (over 11,000), indicating that there are very many words with frequencies far removed from the mean.

- With what meanings is a particular word-form, or group of forms, used? Is 'back' more frequently used with reference to a part of the body or a direction? Do we 'start' and 'begin' the same sorts of things?

- How often does a particular word-form, or group of forms, appear near to other particular word forms, which *collocate* with it within a given distance? Does 'immemorial' always have 'time' as a collocate? Is it more common for 'prices' to 'rise' or to 'increase'? Do different senses of the same word have different collocates?

- How often does a particular word-form, or group of forms, appear in particular grammatical structures, which *colligate* with it? Is it more common to 'start to do something', or to 'start doing it'? Do different senses of the same word have different colligates?

- How often does a particular word-form, or group of forms, appear in a certain semantic environment, showing a tendency to have positive or negative connotations? Does the intensifier 'totally' always modify verbs and adjectives with a negative meaning, such as 'fail' and 'ridiculous'?

- How often does a particular word-form, or group of forms, appear in a particular type of text, or in a particular type of speaker or author's language? Is 'little' or 'small' more common in conversation? Do women say 'sort of' more than men? Does the word 'wicked' always have positive connotations for the young? Is the word 'predecease' found outside legal texts and obituaries? Do lower-class speakers use more (or different) expletives?

- Whereabouts in texts does a particular word form, or group of forms, tend to occur? Does its meaning vary according to its position? How often does it occur within notes or headings, following a pause, near the end of a text, or at the beginning of a sentence, paragraph or utterance? And is it in fact true that 'and' never begins a sentence?

A corpus can also be analyzed to provide the following kinds of morphosyntactic information:

- How frequent is a particular morphological form or grammatical structure? How much more common are clauses with active than with passive main verbs? What proportion of passive forms have the agent specified in a following 'by' phrase?

- With what meanings is a particular structure used? Is there a difference between 'I hope that' and 'I hope to'?

- How often does a particular structure occur with particular collocates or colligates? Is 'if I was you' or 'if I were you' more common?

- How often does a particular structure appear in a particular type of text, or in a particular type of speaker or author's language? Are passives more common in scientific texts? Is the subjunctive used less by younger speakers?
- Whereabouts in texts does a particular structure tend to occur? Do writers and speakers tend to switch from the past tense to the 'historic present' at particular points in narratives?

And, finally, a corpus can be analyzed to provide semantic or pragmatic information. Rather than examining the meanings and uses of particular forms, we can use it to identify the forms associated with particular meanings and uses:

- What tools are most frequently referred to in texts talking about gardening?
- What fields of metaphor are employed in economic discourse?
- Do the upper-middle classes talk differently about universities from the working classes?
- How do speakers close conversations, or open lectures? How do chairpersons switch from one point to another in meetings?
- Are pauses in conversation more common between utterances than within them?
- What happens when conversationalists stop laughing?

Not all of these types of information are equally easy to obtain. In using concordancing software, specific strings of characters have to be searched for. In order to disambiguate homographs or to identify particular uses of words or structures, it may be necessary to inspect the lines in the output, classifying them individually. Thus while it is relatively easy to calculate the frequency of a word-form and of its collocates, it may be more difficult to calculate its frequency of use as a particular part of speech, with a particular sense, or in a particular position or particular kind of text.

To help in such tasks, computer corpora are increasingly *marked up* with a detailed encoding which encompasses both external characteristics of each text and its production, and internal characteristics such as its formal structure. Such information will typically include details of what kind of text it is and where it comes from, details relating to the structure of the text and the status of particular components — division into chapters, paragraphs, spoken utterances, headings, notes, references, editorial comments etc., as well as any linguistic annotation, indicating for instance the part-of-speech value or the root form of each word. Such encoding permits the user to search for strings or patterns in particular kinds, parts or positions of texts, or with particular types of linguistic annotation.

It can be equally difficult to find instances of particular syntactic, semantic or pragmatic categories unless these happen to have clear lexical correlates, or the corpus markup clearly distinguishes them. For instance, the markup of the BNC might be used to find occurrences of highlighting (typically through italics or underlining in the original), to investigate headings and captions, to generate a list of the publishers responsible for the texts in the corpus, or to identify those texts published by specific publishers.

While the examples just cited have all concerned analyses within a particular corpus, it is evident that all these areas can also be examined contrastively, comparing data from corpora of different languages, historical periods, dialects or geographical varieties, modes (spoken or written), or registers. By comparing one of the standard corpora collected twenty years ago with an analogous corpus of today, it is possible to investigate recent changes in English. By comparing corpora collected in different parts of the world, it is possible to investigate differences between, for instance, British and Australian English. By comparing a corpus of translated texts with one of texts originally created in the target language, it is possible to identify linguistic properties peculiar to translation. By comparing a small homogeneous corpus of some particular kind of material with a large balanced corpus (such as the BNC), it is possible to identify the distinctive linguistic characteristics of the former.

1.3   How have corpora been used?

This section describes a few major corpora which have previously been created and discusses some of the work done with them, to illustrate current concerns in the field.

1.3.1   What kinds of corpora exist?

We begin by listing some of the main corpora developed for English in the past, grouped according to the main areas of language use they sample. For a fuller annotated list, see Edwards (1993) or Wichmann et al (in press).

geographical varieties The earliest corpus in electronic form, compiled at Brown University in 1964, contained 1 million words of written American English published in 1961 (Kucera and Francis 1967). The Brown corpus has since been widely imitated, with similarly-designed corpora being compiled for British (the Lancaster-Oslo-Bergen corpus or LOB: Johansson 1980), Indian (the Kolhapur Corpus of Indian English: Shastri 1988), Australian (the Macquarie Corpus of Australian English: Collins and Peters 1988) and New Zealand varieties (the Wellington corpus:

Bauer 1993). The International Corpus of English project (ICE) is currently creating a corpus with similarly-designed components representing each of the major international varieties of contemporary English (Greenbaum 1992).

spoken language corpora The earliest computer corpora, such as Brown and LOB, were collections of written data. A number of corpora consisting of transcripts of spoken English have since been developed. These vary enormously both in the types of speech they include and in the form and detail of transcription employed (see 1.4.2 on page 26). The best-known is probably the London-Lund Corpus, a computerised version of just under half-a-million words of the Survey of English Usage conversational data (Svartvik 1990; Svartvik and Quirk 1980), which has been widely used in comparisons with the LOB corpus of written English. The Corpus of Spoken American English under development at Santa Barbara (Chafe *et al* 1991) is collecting a similar quantity of American conversational data.

mixed corpora The major large mixed corpus to precede the BNC was the Birmingham collection of English texts, developed at the University of Birmingham with the dictionary publishers Collins during the 1980s as a basis for the production of dictionaries and grammars (see e.g. Sinclair 1987). This originally contained 7.5 million words, growing eventually to nearly 20 million, of which approximately 1.3 million were transcripts of speech. The collection has continued to grow since, having now been incorporated into the 300 million word Bank of English (see 1.4.1 on page 21).

historical varieties The most extensive corpus of historical English is probably the Helsinki corpus of English texts: diachronic and dialectal (Kytö 1993). The corpus has three parts, corresponding with three historical periods (Old, Middle, and Early Modern English); within each period, there are samples of different dialects, permitting not only diachronic comparisons but also synchronic comparisons of different geographical varieties.

child and learner varieties A number of corpora have been compiled relating to particular categories of language users, in particular children who are acquiring English as their first language, and foreign learners of English. They are sometimes termed *special corpora* (Sinclair 1996), because they document uses of language which are seen as deviant with respect to a general norm. Instances include the Polytechnic of Wales corpus of child language (O'Donoghue 1991), and the International Corpus of Learner English (ICLE) being created at Louvain (Granger 1993).

genre- and topic-specific corpora Other corpora have been designed to include only samples of language of a particular type, for example dealing with a particular topic, or belonging to a particular genre or *register*. There are many examples, ranging from psycholinguistically motivated experiments such as the HCRC map task corpus (Anderson *et al* 1991), consisting of 128 transcribed performances of map-reading tasks, to corpora created for other purposes, such as the Hong Kong corpus of computer science texts, designed to support analysis of technical vocabulary (Davison 1992). In the USA, the Linguistic Data Consortium has produced a large number of corpora of specific genres of speech and writing on CD-ROM, ranging from telephone conversations to stock-exchange reports.

multilingual corpora Monolingual corpora of languages other than English are not mentioned here for reasons of space, but a number of multilingual corpora containing texts in both English and one or more other languages have been developed. Some are fairly heterogeneous collections, while others are carefully constructed ensembles of texts selected on the basis of similar criteria in each language. In the former category, the European Corpus Initiative (ECI) has produced a multilingual corpus of over 98 million words, covering most of the major European languages, as well as Turkish, Japanese, Russian, Chinese, Malay and more (Armstrong-Warwick *et al* 1994). In the latter category, an EU-funded project called PAROLE is currently building directly comparable corpora for each major European language.

1.3.2   Some application areas

The range of corpus-based descriptive work is well documented by Altenberg's bibliographies of corpus linguistics (Altenberg 1990, 1995), and is also covered in a number of introductory textbooks on the field. Recent examples include Sinclair (1991), Stubbs (1996) and McEnery and Wilson (1996); Leech and Fligelstone (1992) and Biber *et al* (1996) provide accessible short introductions. In this section, we review a handful of studies in order to illustrate some of the areas in which corpus-based work has been carried out, and to raise some of the key methodological issues. No claim to completeness of coverage is intended, as the field is both very varied and rapidly expanding. For up-to-date information, and for a wider (more corpus-like!) perspective, the reader could do a lot worse than to search the World Wide Web for pages on which the phrase 'corpus linguistics' appears.

Corpus-based research naturally grounds its theorizing in empirical obser-vation rather than in appeals to linguistic intuition or expert knowledge. It thus emphatically rejects one of the major tenets of Chomskian linguistics, namely that the linguist's introspection provides the only appropriate basis for describing language, insofar as "information about the speaker-hearer's competence ... is neither presented for direct observation nor extractable from data by inductive procedures of any known sort" (Chomsky 1965: 18). Corpus users have taken varying positions on these issues, ranging from the 'weak' view, that sees corpus data as complementing the 'armchair' linguist's intuitive insights by providing real-life examples and a reliable testbed for hypotheses (see 8.1 on page 143), to the 'strong' view, according to which corpus data should always override intuition, and discussion should be confined solely to naturally-occurring examples. In either case, corpus-based work has wider affinities than many other branches of linguistics, since the study of language-in-use has something to offer historical, political, literary, sociological, or cultural studies, and has profited from the resulting synergy.

Our discussion focuses on four application areas: the emergence of *collocation* as a key component in linguistic description; the opportunities afforded by corpus-based methods for *contrastive* studies of different languages, varieties and registers; the use of corpora in *natural language processing* (NLP); and finally, their use in *foreign language teaching*.

1.3.3   Collocation

One of the forefathers of contemporary corpus linguistics, J.R. Firth, observed that part of the meaning of the word 'ass' consists in its habitual collocation with an immediately preceding 'you silly' (Firth 1957: 11). (Whether this use is still current some fifty years later is a question the BNC can answer: there are in fact only 8 occurrences of 'silly ass' in the corpus, none of them preceded by 'you'.) There are a great many cases in English where the occurrence of one word predicts the occurrence of another, either following or preceding it. Kjellmer (1991) notes such examples as 'billy', which predicts 'goat' or 'can' following, and 'bail', which predicts 'jump' or 'stand' preceding. Such collocational patterns tend to be highlighted by KWIC concordances, since these show just the few words which precede and follow the keyword or focus, and can typically be sorted according to these words. It is also relatively easy to calculate the frequency with which a particular collocate appears within a certain range of the focus — its *collocation frequency* within a given *span* — and to compare such frequencies to find the most common collocates occurring, say, up to two words before 'ass'.

Jones and Sinclair (1974) claim that the probabilities of lexical items occurring in English are generally affected by collocational norms within a span of up to four words. Co-occurrence of two or more words within a short space can be important insofar as that co-occurrence is expected and typical (whether in the language in general, in a particular text-type, or in the style of a particular speaker or author), or insofar as it is unexpected and atypical. Sinclair (1991) argues that recurrent collocational patterns effectively distinguish different senses of the same word — a 'silly ass', while potentially a quadruped, is statistically a biped — and that consequently collocational frequencies can be used to disambiguate word senses. In this he builds on Firth's view that for the lexicographer, "each set of grouped collocations may suggest an arbitrary definition of the word, compound or phrase which is being studied" (Firth 1957: 196). From a converse perspective, deviation from a collocational norm — 'since breakfasts immemorial', say — can be a means of generating particular effects, such as irony (Louw 1993).

The tendency for one word to occur with another has both grammatical and semantic implications. The collocation of a word with a particular grammatical class of words has been termed *colligation*. For instance, unlike 'look at', the verb 'regard' appears always to colligate with adverbs of manner, as in 'She regarded him suspiciously' (Bolinger 1976). From a semantic perspective, the habitual collocations of some words mean that they they tend to assume the positive or negative connotations of their typical environments — a particular *semantic prosody*. For example, Sinclair (1991) notes that the verb 'set in' has a negative prosody, because things which typically set in are 'rot', 'decline' etc., making it extremely difficult to use this verb with positive implications. In the same way, the typical collocations of many apparently neutral terms may reveal deep-seated cultural prejudices: Stubbs (1996: 186ff.) notes how the high-frequency collocates of terms such as 'Welsh' or 'Irish' tend to reinforce nationalistic stereotypes.

Other than in set phrases, collocations and their frequencies are not generally accessible to intuition. They can however be easily identified and quantified by computational methods, in corpora which are sufficiently large for the purpose. Work based on the Birmingham collection of English texts, revealing the extent of collocational patterning in English, has contributed to change current views of psycholinguistic organization, by providing important evidence that lexical items are to a large extent co-selected rather than combined individually, following what Sinclair terms an *idiom principle* rather than an *open-choice* one. A collection of concordances showing the most frequent collocates of some 10,000 words in the Bank of English has recently been published on CD-ROM (Cobuild 1995). Much discussion and research has also been dedicated to the development of appropriate measures of the strength of collocational links (Dunning 1993; Stubbs 1995), and to the automatic listing of significant collocations.

1.3.4 Contrastive studies

The construction of the LOB corpus of British English, on closely parallel lines to the Brown corpus of American English, and their subsequent morphosyntactic annotation (see 1.4.2 on page 24), stimulated a variety of comparative studies, facilitated by the wide distribution of both corpora on a single CD-ROM by ICAME, a highly influential organization of European corpus linguists based at the University of Bergen in Norway. This section reviews some examples of contrastive studies, involving both different corpora and different components of a single corpus, with the purpose of illustrating some of the methodological issues involved.

Comparing geographical varieties and languages Hofland and Johansson (1982) and Johansson and Hofland (1989) report detailed studies of word frequencies in the Brown and LOB corpora, showing, for instance, that 49 of the 50 most frequent words in each corpus are the same. Contrasts concern not only such areas as spelling (e.g. 'colour' vs. 'color'), and different choices of synonyms (e.g. 'transport' vs. 'transportation', 'film' vs. 'movie'), but also different subject matter (e.g. 'tea' vs. 'coffee', 'London' vs. 'Chicago'). Leech and Falton (1992) suggest that some of these differences in frequency may indicate cultural, rather than simply linguistic differences. Noting, for instance, the considerably more frequent use in Brown of military terms, such as 'armed', 'army', 'enemy', 'forces', 'missile(s)', 'warfare', they suggest that this may reflect a greater concern in the US with military matters (remembering that 1961, the year of the Brown texts, was also that of the Cuban missile crisis). And faced with the greater frequency in LOB of conditional and concessive conjunctions ('if', 'but', 'although', 'though') and words denoting possibility or uncertainty ('possible', 'perhaps', 'unlikely' etc.), they speculate that this may conform to the stereotype of the "wishy-washy Briton who lacks firmness and decisiveness" (Leech and Falton 1992: 44).

In reaching these (tentative) conclusions, they note that a relatively small number of words can be analyzed in this way. The LOB and Brown corpora each contain only 50,000 word types (less than the number of headwords in a single-volume dictionary), and among the less frequent words, relative frequency or infrequency may be due to sampling bias. Even at higher frequency levels, differences may be the product of a skewed distribution across texts. While the influence of these sources of error can be reduced by comparing groups of words identified by semantic or other criteria, careful examination of concordances remains necessary to check how often the word or words in question are in fact used with a particular sense — not all occurrences of the word 'film' refer to cinema, and 'tea' is a meal in some parts of Britain, as well as a drink.

Multilingual, comparable and parallel corpora   There is an increasing tendency to apply corpus techniques to the task of comparing different languages. Where a corpus consists of texts selected using similar criteria in two or more languages, comparisons can be made at many different levels, ranging from lexicogrammatical preferences to rhetorical organization. One particularly interesting type of multilingual corpus is the *parallel corpus*, consisting of texts that are actually translations of each other: prototypical instances are official documents produced in multilingual environments, such as the UN and EU, or the Canadian *Hansard*, which is published in both English and French. Such corpora have clear utility for the study of translation itself, as well as providing a useful focus for contrastive studies of the differences between particular languages.

To facilitate comparison, the texts in parallel corpora may be *aligned*, identifying equivalences on a sentence-by-sentence, phrase-by-phrase, or word-by-word basis, and much effort has gone into the development of software to align parallel texts automatically. The major fields of application have so far been in developing and testing machine translation packages and producing computerized translation aids (such as bilingual dictionaries and terminology databanks), but such corpora also have much to teach about the universals and specifics of language, and the process of translation. For instance, the English–Norwegian parallel corpus project (Johansson and Hofland 1993; Johansson and Ebeling 1996; Aijmer *et al* 1996) lists among its fields of investigation not only the similarities and differences in the lexicogrammatical, rhetorical, and information structure of texts in the two languages, but also such questions as:

- To what extent are there parallel differences in text genres across languages?
- In what respects do translated texts differ from comparable original texts in the same language?
- Are there any features in common among translated texts in different languages (and, if so, what are they)?

Comparing diachronic varieties   English-language corpus-building dates back at least thirty years. The continued availability of these pioneering corpora has made possible a range of contrastive studies investigating changes in the English language over time. There is also a growing interest in the construction of specifically designed *diachronic corpora* which sample language production over much longer time periods.

Examples of the first kind include a 1991 version of LOB, using identical sampling criteria as far as possible, recently completed at Freiburg (Mair 1993). As well as facilitating diachronic comparison of particular linguistic features, such corpora may also provide a useful yardstick for comparing studies based on the larger corpora of recent years with ones based on the smaller corpora which preceded them.

Notable examples of the second kind include the Archer corpus (Biber, Finegan and Atkinson 1994), which contains samples of eleven different registers from different historical periods, and the Helsinki corpus of English texts: diachronic and dialectal (Kytö 1993: see 1.3.1 on page 10). Kytö *et al* (1995) provides a useful checklist of new projects in this expanding field.

Change over time can also be investigated by contrasting the usage of different age groups, as further discussed in the next section.

Comparing categories of users   Where corpora provide information as to the social and linguistic provenance of speakers and hearers, or of writers and readers, they can be used to compare the language of different groups according to such variables as region, age, sex, and social class, provided that a demographically balanced sample of language users has been taken. For instance, Stenström (1991) used the London-Lund corpus to study the relationship between gender and the use of expletives relating to religion, sex and the body in speech. She found that while female speakers tended to use such words more often than male, they tended to choose expletives from a 'heaven' group, while male speakers used ones relating to 'hell' and 'sex'. Investigating the function of these words in the light of their position in the utterance, she also found that the male speakers used them to emphasize their own contributions, whereas female speakers used them to give responses and invitations to continue.

Comparing different uses of language   The construction of the London-Lund corpus of spoken English spawned a large number of studies comparing speech with writing, generally using the LOB corpus as evidence of the latter. These have highlighted differences in the relative frequencies of words and structures in the two modes (in speech the most common word is 'I', while in writing it is 'the'), as well as facilitating the identification and description of features whose use appears to be specific to the spoken language, most notably discourse-structuring elements such as 'well', 'I mean', and 'you know'.

Corpora have also been extensively used to investigate the ways in which genres differ linguistically, attempting to characterize genres by the relative frequency of particular features. Conversely, insofar as texts can be categorized statistically according to linguistic features, what correspondence is there between those categorizations and the lists of text-types employed, for instance, in corpus design? Biber (1988) compared the frequencies of a range of linguistic features which can be automatically counted (word length, type/token ratio, nouns, prepositions, first/second/third person pronouns, tense, voice, aspect, 'wh-' relative clauses, synthetic vs. analytic negation, 'private' vs. 'public' verbs, etc.) in samples from texts of different types in the LOB and London-Lund corpora, using cluster and factor analysis to identify eight basic classes of text, grouped by similar scores on five dimensions of variation. Biber and Finegan (1994) employ similar methods to investigate variation within texts, showing that in medical research articles, frequencies of a number of lexicogrammatical phenomena vary according to the section of the article sampled.

1.3.5 NLP applications

There has recently been an increased awareness of the potential which corpus methods offer for tackling a number of problems in the field of *natural language processing* (NLP), that is, the development of automatic or semi-automatic systems for analyzing, 'understanding', and producing natural language.

Corpora are increasingly used in the development of NLP tools for applications such as spell-checking and grammar-checking, speech recognition, text-to-speech and speech-to-text synthesis, automatic abstraction and indexing, information retrieval, and machine translation. A major problem to be faced by all NLP systems is that of resolving ambiguity, be this selecting which of two or more possible orthographic transcriptions might match a given acoustic input ('whales', 'Wales', or 'wails'?), or deciding whether an instance of the word 'bank' refers to a financial institution or a landscape feature, and hence how it should be translated into, say, French, or how the text that contains it should be classified for retrieval purposes.

The limited results achieved in such areas using traditional rule-based models of language have led to an increasing interest in *probabilistic models*, where probabilities are calculated on the basis of frequencies in corpus data (Church and Mercer 1993). Traditional spell-checkers, for instance, are based only on a dictionary of possible orthographic forms in the language, so that they fail to recognize errors which are nonetheless acceptable forms (such as 'form' for 'from'). Performance in such cases can be improved by considering the probability that the form typed by the user will occur after the previous word, where this probability has been calculated by analyzing a corpus for the language concerned. (For instance, it is highly unlikely that the word between 'the' and 'typed' in the previous sentence could be 'from'.)

The analysis of frequencies of particular features in corpora underlies a wide variety of NLP applications based on probabilistic techniques, such as:

- categorization of specific texts, for instance by identifying their type, semantic field, and keywords as a basis for automatic indexing and abstracting, or extracting terminology;
- refinement of question-answering and information retrieval systems, enabling them to employ or suggest additional or alternative search terms to interrogate textual databases, on the basis of collocational regularities in corpus data, and to filter retrieved information by checking its conformity to the typical collocational patterns of the search terms proposed;
- improvement of multilingual retrieval of texts, and identification of terminological equivalents in different languages, on the basis of lexical and collocational equivalences identified in parallel multilingual corpora (see 1.3.4 on page 15).

A further use of corpora in NLP is as testbeds to evaluate applications, be these theoretically motivated or probabilistic. Probabilistic models of language can, to a certain extent, be self-organizing, and in this respect corpora can provide training instruments for software which learns probability through experience, or refines an initial model in a bootstrapping process (Atwell 1996). A system which needs to disambiguate the term 'bank', for instance, can analyze a corpus to learn that the landscape sense generally collocates with 'river', 'flower', etc., while the financial one collocates with 'merchant' and 'high street'. Such uses typically call for substantial annotation of corpora in order to reduce ambiguity in the training materials, and NLP applications in many cases overlap with applications designed to annotate corpora in various ways (see 1.4.2 on page 24).

1.3.6   Language teaching

The growing variety of corpus applications in the field of English language teaching is reviewed by Murison-Bowie (1996). Corpora have already had a considerable influence in the creation of new dictionaries and grammars for learners, where the use of corpus data has allowed:

- more accurate selection of words and senses for inclusion, based on frequency of occurrence;
- introduction of information concerning the relative frequency of each word and of the different senses of each, and their use in different genres and registers;
- citation of actual rather than invented examples, selected to illustrate typical uses and collocations.

Sinclair (1987) provides a detailed discussion of these issues in reference to the creation of the *Collins Cobuild Dictionary*.

Kennedy (1992) reviews the long tradition of pre-electronic corpus work in language teaching. Many of the studies he discusses aimed to identify the most frequent words and grammatical structures in the language, with a view to optimizing the design of syllabuses and the grading of materials. Such goals have received new impetus from the availability of electronic corpora. Analysis of the Birmingham collection of English texts underlay the selection of the 'lexical syllabus' proposed by Willis (1990); Grabowski and Mindt (1995) used the Brown and LOB corpora to create a list of irregular verbs ordered according to frequency, arguing that by following this order in syllabus design, teaching should achieve maximum yield for the student's effort, irrespective of when the learning process is broken off.

Corpus data have also provided a means of evaluating conventional syllabuses. Ljung (1991) compares the lexis of textbooks of English as a foreign language with that of a corpus of non-technical writing, while Mindt (1996) compares the treatment of future time reference in textbooks and learner reference grammars with corpus data. Such studies use corpora to highlight actual frequency of occurrence, which, while not the only criterion for deciding syllabus content or the form of materials (Widdowson 1991), can clearly provide teachers and textbook writers with an important tool to assess the pedagogic suitability and adequacy of particular choices (Biber *et al* 1994).

There is also a growing interest in providing teachers and learners with direct access to corpora as resources for classroom or individual work. Fligelstone (1993) suggests that learners can use corpora to find out about the language for themselves and hence to question prescriptive specifications, for instance by exploring the nature of idioms and collocations, rhetorical questions, the use of sentence-initial 'and', etc. Similarly, Aston (in press) argues that with appropriate training, advanced learners can use large corpora as reference tools which overcome many of the limitations of existing dictionaries and grammars by providing a much larger number of more contextualized examples. Corpora may not only be a source of information about the language in question: Fligelstone notes that they can also provide encyclopedic knowledge, making them a useful tool to gather ideas about a subject in order to write or talk about it, while Aston (1995) suggests that concordancing software enables learners to browse the corpus texts in a serendipitous process where they not only analyze language but experience it as communicative use. In such ways the growing availability of corpora offers learners a new kind of resource which can complement the traditional dependency on teacher, textbook, and reference book.

1.4   How should a corpus be constructed?

We noted above that a corpus is not a random collection of text. In this section, we review some of the major issues relating to corpus construction. We discuss first some basic design principles, concerning size, sampling practice, and composition, and then consider the various kinds of encoding, annotation, and transcription policies which may be adopted.

1.4.1   Corpus design

In designing a corpus to address a particular purpose, two groups of criteria must be considered. On the one hand the size of the corpus and of its component parts, and on the other the material actually selected for inclusion, may each have crucial effects on its usability.

Corpus size and sample size   The frequency of different word forms in a corpus generally follows a *Zipfian distribution* (Zipf 1935), whereby the second most frequent word occurs approximately half as often as the most frequent one, the third most frequent word approximately one third as often, and so on. All but the most frequent words are extremely rare. Corpora therefore need to be very large and heterogeneous if they are to document as wide as possible a range of uses of as many linguistic features as possible.

Even where they are relatively frequent, features which are unevenly distributed across different types of text in the corpus may not be adequately represented. Sinclair (1991: 24) notes of the Brown and LOB corpora that they only provide reliable sources of information concerning relatively frequent words that occur in a wide range of texts. They are much less reliable for words which occur only in certain text-types, because "the sub-categories necessary to balance the sample are not in themselves reasonable samples because they are too brief". Increasing corpus size can go some way to solving these problems by providing larger samples for each sub-category.

While an increase in size provides more data, it also tends to entail less detailed analyses: it is striking how many descriptive studies have analyzed only small corpora (or small samples of larger ones), often because of the need to inspect and categorize data manually. The analysis of larger corpora is heavily dependent on the use of automatic or semi-automatic procedures able to identify particular linguistic phenomena (see 1.4.2 on page 24). The availability of such procedures is still limited in many areas.

Sinclair (1991: 24ff.) has argued that the static *sample corpus* consisting of a fixed collection of data should ideally give way to the *monitor corpus* where information could be gleaned from a continuous stream of new text "as it passes through a set of filters which will be designed to reflect the concerns of researchers." In the lexicographical field, for instance, procedures might be designed to capture new word forms or usages, and shifts in frequency of use. Such a corpus would allow the user to detect phenomena which would be inadequately represented in even a very large sample corpus, and to monitor changes in the language as they took place. The Bank of English project at the University of Birmingham puts this idea into practice (Sinclair 1992). At the time of writing, this corpus contains over 300 million words, but is continually expanding and being monitored by a set of software tools which categorize incoming data automatically for particular purposes.

In order to include both a wide range of text-types and a large number of different texts of each type, early corpora included relatively brief extracts from each text sampled: the one million-word Brown and LOB corpora each consisted of randomly-selected 2000-word samples from 500 texts, of 15 different types. A corpus composed of short samples of equal length is less likely to give skewed results due to the influence of particular source texts, but is of little use for the study of large textual features such as narrative organization, or of within-text variation (Biber and Finegan 1994). To permit the study of such phenomena, Sinclair (1996) has argued that large corpora should be composed of whole texts wherever possible.

The continued growth in the size of corpora has generally implied an increase in sample sizes as well as in the number of samples. However, the inclusion of complete texts may not always be possible, either for copyright reasons, or because the notion of 'completeness' is inappropriate or problematic (Is a newspaper a complete text? Is each story in a newspaper a complete text?). Complete texts may also vary greatly in size, giving rise to problems of balance.

Corpus composition   A corpus which claims to 'characterize the state of a language' must define both the linguistic universe which has been sampled and the sampling procedures followed. Is it intended to characterize only the speech and writing of competent native-speakers? If so, how are the latter to be defined? Is it to include as wide a variety of different types of language as possible? Should its composition reflect the relative frequencies with which these different types occur? And if so, should these frequencies be calculated on the basis of *reception* (the language people hear and read), *production* (the language people speak and write), or both? In the first case priority will be given to those text-types which are most widely and frequently experienced, such as casual conversation, everyday workplace and service encounters, television, radio and the popular press. In the second case, while much of the everyday dialogue content may be similar, the rest of the corpus may look very different, since most texts are produced for small audiences.

Many of the criteria for the composition of a corpus are determined by its intended uses. The Survey of English Usage aimed to describe the grammatical repertoire of adult educated speakers of English with the aid of a corpus which was "reasonably representative of the repertoire of educated professional men and women in their activities, public and private, at work and at leisure, writing and speaking" (Quirk 1974: 167). Given these goals, it was designed to sample a wide range of text types, deciding the proportions of each largely on their assumed frequency of production in the language as a whole. Most large mixed corpora have tended to follow the Survey in aiming to cover users' production repertoires (though not merely the educated, professional and adult) by drawing up a list of text types to be included, deciding the proportions of the corpus to be constituted by each, and then selecting texts for each type using a combination of random and controlled sampling techniques.

There are, of course, many different ways of characterizing texts, and hence many text typologies. One of the more fundamental distinctions is between spoken and written materials. The Survey of English Usage contained equal quantities of each, and subsequent compilers of mixed corpora have generally agreed that ideally this proportion should be respected — though there is no particular reason for thinking that writing and speech are equally present in either production or reception of the language as a whole. However, since it is for the moment much more expensive to obtain speech data, which has to be recorded and transcribed, than written texts, many of which are already available in machine-readable form, large mixed corpora generally contain much smaller proportions of speech.

More complex text typologies have been based on such concepts as the *field* (that is, the topic and purpose) of the text; on sociolinguistic factors determining its *tenor* (for example, the context in which the text is produced or received, the participants and their inter-relationships, etc.); or on its *mode* (that is, whether speech is monologue or dialogue, face-to-face or broadcast, prepared or spontaneous; or whether writing is published or unpublished). Atkins *et al* (1992) list as many as 29 parameters to be considered in constructing a 'balanced' corpus. Within each category, reception criteria may be used to complement production ones, for instance by preferring bestsellers to remaindered novelettes when sampling published fiction.

There is ample evidence that word frequencies and other linguistic features vary widely within different text-types, both with respect to each other, and with respect to the whole of a corpus, whatever typology is employed. For instance, in most forms of speech, 'sure' is more common than 'certain', while in written social science texts the opposite is the case (Biber and Finegan 1989).

Biber (1993) demonstrates that analyses based on restricted samples cannot be generalized to language as a whole. It has consequently been argued that a balanced corpus is useful in a specific application only to the extent that it includes an adequate sample of the category in question, which can be separated out and treated as a corpus in its own right. However, balanced corpora can at least provide a baseline against which variation amongst pre-defined categories can be measured. Halliday (1992: 69) argues "if we recognize departure from a norm, then there has to be a norm to depart from. If we characterize register variation as variation in probabilities, as I think we must, it seems more realistic to measure it against observed global probabilities than against some arbitrary norm such as the assumption of equiprobability in every case."

1.4.2 Encoding, annotation, and transcription

Simple lexical analysis of a corpus of written texts requires only a computer-processable version of the text. However, for the full range of analytic possibilities sketched out in section 1.2 on page 5 above, some thought must also be given to the ways in which the text and its context are to be *encoded*, that is, the way in which particular features of them can be made explicit and hence processable. This is especially important for corpora derived from spoken language, where the process of transcription immediately confronts the analyst with many difficult theoretical and methodological issues.

Encoding and annotation A corpus may simply consist of sequences of orthographic words and punctuation, sometime known as *plain text*. However, texts are not just sequences of words; they have many other features worthy of attention and analysis. At the very least, we want to distinguish and describe the different texts in the corpus, as well as their different components. Such text descriptions may include bibliographic details, details of the nature of the sample (complete or otherwise), or classification in terms of the parameters employed in designing the corpus.

When describing the components of written texts (other than words), it is useful to indicate the boundaries of chapters, sections, paragraphs, sentences, etc., and the specialized roles of headings, lists, notes, citations, captions, references, etc. For spoken texts, indications of the beginnings and ends of individual utterances are essential, as is an indication of the speaker of each. It may also be desirable to encode *paralinguistic* phenomena such as pausing and overlap, and *non-verbal* activity such as laughter or applause. For either kind of text, it may be helpful to include editorial information about the status of the electronic text itself, for example to mark corrections or conjectures by the transcriber or editor.

A further type of information which may be provided is *linguistic annotation* of almost any kind, attached to components at any level from the whole text to individual words or morphemes. At its simplest, such annotation allows the analyst to distinguish between orthographically similar sequences (for example, whether the word 'Frank' at the beginning of a sentence is a proper name or an adjective), and to group orthographically dissimilar ones (such as the negatives 'not' and '-n't'). More complex annotation may aim to capture one or more syntactic or morphological analyses, or to represent such matters as the thematic or discourse structure of a text.

Types of linguistic annotation that have been employed with corpora include the following:

part-of-speech or word-class Placing a *tag* alongside each word in the corpus to indicate its word-class can disambiguate different grammatical uses of a word such as 'works', which may be a plural noun or a singular verb. Such *part-of-speech tagging* can also help identify grammatical patterns. While many existing corpora have been manually or automatically tagged in this way, no standard set of part-of-speech tags has yet been defined.

lemmatization and morphological analysis *Lemmatization* involves the use of tags to indicate the relationship of each word-form to its root (e.g. that 'took' is the past tense form of 'take'). It enables derived and inflected forms of a word to be retrieved and counted along with its root. While lemmatization provides a useful way of grouping data for many descriptive purposes, particularly in languages with many declensions and conjugations, corpus-based research suggests that different forms of lemmas do not always share the same meaning, but tend to occur in distinctive contexts (Sinclair 1991).

word-sense Tags can also be used to distinguish different senses of the same word (e.g. 'table' meaning 'piece of furniture' as opposed to 'data in rows and columns'), on the basis of an existing dictionary or thesaurus. While *word-sense annotation* is quite extensively used in the fields of machine translation and information retrieval (Guthrie *et al* 1994), it clearly prejudges the issue for corpora whose goals include lexicographic description.

syntactic role The *parsing* of corpora involves the addition of annotation to indicate the grammatical function of each word, describing the structure of each sentence as a set of labelled bracketings or tree. A number of small parsed corpora have been derived from pre-existing larger corpora. These include the Gothenberg corpus (Ellegård 1978) derived from parts of Brown; the LOB corpus treebank (Leech and Garside 1991) derived from LOB; and the Susanne corpus (Sampson 1994), which combines results from both. While most parsing has been done by hand, considerable research effort has gone into the development of automatic parsers. Notable examples include the English Constraint Grammar Parser developed at Helsinki (Karlsson 1994) and the TOSCA system developed at Nijmegen (van Halteren and Oostdijk 1993). As syntactic analysis is often necessary to decide who did what to whom in English, parsed corpora have an important role in many NLP applications. Parsing schemes are, however, highly theory-dependent, and there is relatively little consensus in the field.

pragmatic annotation In a sentence like 'Not there they won't', pronouns, deixis, and ellipsis refer to concepts which are (probably) more fully expressed elsewhere in the text. Identifying those concepts is often important for natural language understanding systems and for machine translation. Substantial work has been carried out on procedures to insert *pragmatic annotation* linking such anaphoric features to their antecedents (Fligelstone 1992; Garside 1993). Annotation indicating other pragmatic features such as the function of individual speech acts and overall discourse structure (Coulthard 1994) has been so far limited to very small samples, given the lack of consensus as to relevant units and categories, and of explicit algorithms for their identification.

Much of the concern with annotated corpora derives from the need to provide training materials and testbeds for software which will annotate text automatically for various NLP applications (see 1.3.5 on page 18). Some descriptive linguists have on the other hand argued that corpora should only be made available as plain text, given that annotation always involves introducing an interpretation of some kind (Sinclair 1991).

Transcribing speech No transcript, however detailed, is able to provide all the information on which hearers draw when understanding speech (Cook 1995). French (1992) proposes four levels of transcription, ranging from a broad orthographic representation of the words spoken, to a narrow phonetic transcription with detailed prosodic information. The act of transcribing spoken data is in itself a kind of encoding, making explicit an interpretation of the original sound wave. Even a broad transcription generally implies, for instance, distinguishing different speakers' utterances, dividing these into sentences or prosodic units, and dividing the latter into words, with a disambiguation of homophonous elements with distinct orthographic forms. Narrower transcription involves additional encoding of prosodic features, such as stress and intonation, as well as of paralinguistic ones such as changes in voice quality, pausing, and non-vocal events (phone rings, applause, shifts in position and eye-contact, etc.).

For studies of phonology and dialectology, an orthographic transcription is clearly unlikely to be adequate unless supported by more detailed phonemic or phonetic data. Such coding systems are not discussed here. Their complexity, requiring highly-specialized expertise, has meant they are only currently available for relatively small corpora of speech. Given its costs, there has generally been a trade-off between size and detail in corpus transcription. Edwards and Lampert (1993) provide a detailed survey of different transcription systems, both in terms of the features encoded and their representation (for a summary, see Edwards 1995).

2 The British National Corpus

2.1 How the BNC was constructed

Here we review the status of the British National Corpus with respect to the corpus construction issues discussed in the previous section. The discussion follows the same order as that used above.

2.1.1 Corpus design

Corpus size and sample size   Looking back over the history of computer corpora, we can see that corpus sizes have increased by roughly one order of magnitude per decade. It has been estimated that the 100 million word BNC would take 4 years to read aloud, at 8 hours a day. The Associated Press newswire, by comparison, generates some 50 million words per year. The overall size of the BNC corresponds to roughly 10 years of linguistic experience of the average speaker in terms of quantity — though not, of course, in quality, given that it aims to sample the language as a whole, rather than that experienced by any particular type of speaker.

Most samples in the BNC are of between 40,000 and 50,000 words; published texts are rarely complete. There is, however, considerable variation in size, caused by the exigencies of sampling and availability. In particular, most *spoken demographic* texts, which consist of casual conversations, are rather longer, since they were formed by grouping together all the speech recorded by a single informant. Conversely, several texts containing samples of written unpublished materials such as school essays or office memoranda are very short.

Corpus composition   The BNC was designed to characterize the state of contemporary British English in its various social and generic uses. A more detailed discussion of the design criteria and their implementation is provided in chapters two and three of the *BNC Users' Reference Guide* (Burnard 1995). In selecting texts for inclusion in the corpus, account was taken of both production, by sampling a wide variety of distinct types of material, and reception, by selecting instances of those types which have a wide distribution. Thus, having chosen to sample such things as popular novels, or technical writing, best-seller lists and library circulation statistics were consulted to select particular examples of them.

Although the BNC distinguishes several different geographical, sociological, and generic varieties, it does not necessarily provide a reliable sample for any particular set of such criteria. Different considerations applied to the procedures used when choosing material for inclusion in the written and spoken parts of the corpus, which are therefore discussed separately.

Written texts Ninety per cent of the BNC is made up of written texts, chosen according to three *selection features*: *domain* (subject field), *time* (within certain dates) and *medium* (book, periodical, unpublished, etc.). In this way, it was hoped to maximize variety in the language styles represented, both so that the corpus could be regarded as a microcosm of current British English in its entirety, and so that different styles might be compared and contrasted.

Each selection feature was divided into classes and target percentages were set for each class. Thus for the selection feature 'medium', five classes (books, periodicals, miscellaneous published, miscellaneous unpublished, and written-to-be spoken) were identified. Samples were then selected in the following proportions: 60 per cent from books, 30 per cent from periodicals, 10 per cent from the remaining three miscellaneous sources. Similarly, for the selection feature 'domain', 75 per cent of the samples were drawn from texts classed as 'informative', and 25 per cent from texts classed as 'imaginative'. The following list illustrates each selection criterion, and indicates the actual numbers of texts and words in each category — words being counted according to the criteria described in 2.1.2 on page 34.

Domain The evidence from catalogues of books and periodicals suggests that imaginative texts account for less than 25 per cent of published output. Correspondence, reference works, unpublished reports, etc. add further to the bulk of informative text which is produced and consumed. Nevertheless, the overall distribution between informative and imaginative text samples in the BNC was set to reflect the influential cultural role of literature and creative writing. The target percentages for the eight informative domains were arrived at by consensus within the project, based loosely upon the pattern of book publishing in the UK during the past 20 years or so.

	texts	percentage	words	percentage
Imaginative	625	19.47	19664309	21.91
Arts	259	8.07	7253846	8.08
Belief and thought	146	4.54	3053672	3.40
Commerce and finance	284	8.85	7118321	7.93
Leisure	374	11.65	9990080	11.13
Natural and pure science	144	4.48	3752659	4.18
Applied science	364	11.34	7369290	8.21
Social science	510	15.89	13290441	14.80
World affairs	453	14.11	16507399	18.39
Unclassified	50	1.55	1740527	1.93

Time Informative texts were selected only from 1975 onwards, imaginative
ones from 1960, reflecting their longer 'shelf-life', though most (75 per
cent) of the latter were published no earlier than 1975.

	texts	percentage	words	percentage
1960–1974	53	1.65	2036939	2.26
1975–1993	2596	80.89	80077473	89.23
Unclassified	560	17.45	7626132	8.49

Medium This categorization is broad, since a detailed taxonomy or feature
classification of text medium would have led to such a proliferation of
subcategories as to make it impossible to represent them all adequately.
The labels used were intended to be comprehensive in the sense that
any text can be assigned with reasonable confidence to these macro categories. 'Miscellaneous published' includes brochures, leaflets, manuals,
advertisements. 'Miscellaneous unpublished' includes letters, memos, reports, minutes, essays. 'Written-to-be-spoken' includes scripted television
material, play scripts etc.

	texts	percentage	words	percentage
Book	1488	46.36	52574506	58.58
Periodical	1167	36.36	27897931	31.08
Misc. published	181	5.64	3936637	4.38
Misc. unpublished	245	7.63	3595620	4.00
To-be-spoken	49	1.52	1370870	1.52
Unclassified	79	2.46	364980	0.40

Written texts are further classified in the corpus according to sets of *descriptive
features* (see 5.2.3 on page 103 for a complete list). This information was
recorded to allow more delicate contrastive analysis of particular sets of texts.
These descriptive features were monitored during the course of data collection,
and, in cases where a free choice of texts was available, text selection took
account of the relative balance of these features. For example, although no
relative proportions were pre-defined for different target age groups, it was

possible to ensure that the corpus contained texts intended for children as well as texts intended for adults.

Spoken texts Ten percent of the BNC is made up of transcribed spoken material, totalling about 10 million words. Roughly equal quantities were collected in each of two different ways:

- a *demographic* component of informal encounters recorded by a socially-stratified sample of respondents, selected by age group, sex, social class and geographic region;
- a *context-governed* component of more formal encounters (meetings, debates, lectures, seminars, radio programmes and the like), categorized by topic and type of interaction.

This dual approach was chosen in the absence of any obvious objective measures that might be used to define the target population or to construct a sampling frame for spoken language. Demographic sampling techniques alone would have resulted in the omission from the corpus of many types of spoken text produced only rarely in comparison with the total output of all speech producers. Examples include broadcast interviews, lectures, legal proceedings, and other texts produced in situations where — broadly speaking — there are few producers and many receivers. Reliance on a previously drawn–up list of spoken text types alone would have been very difficult to justify, given the lack of agreement on ways of categorizing speech and the impossibility of determining the relative proportions of each type..

The following classifications apply to both the demographic and context-governed components:

- Region where text captured

	texts	percentage	words	percentage
South	296	32.34	4728472	45.61
Midlands	208	22.73	2418278	23.33
North	334	36.50	2636312	25.43
Unclassified	77	8.41	582402	5.61

- Interaction type

	texts	percentage	words	percentage
Monologue	218	23.82	1932225	18.64
Dialogue	672	73.44	7760753	74.87
Unclassified	25	2.73	672486	6.48

Crowdy (1995) describes in more detail the procedures adopted both for sampling and for transcribing the spoken part of the BNC. For the demographic component, random location sampling procedures were used to recruit 124 adults (aged over 15) from across the United Kingdom, with approximately equal numbers of both sexes and from each of five age groups and four social classes. Each recruit used a portable tape recorder to record their own speech and the speech of people they conversed with over a period of up to a week. Additional recordings were gathered for the BNC as part of the University of Bergen COLT Teenager Language Project (Stenström and Breivik 1993). This project used the same recording methods and transcription scheme, but selected only respondents aged 16 or below.

As with any sampling method, some compromise had to be made between what was theoretically desirable and what was feasible within the constraints of the BNC project. There is no doubt that recruiting 1000 people would have given greater statistical validity but the practical difficulties and cost implications made this impossible. Nevertheless, the total number of participants in all conversations was well in excess of a thousand, producing a total of 4.2 million words of unscripted conversational English.

The *context-governed* component consists of 762 texts (6.1 million words). As in the written component, the range of text types was selected according to previously-defined criteria, based in the first place on domain:

	texts	percentage	words	percentage
Educational and informative	144	18.89	1265318	20.56
Business	136	17.84	1321844	21.47
Institutional	241	31.62	1345694	21.86
Leisure	187	24.54	1459419	23.71
Unclassified	54	7.08	761973	12.38

Each of these categories was divided into the subcategories *monologue* (40 per cent) and *dialogue* (60 per cent), and within each category a range of contexts defined as follows:

educational and informative Lectures, talks and educational demonstrations; news commentaries; classroom interaction etc.

business Company and trades union talks or interviews; business meetings; sales demonstrations etc.

institutional Political speeches; sermons; local and national governmental proceedings etc.

leisure Sports commentaries; broadcast chat shows and phone-ins; club meeting and speeches etc.

The overall aim was to achieve a balanced selection within each category, taking into account such features as region, level, gender of speakers, and topic. Since the length of these text types varies considerably — news commentaries may be only a few minutes long, while some business meetings and parliamentary proceedings may last for hours — an upper limit of 10,000 words per text was generally imposed.

2.1.2 Encoding, annotation, and transcription

The encoding of the BNC is designed to capture an extensive variety of information. It includes the various design features described in the previous section, bibliographic details, and a great deal of detail about the structure of each text, that is, its division into sections or chapters, paragraphs, verse lines, headings, etc. for written text, or into speaker turns, conversations, etc. for spoken texts.

In the corpus, such information must be represented in a manner which distinguishes it from the words of the plain text. In the BNC this is achieved through the use of special purpose *markup*, following a scheme known as the *Corpus Data Interchange Format* (CDIF), itself strongly influenced by the Text Encoding Initiative's *Guidelines* for the encoding of electronic text (Sperberg-McQueen and Burnard 1994). The purpose of CDIF is to allow the portability of corpora across different types of hardware and software environments, and the comparability of different corpora, as well as to make it easy to search for occurrences of particular encoded features, or for linguistic phenomena which occur in particular contexts.

Contextual information common to all texts is described in an initial *corpus header*. Contextual information specific to a given text is listed in a *text header* which precedes each text. Detailed structural and descriptive information is marked at appropriate positions within each text. The *BNC Users' Reference Guide* includes a full description of the markup conventions employed, from which the following brief description is taken.

CDIF uses an international standard known as *SGML* (ISO 8879: Standard Generalized Mark Up Language), now very widely used in the electronic publishing and information retrieval communities. In SGML, electronic texts are regarded as consisting of named *elements*, which may bear descriptive *attributes* and can be combined according to a simple grammar, known as a *document type definition* (Goldfarb 1990). In an SGML document, element occurrences are delimited by the use of *tags*. There are two forms of tag, a *start-tag*, marking the beginning of an element, and an *end-tag* marking its end. Tags are delimited by the characters < and >, and contain the name of the element, preceded by a solidus (/) in the case of an end-tag. For example, a heading or title in a written text will be preceded by a tag of the form <HEAD> and followed by a tag in the form </HEAD>. Everything between these two tags is regarded as the *content* of an element of type <HEAD>.

Instances of elements may also be assigned particular *attributes*. If present, these are indicated within the start-tag, and take the form of an attribute name, an equal sign and the attribute value. For example, the <HEAD> element may take an attribute TYPE which categorizes it in some way. A main heading will thus appear with a start-tag <HEAD TYPE=MAIN>, and a subheading with a start-tag <HEAD TYPE=SUB>. Attribute values are used for a variety of purposes in the BNC, notably to represent the part of speech codes allocated to particular words by the CLAWS tagging scheme, described below.

End-tags are omitted for the elements <s>, <w> and <c> (i.e., for sentences, words, and punctuation). For all other non-empty elements, every occurrence in the corpus has both a start-tag and an end-tag. In addition, attribute names are omitted for the elements <w> and <c> to save space. A list of the elements employed in the BNC is provided in the *BNC Users' Reference Guide*.

A restricted range of characters is used in element content: specifically, the upper- and lower-case alphabetics, digits, and a subset of the common punctuation marks. All other characters are represented by SGML *entity references*, which take the form of an ampersand followed by a mnemonic for the character, and terminated by a semicolon where this is necessary to resolve ambiguity. For example, the pound sign is represented by the string £, the character é by the string é and so forth. The mnemonics used are taken from standard entity sets, and are also listed in the *BNC Users' Reference Guide*.

Since the publication of the BNC, its encoding scheme, or derivations from it, have been widely adopted by other corpus building projects. It also forms the basis of the 'Corpus Encoding Standard' (CES) recommended by the European Union's Expert Advisory Group on Language Engineering Standards (EAGLES).

Part-of-speech annotation   Leech *et al* (1994) describe how the 100 million words of the BNC were automatically tagged, using the CLAWS4 system developed at Lancaster University, originally by Roger Garside, with additional software developed by Michael Bryant. CLAWS was first used for the tagging of the LOB Corpus (Garside *et al* 1987) using an annotation scheme described in Johansson *et al* (1986). The CLAWS system automatically attaches a tag to each word indicating its grammatical class, or part of speech (POS), and to each punctuation mark. The aim is to provide distinct codings for all classes of words having distinct grammatical behaviour. A set of 58 POS codes, known as the C5 tagset, is used in the first release of the BNC; these are listed in section 2.1 on page 230.

CLAWS generally assumes that an orthographic word (separated by spaces from the adjacent words) is the appropriate unit for tagging. The following particular cases should however be noted:

- A single orthographic word may contain more than one grammatical, or *L-word*: thus in the case of contractions, such as 'she's', 'they'll', 'we'd', 'don't', 'won't', 'd'ya', 'gotta', ' 'twas', and of possessives ('John's', 'pupils'' etc.), separate tags are assigned to each grammatical component of the orthographic word. A list of cases where orthographic words are treated as multiple L-words is given in the *BNC Users' Reference Guide*.

- The opposite circumstance is also quite common, where two or more orthographic words behave as a single grammatical word: for example, compound prepositions such as 'instead of' and 'up to' are assigned a single preposition tag. Foreign phrases such as 'hoi polloi' or 'viva voce' are also tagged as single items. Again, a list of such multi-word L-words is given in the *BNC Users' Reference Guide*.

Otherwise, spaces determine treatment as single or multiple L-words. Note that compounds, where orthographic practice is often uncertain (for example 'fox holes', 'fox-holes', and 'foxholes', all of which appear in the BNC), may occur tagged as two words (if they are separated by spaces), or as one (if they appear as a single word, or with a hyphen). Truncated words in spoken data are also tagged as separate L-words which are unclassified.

For approximately 4.7% of the L-words in the corpus, CLAWS was unable to decide between two possible POS codes. In such cases, a two-value POS code known as a *portmanteau* is applied. For example, the portmanteau code VVD-VVN means that the word may be either a past tense verb (VVD), or a past participle (VVN).

The automatic tagging system had an overall error-rate of approximately 1.7%, excluding punctuation marks. With such a large corpus, there was no opportunity to undertake post-editing to correct annotation errors. However, in a successor project, due to complete in 1997, the Lancaster team has been refining the tagging of the whole corpus, using as input a new set of data derived from a 2% sample of the BNC which was manually checked and corrected.

Speech transcription   The spoken texts of the BNC are transcribed at a level roughly corresponding to French's (1992) level 2 (see 1.4.2 on page 26). It is an *orthographic transcription*, rather than a phonological or prosodic one, in which changes of speaker, pausing, overlap, and a variety of non-verbal and non-vocal events identified by the transcribers are made explicit by means of SGML markup.

The basic unit is the utterance, marked as a <u> element, with an attribute WHO whose value specifies the speaker, where this is known. Overlapping speech is marked using a system of pointer elements, explained in 9.2.4 on page 172. Pausing is marked using a <PAUSE> element, with an indication of its length if this seems abnormal. Gaps in the transcription, caused either by inaudibility or the need to anonymize the material, are marked using the <UNCLEAR> or <GAP> elements as appropriate. Truncated forms of words, caused by interruption or false starts, are also marked, using the <TRUNC> element.

A semi-rigorous form of normalization is applied to the spelling of non-conventional forms such as 'innit' or 'lorra'; the principle adopted was to spell such forms in the way that they typically appear in general dictionaries. Similar methods are used to normalize such features of spoken language as filled pauses, semi-lexicalized items such as 'um', 'err', etc. Some light punctuation was also added, motivated chiefly by the desire to make the transcriptions comprehensible to a reader, by marking (for example) questions, possessives, and sentence boundaries in the conventional way.

Paralinguistic features affecting particular stretches of speech, such as shouting or laughing, are marked using the <SHIFT> element to delimit changes in voice quality. Non-verbal sounds such as coughing or yawning, and non-speech events such as traffic noise are also marked, using the <VOCAL> and <EVENT> elements respectively; in both cases, the values supplied for the DESC attribute specifies the phenomenon concerned. It should, however, be emphasized that the aim was to transcribe as clearly and economically as possible rather than to represent all the subtleties of the audio recording.

2.2   Using the BNC: some caveats

Although the BNC was designed to represent the full variety of the English language at a particular point in time, users of the corpus should be cautious in generalizing from the evidence it provides about the frequency of particular linguistic phenomena in the language. The very all-inclusiveness of the BNC means that it necessarily contains instances of untypical, irregular, accidental, and possibly erroneous phenomena. Defining 'erroneous' in the context of corpus linguistics is not methodologically neutral, for no corpus is error free, and indeed to decide finally that some aspects of a corpus *are* erroneous may be a non-trivial operation.

We list some features of the BNC which may mislead the unwary, relating to

- the nature of the materials included in the corpus;
- the sampling, encoding and annotation procedures adopted;
- the division of the corpus data into separate documents, and the division of those documents into text headers and the texts themselves.

Many of these difficulties are inherent in the materials making up the BNC. Others are attributable to errors or inconsistencies in the process of sampling, encoding, and annotating the corpus. Corrigible errors of these kinds will be corrected, as resources permit, in later versions of the BNC.

2.2.1 Source materials

As with any other large corpus, the texts themselves contain a wide variety of potentially deceptive features. These include:

orthographic error and variation Texts were not systematically proof-read or corrected prior to inclusion in the corpus, with the result that any errors in the original will normally be reproduced in the BNC. In particular, printing errors in the original may lead to incorrect division of the text into words, as when a dash is printed as a hyphen, or a full stop without a following space is interpreted as an abbreviation rather than a sentence boundary. Written English also accepts a wide range of spelling variants, as with '-ise' and '- ize' forms. This is particularly problematic where compounds are concerned, since the number of words may also vary: for instance, the forms 'busybody', 'busy-body' and 'busy body' are all present in the BNC.

features of spoken performance Spontaneous speech not only involves a range of conventionally 'non-verbal' elements whose orthographic transcription is relatively unstandardized ('uhuh', 'haha', 'heheh' and the like), but also what are (by written standards) lexical and grammatical errors. False starts, changes of mind etc. may be cut short or subsequently corrected by their producers, with the effect that the transcript retains both the original and its repetition or reformulation.

variation in transcription practice Every effort was made to achieve accuracy and consistency in transcriptions, but unquestionably some errors remain. It should not be assumed, for example, that one transcriber's 'erm' or 'going to' is necessarily phonetically distinct from another's 'um' or 'gonna'.

non-standard usage Although a check was made that all identifiable authors represented in the corpus were native speakers of British English, no such check was (or could have been) applied to the authors of unattributed material, or to all speakers in the spoken part of the corpus. In fact there are many non-standard usages, not all of them produced by non-native speakers or writers. It should also be borne in mind that both speech and writing contain wilfully deviant forms, as in puns or poetry. The demographically sampled part of the corpus contains a number of jokey discussions of the likely use of the tape recordings. In the written part of the corpus, extracts from electronic mail discussion lists, and personal letters, contain equally informal and unorthodox usages.

quotation and allusion Apparent inconsistencies may also be due to the presence of quotations or allusions, or of explicit references to linguistic features. Quotations in languages other than English are also occasionally to be found, which may lead to confusion where they include forms which are identical to English words — for example, a fragment in German may contain many occurrences of the word 'die' but have nothing to do with mortality.

homographs Foreign words are only one category of unexpected homographs in the corpus: others include names, abbreviations, and acronyms, as well as misprints. The wide range of material included in the BNC means that almost any possible variant is likely to appear. Analyses of word frequency should pay particular attention to homographic forms: for example, any attempt to repeat Holmes' (1994) study of changes in gender-related usages with the BNC data, would need to take as much care as she does to separate out occurrences of 'Miss' as a term of address from the verbal and nominal usages, and to distinguish 'Ms' from the disease 'MS' and the abbreviation 'ms' before attempting to tabulate their relative frequencies.

2.2.2 Sampling, encoding, and tagging errors

The BNC is probably more richly encoded and annotated than any other corpus of comparable size. Despite the best endeavours of all involved, the need to complete the project on time and within a tight budget meant that errors and inconsistencies remain in the corpus. Some typical errors are listed:

sampling errors Some texts, or parts of texts, appear in the corpus more than once. This particularly applies to newspaper materials, and is a consequence of the way such texts were prepared and selected for inclusion in the corpus.

encoding errors Not all structural features of the texts are consistently encoded. For instance, not all quotations are marked as SGML <Q> elements, many being simply implied by the appearance of inverted commas; list items are sometimes tagged as <P> (paragraph) elements; not all headings are correctly identified, and so forth. In general, items which are tagged at all are tagged correctly, but inferences about the frequency distribution of structural elements in the BNC should be made only with great caution.

tagging errors There are part-of-speech tagging errors and inconsistencies. Although the part-of-speech tagging has high overall accuracy, errors in part-of-speech assignment to words which have more than one possible POS value can still be frequent. Furthermore, the parameters of the tagging system were modified during the tagging process, in the light of experience. This means that in the first release of the corpus some instances of the same sequence of words have received different taggings. Similar inconsistencies may be observed in the case of phrases which are treated as a single L-word, or of orthographic words which are treated as two or more L-words: for example, the phrase 'innit' (for 'isn't it') appears in the first release of the corpus both as a single lexical item, with a single POS code, and (correctly) as a phrase, with three.

It is hoped to correct many of the errors listed in these three categories in later versions of the BNC.

2.2.3 What is a BNC document?

The overall organization of the BNC entails the following problems:

BNC documents None of the 4124 *BNC documents* making up the corpus should properly be regarded as a complete written or spoken text. Either for reasons of length or, more frequently, for reasons of copyright, only samples of original written texts are included, of size between 40 and 50 thousand words. Care should therefore be exercised when interpreting such features as co-occurrence and position within a document. The sampling method (beginning, middle, or end) is included along with other text classification information provided by the <CATREF> element in the header of each text. Some BNC documents, by contrast, contain more than one text in the everyday sense of the word. Documents taken from newspapers and periodicals, for example, are likely to be composed of a considerable number of articles. For spoken demographic material, all the conversations recorded by a particular respondent are combined to form a single document. In these cases co-occurrence within the document clearly does not imply co-occurrence within the same article or conversation. For spoken texts in general, the notion of completeness is rather hard to define: it cannot be assumed that an entire speech event has been successfully recorded in every case. Even where an entire event was recorded, it may have been only partially transcribed, whether for ethical or technical reasons.

Text headers Each BNC document contains a *header* as well as the text itself. The header contains information about the text of a largely repetitive nature. Consequently, searches which include headers in their scope may find a surprisingly high number of occurrences of words such as 'publication' or 'press'. The amount of information provided in headers varies considerably from text to text: for instance only a few texts have lists of *keywords* included in the header.

2.2.4   *Miscellaneous problems*

Further sources of potential misinterpretation have to do with the composition of the BNC. Some results may be biassed by the fact that the corpus was collected at a particular time, with the result that certain 'buzzwords' occur more frequently than might otherwise have been the case. Others may be influenced by atypically frequent recurrences in one or a few particular texts.

Although the BNC contains many different kinds of text, it should not be assumed that it contains every possible kind of material. There are almost as many ways of classifying texts as there are text-classifiers; if therefore you are seeking texts in a category not specifically identified by the BNC's own classification scheme, you may find it very hard to identify them, even if they are present in the corpus, or they may be present in only very small quantities.

In general, it should be borne in mind that numbers of occurrences in a corpus are quite likely to be too small to be interpreted with confidence: half the word-forms in the corpus occur only once. Nor should it be assumed, where higher frequencies are involved, that these are necessarily adequate for any statistical procedure. In principle, corpora lend themselves to quantitative analysis: it is relatively easy to draw up frequency lists of words, collocations, or grammatical patterns, and to compare these in particular categories of use or user. It may also seem obvious to use traditional statistical tests (such as *chi-square* or *t-test*) to assess whether such frequencies, or the differences between them, are significant. However, the use of such tests involves some questionable assumptions:

- The statistics traditionally used in frequency-based analyses assume that observations are *independent* of each other (i.e. that the probability of seeing a particular event is constant — such as the probability of seeing a head or a tail when tossing a coin). In texts, however, the likelihood of a particular word occurring at any point is heavily constrained by neighbouring choices and by the nature of the text — indeed probabilistic tagging techniques such as those employed by the CLAWS program (see 2.1.2 on page 34) are based precisely on the failure of this assumption. This calls into question the use of statistics based on this assumption to interpret language data. It is a separate decision, perhaps carried out after consideration of non-statistical data, whether or not particular statistical values are 'linguistically interesting' (Stubbs 1995: 33).

- Many statistical procedures assume that the events being analyzed are *normally distributed*, an assumption which can only be made for relatively common events. The reliability of the assumption of normal distribution can be calculated using the formula $np(1-p)>5$, where n is the number of events in the sample, and p the probability of the event in question occurring as the next event. As most words, and even more so phrases and collocations, are extremely rare, the value of this formula is near enough to np, meaning that a reliable inference can only be made when the expected frequency of an event is 5 or more. This condition is quite likely not to be satisfied even in the case of very large corpora, particularly where occurrences in limited sections of the corpus are concerned, or specific collocations required.

3 Future corpora

It may not be too soon to ask how the widespread use of computer-held corpora has changed and is changing the study of language in its widest sense, and to hazard some practical consequences. We have already commented on the way in which corpus usage encourages a probabilistic rather than a rule-based approach to fundamental issues of language description. However the question of how these two approaches can best be integrated into a consistent theoretical framework, as well as practically combined in order to maximize the advantages of each for NLP work, remains largely open. Another widely-noted trend is the blurring of traditional linguistic categories as corpus-based analyses reveal complex patternings of language. For instance, the categorical distinction between lexis and grammar is being increasingly questioned, as the extent of collocational patterning of lexis, and the idiosyncracy of the grammar of individual words, are revealed (Sinclair 1991; Francis 1993). Understanding of such features will predictably increase with growth in the number and the size of corpora available. The progressive accumulation of corpus evidence is also providing material that enables linguists to chart changes in the language as they occur, and to understand more deeply the diachronic processes involved.

Natural language processing applications currently provide much of the momentum for new developments in corpus creation, with a trend towards ever-larger corpora, towards greater standardization of sampling procedures and of encoding, and towards more sophisticated and reliable automatic annotation procedures. As the number and the dimensions of available corpora increase, so both the need for more sophisticated automatic analyses, and the feasibility of creating tools to produce them increase.

Advances in computer storage and processing capabilities suggest that it will soon be commonplace to include digital audio along with the transcriptions which make up corpora of speech data. This will help overcome some of the limitations of current transcripts, though the process of automatically aligning the two, or of generating the transcription from the audio, still poses many technical problems. There is an interesting synergy of applications here with recent developments in the computer processing of ancient texts, where there is a need to align a digital image of a manuscript with a 'diplomatic' transcription of it. In both cases, the transcription is an essential indexing aid to the original.

Efforts towards standardization, going hand in hand with efforts to expand the availability of directly comparable corpora for many different languages, are of particular importance in a European context, where there are nine official languages as well as a political commitment to support several other so-called 'minority' languages. Corpus-based techniques are seen by many as central in the development of the European Language Industry, which is attracting significant levels of investment, both private and governmental.

One function served by large reference corpora such as the BNC may be supplied by other resources in the near future. It is already commonplace to comment on the immense quantities of raw electronic text now available from the World Wide Web, and to speculate about ways in which it might be organized as a linguistic corpus resource. It seems probable that as the sophistication of web indexing, search and retrieval systems increases, it will become easier for individuals to create corpora of their own design, representing particular areas of language use by searching for relevant components on the web.

Whatever form corpora of the future may take, it can be predicted that the range and quantity of corpus applications will increase in both academic and everyday fields, with a variety of potential social consequences. Corpus-based analyses may come to influence areas such as public communication, where speakers and writers may begin to rely on demographically-organized corpus evidence as a means of matching their language to a particular target group or groups, or the interpretation of language in legal contexts, either as a means of demonstrating what is generally meant by a particular expression, or of revealing stylistic idiosyncracies in questions of disputed authorship (Coulthard 1993). In language teaching increasing access to corpora may modify the traditional role of the teacher as an authority about the use of the language to be learned, and reduce the sense of inferiority felt by many non-native speaker teachers. More generally, there is much to be said about the way in which thinking about language, particularly the English language, is politicized, and hence about the political implications of changing the basis on which assessments of correctness or appropriateness of usage are made.

II: Exploring the BNC with SARA

Introduction

This part of the *BNC Handbook* contains a series of ten tasks, which introduce you to the main features of the SARA software and illustrate how you can use it to obtain information from the BNC. The tasks investigate several issues which we noted in section 1.2 on page 5 as being important application areas for corpus-based analysis. The topics covered range from the meanings and contexts of particular words and phrases to differences between the language of writing and speech, or of speakers of different ages and sexes. Although these issues are largely linguistic, we have tried to make the discussion as accessible as possible for the non-specialist reader and the tasks do not presuppose any particular competence in linguistics.

Each task has three parts:

- an outline of the problem or issue to be analysed, and the relevant software features to be used;
- step-by-step instructions for performing the analysis;
- a summary of the main points to emerge, together with some suggestions for further practical work of a similar nature.

The tasks are designed as a sequence, progressively introducing different features of the corpus and of the software. You are recommended to work through them in the order they are presented here. Reference information concerning specific features of the software can most easily be found in the final part of this handbook, which provides a summary overview of the program. For more specific details concerning the BNC, you should consult the *BNC Users' Reference Guide*.

The tasks are intended for teaching purposes only, and in no way claim to provide an exhaustive treatment of the linguistic problems discussed, which would in all cases require considerably closer and more extensive analysis. Their primary aim is to familiarize you with the corpus and the software, giving some idea of their potential as a means of investigating such problems. In particular, since SARA can take a long time to provide large sets of results, we have tended to choose examples which involve rather small numbers. These numbers are generally far too small to permit reliable inferences about the language as a whole.

We tested all the exercises described here using version 930 of the SARA system running against release 1.1 of the BNC. In some cases, our results may be different from yours if you run the the same query against a different version of the corpus or of the software. In particular, the frequencies reported for several words in version 1.0 of the BNC (the first released version) are somewhat lower than those for version 1.1. New versions of the corpus and software are announced as they become available at http://info.ox.ac.uk/bnc on the BNC website.

We have assumed that you have some acquaintance with the Microsoft Windows environment, and are familiar with its terminology. If you don't know what a *dialogue box* is, or how to *double-click* your mouse, or how to *re-size* or *iconify* a window, you may find it helpful to have a quick look at any introduction to the Microsoft Windows environment before beginning to work through what follows. The buttons displayed on the screen when using SARA are reproduced and briefly explained on the inside cover of this handbook.

1 Old words and new words

1.1 The problem: finding evidence of language change

1.1.1 Neologism and disuse

One of the most widespread uses of large corpora of contemporary language is to identify changes in vocabulary. Many recently-published dictionaries of English have used corpora to hunt for neologisms, or for evidence that words or senses have fallen into disuse, in order to decide what words and senses they should include. This task takes two examples, using SARA to look in the BNC for evidence of the use of one old word which such dictionaries exclude, and of one new word which they include.

An old word: 'cracksman' In his turn-of-the-century stories about the gentleman-thief Raffles, E.W. Hornung refers to the latter as a 'cracksman'. Cited in the *Shorter Oxford* as a slang term first found in the 19th century, 'cracksman' is absent from recent corpus-based dictionaries such as the *Collins COBUILD*, the *Cambridge International Dictionary of English*, the *Oxford Advanced Learner's Dictionary*, and the *Longman Dictionary of Contemporary English*. This first example examines whether the BNC provides evidence of contemporary use of the term 'cracksman' and its plural, 'cracksmen', with the meaning of burglar.

A new word: 'whammy' The word 'whammy' was introduced in the 1995 editions of all the dictionaries just cited. All define a 'whammy' as an unpleasant or difficult experience, and note the phrase 'double whammy'. This second example examines the BNC for evidence of this use, and looks to see whether 'whammy' is also found in other phrases or with other senses.

1.1.2 Highlighted features

This task shows you:

- how to start and leave SARA, and obtain on-line help;
- how to look for a word in the corpus using the PHRASE QUERY option;
- how to display solutions either on separate pages or as a one-per-line (KWIC) concordance display, using the CONCORDANCE option;
- how to scroll through and select individual solutions;
- how to display bibliographic details of the source of a selected solution and browse the text from which it comes, using the SOURCE and BROWSE options;
- how to copy a selected solution to the Windows clipboard using the COPY option;
- how to change the default display settings using the VIEW PREFERENCES option;

- how to switch between windows showing solutions from different queries using the WINDOW menu.

1.1.3 Before you start

This task assumes that:

- you are familiar with the basic conventions of operation under Microsoft Windows using a mouse, such as moving and sizing windows, starting, exiting and switching between programmes, clipboard operation, and file management;
- the SARA software has been correctly installed on your computer;
- your computer has a TCP/IP connection to the machine running the server;
- you know your SARA username and password, which you should obtain from your local network manager or SARA adviser.

1.2 Procedure

1.2.1 Starting SARA

The BNC icon should be visible on your desktop.

Double-click on the icon and wait for the program to load. The ABOUT SARA box will be displayed, showing the version of the SARA software you are using.

Click on OK (or press ENTER). The LOGON dialogue box should be displayed, showing the server version of the SARA software installed, and prompting you for your username and password. *SARA works by linking your computer to the one where the corpus is stored, which functions as a server. You use your computer (the client) to formulate queries about the BNC and send them to the server, and to manipulate the solutions to these queries returned by it. To start the program, a connection between the client and server must be established. If this cannot be done, a 'Cannot connect to server' message will be displayed. Clicking on OK will then display the COMMUNICATIONS dialogue box, which allows you to RETRY the connection, if necessary changing the server specification, or to CANCEL the display and exit from the program. You should not normally alter the settings in this dialogue box without consulting your network manager.*

1.2.2 Logging on

Type in your username, then press TAB and type in your password. Your password will not be displayed as you type it.

Click on OK (or press ENTER). If you entered an incorrect username or password, the LOGON dialogue box will be re-displayed. Otherwise a message box will confirm that you are logged on to the SARA server. It may also provide messages from the network manager about the system you are using. *If you make a mistake while entering your username and password, clicking on the* CANCEL *button will clear the contents of the dialogue box.*

If you repeatedly enter an incorrect username or password, a 'Cannot log on to server' message will be displayed. Clicking on OK *will clear this message and take you to the* COMMUNICATIONS *dialogue box (see 1.2.1 on the preceding page).*

You can change your password using the VIEW *menu* PREFERENCES *option (see 1.2.8 on page 56) — but only after you have logged on using your current password.*

(5)   **Click on OK (or press ENTER) to remove the message box.** The main window will now be revised to display the title *SARA-bnc*. A BNC icon will also appear in the bottom left-hand corner: you should resist the temptation to click on this icon. *The purpose of this icon is to show which corpora or subcorpora are currently available for searching. In the current version of this software, only the full BNC corpus is available. Clicking on the icon will simply open a view of the first text in the corpus; closing this will close the corpus and SARA will have nothing to search!*

(6)   **If necessary, use the Windows buttons to enlarge the *SARA-bnc* window to full screen size.**

(7)   **Click on the VIEW menu, and check that TOOLBAR and STATUS BAR are both ticked.**

   You are now ready to formulate queries about the contents of the BNC. When you use SARA, you will usually be asking it to find examples of the occurrences of particular words, phrases, patterns, etc. within the BNC. We refer to the request you make of the system as a *query*; the set of examples or other response which this request produces we refer to as the *solutions* to the query. The distinction is important, because SARA allows you to save and manipulate queries and their solutions independently.

1.2.3   Getting help

At the bottom of the screen, on the status bar, is a reminder that you can get help at any point by pressing F1. You can also do this from the HELP menu, or by clicking on the CONTEXT HELP button situated at the right-hand end of the toolbar. Clicking on this button creates a cursor which you can move to any button or box and then click to display help concerning that object. The buttons on the toolbar and their names are shown on the inside cover of this handbook

1.2.4   Quitting SARA

When you want to leave the program, select EXIT under the FILE menu (or press ALT+F4).

1.2.5   Using Phrase Query to find a word: 'cracksmen'

Let us begin by investigating which forms of the word 'cracksman' appear in the BNC. We will start by looking for occurrences of the plural form 'cracksmen'.

Move the mouse to the toolbar, and click on the PHRASE QUERY button. The Phrase Query dialogue box will be displayed. *You can also reach this dialogue box by selecting* NEW QUERY *then* PHRASE *from the* FILE *menu.*

Type in the string cracksmen, **then click on OK (or press ENTER) to send the query to the server.** *The options in the Phrase Query dialogue box are described in 1.3.3 on page 202. They allow you to* CANCEL *the dialogue box and return to the previous window, losing any input you have entered; to* SEARCH HEADERS, *looking for solutions to the query within both the texts and the text headers, which contain information about the corpus and its component texts (for fuller details, see 5.1.1 on page 98); and to* IGNORE CASE *(the default setting), searching for solutions regardless of their use of upper and lower case letters. If the Ignore case box is unchecked, SARA searches only for solutions which match the case pattern used in the input string — a considerably slower process (for examples see 1.3.2 on page 61 and 10.2.4 on page 184).*

Wait while the server searches for solutions and downloads them to the client. A new window called *Query1* will open to display them. *You may briefly see a red* BUSY *dot flashing on the status bar at the bottom of the window as text begins to appear. The red dot means that your computer is exchanging data with the server: it will stop flashing as soon as downloading is complete. You should not attempt to give new commands while the red dot is flashing, but if you want to abandon a search you can either press* ESC *before downloading begins, or simply close the query window after downloading has commenced.*

1.2.6   Viewing the solutions: display modes

Enlarging the context   There is exactly one occurrence of the word 'cracksmen' in the BNC, which you are currently looking at. However the amount of context displayed is probably too small for you to understand how the word is being used.

Position the mouse on the solution and double-click the right mouse button. The amount of context will be increased, up to the *maximum download length* (see 1.2.8 on page 55).

Page and Line display modes   Depending on the default settings being used to display solutions, you will see either:

• a *page* display, showing this solution with a few lines of context, or

- a *line* display, showing this solution on a single line, with a dashed surround.

In both display modes, the *query focus* (the word 'cracksmen') will be shown in a highlight colour: in Line display mode, it will be in the centre of the line.

(12) **Click on the CONCORDANCE button on the toolbar to change the display mode (or select CONCORDANCE under the QUERY menu).** *The CONCORDANCE button allows you to switch between Page and Line display modes. Whichever of the two modes you are in, clicking on the button will change to the other. Clicking on it a second time will return you to your original display mode. You can also toggle the display mode by checking or unchecking the CONCORDANCE option under the QUERY menu. For full details, see 1.6.4 on page 218.*

To change the default display mode and the highlight colour, use the VIEW menu (see 1.2.8 on page 54).

Character display   You will see that in Page display, the solution contains the sequence 'wrong …' at the end of the sentence following that containing 'cracksmen'. All characters outside the basic alphabet are represented in the BNC by SGML *entity references* (see 9.2.2 on page 165, 2.4 on page 239), which SARA converts into appropriate symbols as far as possible when displaying solutions. There is no way of displaying three dots (horizontal ellipsis) as a single character under Microsoft Windows, and so here SARA displays the unconverted entity reference. *You can change the way in which entity references are displayed by configuring your own CUSTOM display format (see 1.2.8 on page 55, 9.2.2 on page 165).*

1.2.7   Obtaining contextual information: the Source and Browse options

On the status bar you will see the code ANL, followed by the number 368. The source text from which the current solution is taken is indicated by the three-character *text identifier* code, displayed in the third box from the left on the status bar. In each text in the BNC, sentences are consecutively numbered, and the number of the sentence from which the current solution comes is shown in the fourth box on the status bar.

The codes used for text identifiers do not provide any information about the nature of the source text. To see the full bibliographic details (author, title, and publication details for written texts; participant details for spoken texts), you can use the SOURCE option. This also allows you to browse the whole of the source text. *A complete bibliographical listing of the texts in the BNC, in order of their text identifier codes, is provided in the BNC Users' Reference Guide.*

Click on the SOURCE button on the toolbar (or select SOURCE from the QUERY menu). The BIBLIOGRAPHIC DATA box will be displayed, showing that this solution comes from a written text, taken from a murder story published in 1991. *The OK button in the Bibliographic data box returns you to the solutions display.*

Click on the BROWSE button in the Bibliographic data box to display the source text. SARA will switch to *browse mode*, opening a *bnc* window to display the source text. This will be represented as a series of SGML elements between angle brackets. Initially only the element identifying the *BNC document* or <BNCDOC> (the highest level of structure) will be shown, followed by a red line and box indicating the point in the document structure at which the solution occurs.

Click in the red box to show the portion of text which contains the solution. The text will start to be expanded, showing its header and various subdivisions (such as chapters or sections). When the whole text has been downloaded from the server, the paragraph which contains the current solution will be displayed in its fully expanded form, with the query focus highlighted. Every word in this paragraph should have a *tag* next to it (shown between angle brackets).

If you cannot see these tags, select the BROWSER menu and check TAGS. If you look carefully, you will see that each sentence is preceded by an <s> tag with its consecutive number; each word is preceded by a <w> tag with its part-of-speech code (see 7.1.2 on page 129), and each punctuation mark by a <c> tag.

The text will be easier to read if these tags are removed from the display.

Select the BROWSER menu and uncheck TAGS. Then scroll through the text till you find the highlighted query focus. The <P> element containing the solutions will be expanded as formatted text, with each sentence beginning on a new line. The <s>, <w> and <c> tags have been removed from the display. *You can choose to have these tags omitted from browse mode displays the next time you start SARA by unchecking SHOW TAGS in the BROWSER section of the USER PREFERENCES dialogue box (see 1.2.8 on the following page).*

Use the scroll bar to show the text immediately preceding the expanded paragraph. You will see that the preceding text is represented as a series of <P> elements, each of which represents a paragraph of the text. These unexpanded elements are preceded by plus signs; whereas the <P> element which has been expanded to show its internal structure is preceded by a minus sign.

(19) **Click on the minus sign to remove the expansion of this paragraph.**
The minus sign will be replaced by a plus, showing that this element is not
expanded, and a red box will be added to the display, to indicate the position of
the solution.

(20) **Use the scroll bar to scroll back to the beginning of the browser display.**
You will see that the fifth <DIV1> element in the text (the one which contains
the solution) is expanded to show its internal structure as a <HEAD> element
(i.e. a heading) followed by a series of <P> elements.

(21) **Click on the plus sign next to the <HEAD> element.** You will see that
the heading to this section of the text reads '5' — it is in fact the fifth chapter
of the book. *The BROWSE option is the only way in which you can examine the whole
text from which a particular solution is taken, rather than just the context immediately
surrounding the query focus. You cannot save or print Browse displays.*

(22) **Click in the *Query1* window (or select QUERY1 from the WINDOW
menu) to return to the solutions display.** You will be returned to the
solutions to your query for 'cracksmen'.

Copying solutions to the Windows clipboard   When using SARA, you
may often want to save a particular solution in order to analyze or quote it
elsewhere. Start by saving the current solution.

(23) **Click on the COPY button on the toolbar (or select COPY from the
EDIT menu).** You can now paste this solution into a Windows word processor,
such as *Word, Notepad* or *Write*.   *Solutions are copied together with the source
information displayed on the status bar. The amount of context copied and the format
will generally correspond to those visible in Page display mode (see 8.2.5 on page 154).
Remember that copying to the clipboard deletes the clipboard's previous contents.*

*To save an entire set of solutions to file, use the LISTING option (see 8.2.5 on page 154);
to print a Line mode display use the PRINT option (see 3.2.3 on page 81).*

1.2.8 Changing the defaults: the User preferences dialogue box
Before formulating any further queries, let us change the default query display
settings, so that solutions will from now on automatically be downloaded in an
appropriate format.

(24) **Under the VIEW menu, select PREFERENCES.** The USER PREFERENCES
dialogue box will be displayed.

From this box you can change SARA's default settings for a variety of
features. We will start by requesting a maximum amount of context (1000
characters) and a maximum number of hits (100).

Download parameters   These specify the maximum amounts of data that should be sent from the server to your computer in response to a query.

Click on the MAX DOWNLOAD LENGTH box and type in 1000. The greatest maximum download length that can be specified is 2000 characters. This includes SGML markup, and corresponds to around 150 words of plain text.

Click on the MAX DOWNLOADS box and type in 100. There is no intrinsic limit to the maximum number of solutions that can be downloaded, but the current version of the software cannot display more than 2000 solutions. On most systems, it will take a long time to download more than a few hundred.

Default query options: Format   These specify the way in which SGML markup is to be displayed on the screen.

Click on the PLAIN radio button. PLAIN is the fastest display format. It shows words and punctuation only. Entity references (see 1.2.6 on page 52) are converted to their conventional typographical equivalents. The query focus is shown in the highlight colour selected under the VIEW FONT and COLOURS options (see 1.7.4 on page 227). *Format options are fully described in 1.6.4 on page 219. POS displays different parts of speech in different fonts and colours (see 7.2.4 on page 137), according to the default FONT and COLOURS selections. The default CUSTOM format behaves differently in Line and Page display modes: in Line mode, paragraph and utterance boundaries are shown as vertical lines, whereas in Page mode the appearance of a printed page is reproduced (see 6.2.2 on page 116). You can edit Custom format to display particular features as you wish (see 9.2.2 on page 165). SGML displays the text with full SGML markup, showing all elements and attributes in angle-bracketed tags, and entity references in their coded form (see 1.2.6 on page 52; for an example see 5.2.3 on page 103).*

Default query options: Scope   These specify the amount of context to be displayed for each solution, within the limits set by the Max download length as defined in the Download parameters (see above).

Click on the PARAGRAPH button. This will display one paragraph of written text, or one utterance of spoken text. It will generally provide enough context to understand the sense in which the query focus is used, and the nature of the source text. *The SCOPE options are fully described in 1.6.4 on page 219. AUTOMATIC will normally display the sentence (or a similarly-sized unit) in which the query focus occurs, unless the query has to be satisfied within the span of a given number of words, in which case as many sentences as are necessary to show that span will be displayed (see 8.2.3 on page 152); SENTENCE displays the sentence in which* the query focus occurs; MAXIMUM *will display the Max download length specified in the Download parameters, trimmed to complete sentences. Since you cannot in any case show more text than specified as the Max download length, you may not see a complete sentence or paragraph if the Max download length is small or the sentence or paragraph is particularly long, regardless of the scope selected.*

Default query options: View These options specify the layout of the window in which solutions will be displayed.

⑨ **Check QUERY and ANNOTATION to show the text of the query and a space for notes above the solutions.**

㉚ **Check the CONCORDANCE box so as to display solutions in Line mode.** *The* VIEW *options are fully described in 1.6.5 on page 221.* QUERY *displays the text of the query above the list of solutions. This provides a useful way of checking complex queries, as well as of learning the syntax of CQL (the SARA Corpus Query Language: see 7.2.3 on page 135). It also shows the number of solutions, and details of any thinning which has taken place (see 2.2.3 on page 66).* ANNOTATION *opens a space for notes above the list of solutions, which can be saved with the query and re-displayed when you re-open it (see 4.2.2 on page 94).* CONCORDANCE *indicates whether solutions are to be displayed in Line (i.e. concordance) or Page mode (see 1.2.6 on page 51).*

Browser options The checkbox indicates whether low-level tags (<s>, <w>, <c>) are to be shown in browser displays (see 1.2.7 on page 52). *Changing this setting will only take effect the next time you log on to SARA.*

Other default settings To change the default display font and colours, use the FONT and COLOURS options under the VIEW menu (see 1.7.4 on page 227). *The other options in the* USER PREFERENCES *dialogue box are fully described in 1.7.5 on page 227.* COMMS *enables you to change the server address, port and timeout interval, while* PASSWORD *enables you to change the password you use to log on to SARA.* CANCEL *returns you to the current solutions window without changing the current defaults.*

Applying changed defaults Any change you make in the USER PREFER-ENCES dialogue box will apply to all further queries in this session, as well as the next time you log on to SARA. It will not however affect queries for which solutions have already been downloaded and displayed on the screen, nor will it affect the BROWSER display in the current session (see above). You can change the settings for individual sets of solutions after they have been downloaded by using the OPTIONS (see 5.2.3 on page 103), QUERY TEXT (see 2.2.3 on page 67), ANNOTATION (see 2.2.3 on page 67) and CONCORDANCE options (see 1.2.6 on page 51) under the QUERY menu.

Click on OK to return to the solutions window. Since the alterations made to the defaults only affect the display of solutions to subsequent queries, the display in the current solutions window (*Query1*) will be unchanged.

1.2.9   Comparing queries: 'cracksmen' and 'cracksman'
We are now ready to perform another query, this time looking for occurrences of the singular form 'cracksman'.

Click on the PHRASE QUERY button on the toolbar. The Phrase Query dialogue box will be displayed.

Type in the string cracksman **and click on OK (or press ENTER).** SARA will open a new solutions window entitled *Query2*.

If you have changed the default options according to the instructions in the last section, you should find that:

- the text of the query ('cracksman') is displayed at the top of the window;

- this is followed by a space where you can write notes if you click in it;

- the four solutions are displayed in Line mode, the first of them being current.

Click on the CONCORDANCE button on the toolbar to switch to Page display mode. You should find that a full paragraph of context (2-3 lines) is displayed for the first solution.

Press PGDN to show the next solution. Repeat to see the following solutions. Of the four solutions, three are references to the title of Hornung's book.

Apart from the references to the book title, there is thus only one example for each of the forms 'cracksman' and 'cracksmen' in the corpus. Are these occurrences merely idiosyncratic uses of an archaism by an isolated writer? You can see whether these solutions both come from the same source text by comparing their text identifier codes, which are displayed in the third box from the left on the status bar.

Read the last 'cracksman' example and note its text identifier.

Click on the SOURCE button on the toolbar to display the biblio-graphic data for this text.

Click on OK (or press ENTER) to return to the solutions display.

Click in the *Query1* window, if it is visible, or select QUERY1 from the WINDOW menu.

(40) **Check the text identifier and source for this solution.** You will see that
the source texts are two different novels. *A difference in text identifier codes is
not a completely reliable indicator that solutions come from different source texts. For
written materials, each distinct BNC document is a sample of up to 45,000 words from a
distinct text. However, some very large and miscellaneous texts such as the* Dictionary of
National Biography *were sampled more than once, as were newspapers and periodicals,
with a view to representing the wide variety of types of language such texts contain.
Consequently there are a few cases where different text identifiers indicate the same source
text. For spoken texts, the material gathered demographically (i.e. the collections of
spontaneous informal conversation) is grouped so that each respondent's conversations make
up a single text. This has not however been done for other kinds of spoken material, with
the result that such things as radio phone-ins or meetings are occasionally split across several
texts.*

We can perhaps infer that the word 'cracksman' has not totally died out
in contemporary British English, at any rate within the genre of thrillers. It
would however seem to be very very rare, which would justify its absence from
the one-volume dictionaries cited earlier, many of which are designed primarily
with foreign learners in mind.

1.2.10   Viewing multiple solutions: 'whammy'

'Cracksman' and 'cracksmen' are very rare in the BNC. We now look at the
word 'whammy', which we would expect to occur rather more frequently, since
it is included in all the dictionaries cited in 1.1.1 on page 48.

(41) **Click on the PHRASE QUERY button on the toolbar. Wait for the
dialogue box to be displayed, then type in the string** whammy **and click
on OK (or press ENTER) to send the query to the server.** If you have
followed all the steps in this task up to now, the results should be displayed in
a window called *Query3*, using the default display options selected in 1.2.8 on
page 54, i.e. in Line mode.

(42) **Wait until the red BUSY dot on the status bar has stopped flashing,
showing that all the solutions have been downloaded.** The solutions are
displayed in the order they appear in the corpus, i.e. according to their text
identifier code and sentence number. In the second box from the left on the
status bar, you will see the numbers 1:46(31). These numbers indicate that a
total of 46 solutions have been downloaded, taken from 31 different texts, and
that the current solution is 1, i.e. the first in the display. *The difference between the
second and the third numbers provides an indicator of dispersion of solutions across texts:
if the difference is large (relative to the total number of solutions), this implies that the
solutions tend to be concentrated in particular texts, rather than being evenly dispersed.*

If necessary, use the Windows buttons to enlarge the solutions window to full screen size.

Changing the current solution   Many of the solutions contain the expression 'double whammy'. Can a 'whammy' be more than double?

Click on the Windows scroll bar to scroll through the solutions until you reach the final one. You will find a 'triple Conservative tax whammy' in the last solution, and a 'quadruple whammy' twelve lines above it.

Look at the first of the numbers in the second box from the left on the status bar. You will see that the current solution is still number 1. Using the scroll bar (unlike the keyboard cursor keys) to scroll through a Line mode display does not change the current solution.

Click on the last solution in the list to make it the current solution. You will see that the first of the numbers in the second box on the status bar is now the same as the second number, i.e. the current solution is now the last solution in the list.

Scrolling through solutions using the arrow buttons   You can also move through a list of solutions (in either Line or Page display mode) by using the ARROW buttons on the toolbar. The inner pair of arrow buttons take you to the previous or next solutions, while the outer pair take you to the first or last solutions. Clicking on any of these buttons also changes the current solution.

Click repeatedly on the inner backward arrow button to make the current solution number 38. The number of the current solution is displayed on the Status bar, and changes as you click on the arrows.   *In Line mode, the current solution is always displayed with a dashed surround.*

Click on the CONCORDANCE button on the toolbar to switch to Page display mode. Use the inner forward arrow button to look through this and the following two solutions, which give an account of the origins of the expression 'double whammy'. *When looking up a rare word in the corpus, it is quite common to find examples which define or explain the meaning of the word.*

Click on the CONCORDANCE button to return to Line display mode, then click on the outer backward arrow button to return to the first solution. From the number display on the status bar, you can see that the first solution in the display is now the current one.

Look through the initial solutions again to see if they all use the word 'whammy' in the same sense. Following a few 'double whammy' examples, you will see a group of solutions which use the word in such phrases as 'whammy bar' and 'whammy pedal'.

(51) **Unless you already know what a 'whammy bar' is, click on the first of these examples to make it the current solution, then click on the CONCORDANCE button to switch to Page display mode.**

(52) **Use the inside forward arrow button (or the PGDN key) to page through the other solutions in this group, until you have roughly understood this second meaning of 'whammy'.** *While you can use the arrow buttons on the toolbar to scroll through solutions in either Line or Page display mode, the keyboard cursor keys behave differently according to the display mode. To scroll through solutions one at a time, you must use the up and down arrow keys in Line mode, and the PGUP and PGDN keys in Page mode. In Line mode, pressing the PGUP and PGDN keys moves you through the display half a screenful at a time, whereas in Page mode, pressing the up and down arrow keys moves you within the single solution displayed. Scrolling through solutions using the cursor keys or arrow buttons also changes the current solution.*

Results It seems clear from the solutions that as well as the 'double whammy' sense of misfortune, 'whammy' quite often has the sense of 'whammy bar' (or pedal) on an electric guitar. This meaning is not included in any of the dictionaries mentioned — perhaps because it is less frequent, or considered a specialized use.

(53) **Close each of the open windows individually by pressing CTRL-F4, or select CLOSE ALL from the WINDOW menu.** *SARA will switch to browse mode, displaying the beginning of the corpus in a bnc window.*

(54) **Press ALT-F4 to leave SARA, or else iconify the browse window, and proceed to experiment with the queries described in the next section.**

1.3   Discussion and suggestions for further work

1.3.1   Caveats

Before drawing conclusions from frequency data, you should evaluate the *precision* of your query — that is, whether all the solutions being counted concern the phenomenon you are interested in. You should look carefully at the solutions themselves, which may include unexpected proper names, foreign words, quotations, deliberate archaisms, misspellings, or misprints. You should also evaluate the query's *recall* — that is, whether it is likely to have found all the occurrences of the phenomenon you are interested in, or whether the latter may take other forms. Finally, you should consider the texts and the corpus from which the numbers have been derived. Even relatively high frequencies may have limited *dispersion*, being due to the influence of just one or two texts. Conversely, if a word is absent from the corpus, this need not mean it does not occur in the language: at most it may suggest that it occurs relatively infrequently, or in text-types which are *under-represented* in the corpus in question. Such methodological issues are further illustrated in the following exercises.

1.3.2 Some similar problems

'thine' and 'wight'   The first example in this task suggested that the word 'cracksman' is still occasionally used in contemporary English. Perform queries to find evidence in the BNC for contemporary use of two other relatively archaic words, 'thine' (other than in addressing God), and 'wight' (other than in the name 'Isle of Wight'). *To increase precision, type in the search terms in lower case, and uncheck* IGNORE CASE *in the Phrase Query dialogue box. This will avoid references to God and to the Isle of Wight. Read through the solutions to check that the word is not merely mentioned or quoted from an older English text, or an attempt to imitate an archaic style.*

The main non-religious use of 'thine' is in a quoted saying: 'Know thine enemy'. The 'wight' query demonstrates how occurrence in the corpus does not always mean that a word is normally used in contemporary English. Of the 17 solutions, several appear to be misprints of 'might' or 'weight'; some reproduce deliberate mispronunciations in a punning conversation ('Quite wight'); some are mentions of Chaucer's 'gentil wight'; while others are references to the names of creatures in J.R.R. Tolkien's fairy world — based largely on Old English vocabulary.

'Avatars'   Neal Stephenson's novel *Snow Crash* (1993) tells the story of a struggle for power in two worlds, that of twenty-first century America, and that of the Metaverse, a virtual reality where the characters interact assuming computer-generated physical forms.   Stephenson terms these computerized personae their 'avatars'. Does the BNC provide any evidence for the use of 'avatar' in this sense? *If you look up both singular and plural forms, you will find a total of 10 solutions. Using Page display mode to see a full paragraph of context, you will see that the main use of 'avatar' is in relation to gods and demons — arguably a similar use to Stephenson's?*

'Psykers'   Look up the word 'psyker' (and its plural 'psykers') in the BNC. Do you feel there is evidence of sufficient use to warrant its inclusion in a dictionary of contemporary English? *Taken together, the two forms occur a total of 21 times. However if you notice the display of the number of texts from which the solutions are taken on the status bar, you will see that they have zero dispersion. As you can find out by using the* SOURCE *button, they all come from a single science-fiction story.*

'In-your-face'   One of the new words in the 1995 edition of the *Collins COBUILD* dictionary is the adjective 'in-your-face' (or 'in-yer-face'), which is defined as follows: "If you say that someone has an in-your-face attitude, you mean that they seem determined to behave in a way that is unconventional or slightly shocking, and that they do not care what people think of them."

Is this word attested in the BNC? Does it always have this meaning? Which of the spellings is more widely used? *While the COBUILD definition takes 'in-your-face' to refer to people, in the corpus examples it is mainly used to describe drama and music. The 'in-yer-face' spelling occurs only once. However, it is possible that we have not found all the occurrences, since we cannot be sure that 'in your/yer face' is always hyphenated. You will see how to design queries to include orthographic variations of this kind in 10.2.5 on page 186.*

2 What is more than one corpus?

2.1 The problem: relative frequencies

2.1.1 'Corpus' in dictionaries

In the last task we used the BNC to find evidence of the occurrence of particular forms and senses of words. In this exercise, we examine the evidence it provides about the relative frequencies of different forms and senses. There is, of course, a big difference between saying that one form or sense is ten times as common as another in a particular corpus, and saying the same thing of the language as a whole; this issue of the *representativeness* of a corpus is discussed in 2.2 on page 36. Here we are primarily concerned with ways of obtaining numeric information from the BNC rather than with its interpretation.

This task investigates plural forms of the word 'corpus' in the BNC, and the senses in which they are used. According to the entry for 'corpus' in the second edition of the *Oxford English Dictionary* reproduced at the start of this Handbook, the plural form of this noun is 'corpora'. The definitions given include five main senses and several phrasal uses, all of them rather esoteric. This suggests that 'corpus' is likely to be a fairly rare noun in the BNC — we shall see in a moment just how rare.

Three smaller recent dictionaries, the *Collins COBUILD*, the *Longman Dictionary of Contemporary English*, and the *Cambridge International Dictionary of English*, give only the 'text collection' meanings (senses 3 and 4 in the *OED2*), but list both 'corpora' and 'corpuses' as alternative plural forms. What evidence is there of the regularized plural 'corpuses' in the BNC? And is this regularized form only found for the 'text collection' sense?

2.1.2 Highlighted features

This task shows you:

- how to find the frequency of a word or group of words in the BNC using the WORD QUERY option;
- how to look for occurrences of a word or group of words using the WORD QUERY option;
- how to download only one solution from each source text using the options in the TOO MANY SOLUTIONS dialogue box;
- how to mark and delete particular solutions using the THIN option;
- how to save and re-open a query.

It assumes you already know how to:

- log on to SARA and display the toolbar and status bar (see 1.2.1 on page 49);

- change the default settings using the View Preferences option (see 1.2.8 on page 54);
- look up a word using Phrase Query (see 1.2.5 on page 51).

2.1.3   Before you start

Log on to SARA and wait for the *SARA-bnc* window to be displayed (see 1.2.2 on page 49). Under the VIEW menu, check that the TOOLBAR and STATUS BAR options are ticked, and then use the PREFERENCES option (see 1.2.8 on page 54) to set the default settings as follows:

MAX DOWNLOAD LENGTH	1000 characters
MAX DOWNLOADS	100
FORMAT	Plain
SCOPE	Paragraph
VIEW: QUERY and ANNOTATION	checked
CONCORDANCE	checked
BROWSER: SHOW TAGS	unchecked

Click on OK (or press ENTER) to return to the *SARA-bnc* window.

2.2   Procedure

2.2.1   Finding word frequencies using Word Query

The WORD QUERY option allows you to specify a list of one or more words, and to search for occurrences of all of them. It also enables you to find out quickly how often any word or group of words occurs in the BNC.

(1)   **Click on the WORD QUERY button on the toolbar to display the Word Query dialogue box.** *You can also reach the Word Query dialogue box by choosing* FILE *from the menu bar, then* NEW QUERY, *then* WORD.

(2)   **Type in the string** corpus **and click on the LOOKUP button.** An alphabetical list will be displayed showing all the word forms in the BNC which begin with the characters 'corpus'. *Notice that the list contains hyphenated forms like 'corpus-based', as well as some foreign phrases like 'corpus delicti' and 'corpus juris'. Each form in the list is a separate entry in the BNC word index, or L-word. As well as conventional orthographic words, L-words include conventional and foreign phrases which function as single units, such as 'in spite of' or 'corpus juris', as well as clitics, i.e. morphological components used in contracted and possessive forms, such as ''s', 'ca' and 'n't'. For a list of clitics and phrasal L-words used in the BNC, see the BNC Users'* Reference Guide.

If the index contains more than 200 L-words which begin with the string entered, an error message will be returned. Either a longer string or a more precise pattern should be specified (see 8.2.1 on page 147).

Click on the first word in the list, i.e. 'corpus'. Clicking on a word in the list selects it and shows how often it occurs in the BNC. You will see that 'corpus' occurs 724 times, with a z-score of 0.0518. *z-scores indicate how frequent an L-word (or group of L-words) is compared with the mean frequency of all the L-words in the corpus, which is 149.3. The z-score is the number of standard deviations from the mean frequency: a positive score indicates that a word is more frequent than the mean, a negative one that it is less frequent. Thus 'corpus' occurs 0.0518 times the standard deviation more frequently than the mean.*

Use the scroll bar to scroll through the list past 'corpuscle', 'corpuscular', etc. until you come to 'corpuses'. Click on 'corpuses' to select it and display its frequency and z-score. 'Corpuses' occurs 9 times, with a z-score of –0.0126.

The other form we are interested in, 'corpora', does not appear in the current list of matching words, since it does not begin with the characters 'corpus'.

Click in the input box and delete the final us of 'corpus'. Then click on LOOKUP again. *The longer list which now appears contains some very strange L-words, such as 'corp*' and 'corp-apple'. The word index includes compounds, abbreviations, foreign words, and misprints, clitics and phrasal L-words, as well as cases where two words had no space between them in the source text. The more peculiar L-words rarely occur more than a few times in the corpus, so that for most purposes they can be safely ignored.*

Scroll through the list of matching words until you find 'corpora', and click on it to select it. You will see that 'corpora' occurs 111 times in the BNC, over ten times more often than 'corpuses'. The Latin plural form given by *OED2* is thus clearly the more frequent one.

2.2.2 *Looking for more than one word form using Word Query*

While these figures tell us something of the relative frequency of the two forms, they do not tell us if they are both used over the full range of senses. To compare their uses we must examine the contexts in which they occur.

We shall do this by downloading occurrences of both forms. WORD QUERY allows you to select several entries from a list of matching words and combine them into a single query. After selecting a first item, you simply add other items by holding down the CTRL key when you click on them.

⑦ **Check that you have selected 'corpora' (i.e. that it is highlighted), then scroll down the list of matching words till you find 'corpuses'. Hold down CTRL and click on 'corpuses' to add it to the selection.** The total number of occurrences of 'corpora' and 'corpuses' will now be displayed, along with their combined z-score.

⑧ **Now click on OK to send the query to the server.** *You can also select a group of consecutive items in the list by clicking on the first item and then dragging the mouse, or by then holding down the SHIFT key and clicking on the last of the group.*

The options in the WORD QUERY dialogue box are fully described in 1.3.2 on page 200. If the PATTERN box is checked, SARA interprets the string entered as a pattern, which may include alternatives and wildcards (see 8.2.1 on page 147). This means that if you look up 'corpus' with PATTERN checked, the list will contain only the L-word 'corpus', instead of all the L-words beginning with the characters 'corpus' (for an example, see 3.3.1 on page 83). COPY copies the input string to the Windows clipboard (for examples, see 7.2.1 on page 131). CANCEL leaves the dialogue box without starting a query, while CLEAR deletes any previous input and selections from the dialogue box.

2.2.3   Defining download criteria

Selecting from the solutions   If you have set the Maximum downloads number at 100 in the default Download parameters, the TOO MANY SOLUTIONS dialogue box will be displayed.

Where the number of solutions to the query is smaller than the number specified in the default settings, all the solutions are automatically downloaded and displayed. Where, on the other hand, a greater number of solutions is found, the Too many solutions dialogue box is displayed prior to any downloading.

The dialogue box tells you:

- how many solutions to the query have been found by the server;
- in how many different texts these solutions occur;
- the Maximum downloads number specified as a default under VIEW PREFERENCES (see 1.2.8 on page 54). *The number of solutions found will normally be the same as the total frequency of the selected items in the Word Query dialogue box. It may however differ where a selected word also occurs as part of a phrasal L-word. For instance, while the index lists the frequency of 'corpus' as 724, a Word Query for 'corpus' will find 776 solutions, since the latter will also include occurrences of the phrases 'corpus juris', 'habeas corpus', etc.*

You can choose how many and which of these solutions to download, namely:

- the INITIAL *n* solutions found in the corpus, where *n* is any number specified in the DOWNLOAD HITS box (this is the fastest alternative);

- a RANDOM set of *n* solutions;
- ALL the solutions found;
- only ONE PER TEXT (where the number of texts is greater than the number in the DOWNLOAD HITS box, this alternative can be combined with the INITIAL or RANDOM or DOWNLOAD ALL options). *The* ONE PER TEXT *option discards all but the first solution in any text.*

The number initially displayed in the DOWNLOAD HITS box is always that specified in the Max Downloads box under VIEW PREFERENCES (see 1.2.8 on page 54). You can change this number temporarily by typing a new number in the box, or by clicking on the DOWNLOAD ALL radio button. If the ONE PER TEXT box is checked, clicking on the Download all button will change the number to the number of texts. If it is not, the number will change to the total number of hits.

In this example, we shall use One per text as the criterion for downloading. The total number of solutions found (120) is very much larger than the number of different texts in which they appear (17). This limited *dispersion* in the corpus suggests that 'corpora' and 'corpuses' are — at least in some of their senses — highly specialized: they appear in very few texts, but in those texts they appear on average several times. Given publishers' tendencies to standardize spellings, it seems unlikely that both forms will occur in the same text.

For the moment, we will assume that relatively little information will be lost by downloading only one solution per text, thereby reducing the total number of solutions to 17. We will return to check the validity of this assumption in section 2.3.2 on page 72.

Check the ONE PER TEXT box.

Click on OK (or press ENTER) to start downloading the solutions.

The Query Text and Annotation displays Provided you checked the QUERY and ANNOTATION boxes under VIEW PREFERENCES in 2.1.3 on page 64, the text of the query which was sent to the server will be displayed above the solutions, along with details of any thinning procedure adopted in the TOO MANY SOLUTIONS dialogue box. In addition there will be a blank pane for notes below the query text. The query is shown in the SARA *Corpus Query Language*, or *CQL* for short. *While not necessary for simple searches, you may at some stage want to formulate queries directly in CQL (see 7.2.3 on page 135). Displaying the query text as you use SARA is a convenient way of learning the CQL syntax. Thus you will see that the query finding any instance of 'corpora' or 'corpuses' is expressed as* `"corpora"|"corpuses"`. *Each word form is enclosed in double quotation marks, while the vertical line indicates a disjunction. The thinning procedure is shown as* OPT *(one per text), with the number of downloaded solutions (17) and the total number of hits found on the server (120) in brackets.*

⑪ **Click in the Annotation pane between the query text and the solutions.**
A cursor will appear at the point where you can type in notes. For instance, you might like to note the meaning of the query text. Any annotations can be saved along with the query by using the SAVE option under the FILE menu (or by clicking on the SAVE button on the toolbar: see 2.2.5 on page 70). *You can also copy text to the annotation pane from the Windows clipboard using* SHIFT+INSERT.

⑫ **Click anywhere in the solutions display to leave the Annotation pane.**
You can switch the QUERY TEXT *and* ANNOTATION *displays on and off in the current window from the* QUERY *menu.*

Aligning solutions   If this is your first query since starting SARA, the solutions will be displayed in the *Query1* window.   Provided you checked CONCORDANCE under VIEW PREFERENCES in 2.1.3 on page 64, they will be displayed in Line mode, with the query focus ('corpuses' or 'corpora') highlighted in the centre of each line.

If you glance through the solutions, you will see that all the occurrences of 'corpuses' and 'corpora' are aligned to begin in the same column. You can change the alignment to the centre or to the final character of the query focus using the ALIGN button on the toolbar.

⑬ **Click on the ALIGN button on the toolbar.** You will see that the solutions are now aligned around the central point in the focus, and that the pattern on the ALIGN button on the toolbar has changed to a symbol indicating central alignment.

⑭ **Click again on the ALIGN button to see the third possibility, i.e. right alignment.** The pattern on the button changes, and the solutions are aligned on the final character of the query focus. *Where, as in this example, the query focus varies in length, changing the alignment can be a convenient way of highlighting the patterns immediately preceding or following the query focus. For instance, in the right-aligned display, solutions where the word following the query focus is 'of' are now more clearly identifiable.*

⑮ **Click again on the ALIGN button to return to left alignment.**

2.2.4   Thinning downloaded solutions

With such a small number of solutions it is relatively easy to count the instances of each form and sense by inspection. However we shall take the opportunity to divide them up into groups using the THIN option.

Glancing through the 17 solutions, you will see that two main senses of 'corpuses' or 'corpora' are present:

- collections of texts or knowledge;
- body parts ('corpora lutea' etc.).

There is however also one instance which is a citation from the Latin (with an English gloss), "Ne polluantur corpora. Lest our bodies be polluted". Let us start by discarding this solution, as it is irrelevant to a study of the plural forms of 'corpus' in English.

Click on this solution to select it. The dashed surround shows that it is now the current solution.

Mark this solution by double-clicking on it (or pressing the space bar). The solution will now be displayed in reverse video.

From the QUERY menu, select THIN then REVERSE SELECTION. The list of solutions will be re-displayed, this time without the one you marked. You will see that the total number of solutions indicated on the status bar is now only 16, and that the thinning description in the Query Text pane records this further selection as SEL 16/17. *The THIN menu is fully described in 1.6.3 on page 218. While REVERSE SELECTION keeps the unmarked solutions, deleting marked ones, SELECTION does the opposite, keeping the marked solutions and deleting unmarked ones. RANDOM keeps a specified number of randomly selected solutions, while ONE PER TEXT keeps only the first solution from each source text: these options are analogous to those in the TOO MANY SOLUTIONS dialogue box (see 2.2.3 on page 66), with the difference that using THIN allows you to see all the solutions before reducing their number. The RANDOM and ONE PER TEXT options do not distinguish between marked and unmarked solutions, and any previous marking will be lost in the thinned display.*
You cannot recover solutions once they have been removed by thinning, unless you have saved the query in its previous state (see 2.2.5 on the next page).

We now want to divide the remaining solutions according to the sense of the query focus.

Glance through the solutions to decide whether the 'body part' or 'text collection' sense is the less frequent. Overall, there appear to be fewer solutions with the 'body part' sense.

Scroll through the solutions using the arrow buttons on the toolbar. Press the space bar (or double-click) on all those with the 'body part' sense to mark them. *If you mark a solution by mistake, pressing the space bar or double-clicking a second time will unmark it.*

If you are uncertain of the sense used in a particular solution, click on the CONCORDANCE button on the toolbar to display the solution in Page mode and show a larger amount of context. Click on the

CONCORDANCE button a second time to return to Line display mode.
You may also be able to expand the context even further by double-clicking on
the right mouse button (see 1.2.6 on page 51).

2.2.5   Saving and re-opening queries

You should now have marked all the solutions which have the 'body part' sense.
If you were now to use the SELECTION option under the THIN menu, you
would obtain a display of only these solutions. If instead you used the REVERSE
SELECTION option, you would delete them, obtaining a display of only those
solutions with the 'text collection' sense. We shall now create a second copy
of the solutions in another window, so that by thinning each window using a
different criterion, we can obtain separate displays of the two sense groups. As
we cannot display different sets of solutions for a single query, we must first make
a second copy of the query by saving it with two different names, one for each
window.

(22) **Click on the SAVE button on the toolbar.** The File Save As dialogue box
will be displayed, proposing the name `query1.sqy` for the query.

(23) **Click on OK to save the query.**

(24) **If you are asked whether a preceding file with the same name should
be replaced, click on OK (or press ENTER).** When saving is complete, you
will see the solutions window has been renamed *QUERY1.SQY. Where displayed
solutions correspond to a saved query, the window name is that of the query file, and is
displayed in upper case.*

*SARA can save two kinds of files: Query files, which record queries, and Listing files,
which record solutions (see 8.2.5 on page 154). Unless the defaults are overridden, they
are automatically assigned .SQY and .SGM extensions respectively. To save queries and
solutions for future use, you are advised to use these filetype extensions, but to choose
filenames which will act as appropriate mnemonics.*

You now need to save a second copy of the same query, this time with a
different name.

(25) **Select SAVE AS from the FILE menu.** The File Save As dialogue box will
be displayed once more, again proposing to save the file as *query1.sqy.*

(26) **Type in a new name for the query (such as `query1a`) and click on
OK.** You will see that the title of the current solutions window now shows
the new name. *As well as the text of the query itself, saving a query records the
display options selected at the time (including annotations); any bookmarks (see 10.2.2
on page 181); any thinning selections, whether made when downloading solutions or
subsequently (see 2.2.3 on page 66, 2.2.4 on page 68). Saved queries which were
randomly thinned are re-opened with the same randomization.*

Now re-open your first copy of the query in a new window.

Under the FILE menu, click on QUERY1.SQY to open it. (Alternatively, click on the OPEN button on the toolbar, then select query1.sqy from the FILE OPEN dialogue box). A new window will be opened with the title *QUERY1.SQY*. This new window should contain exactly the same solutions as the other window (*QUERY1A.SQY*). *The other options on the* FILE *menu are described in 1.3 on page 199. These allow you to formulate a* NEW QUERY *of any type; to* CLOSE *the current window; to* PRINT *the current solutions display (one-per-line) or to* PREVIEW *and change the* PRINT SETUP *(see 3.2.3 on page 81); and to* EXIT *from SARA.*

We shall now thin the solutions in each window according to their senses.

From the WINDOW menu, select TILE to display both windows. Unfortunately the solutions are now barely visible, the screen being mainly occupied by the Query Text and Annotation panes. Let us therefore remove these from the display.

Under the QUERY menu, click on QUERY TEXT to uncheck it. The Query Text pane will be removed from the window.

Again under the QUERY menu, uncheck ANNOTATION. The Annotation pane will also be removed from the window, which should now show only the solutions.

Click in the other window to make it the active window.

Following the same procedure as above, remove the Query Text and Annotation panes. You should now be able to see most of the solutions, and to scroll through them using the scroll bar.

In the QUERY1A.SQY window, the solutions with the 'body part' sense are marked. Mark the same solutions in the QUERY1.SQY window by double-clicking on them.

Under the QUERY menu, select THIN followed by SELECTION. This window will now include only the marked solutions — those with the 'body part' sense.

Click in the other window to make it the active window (or select it from the WINDOW menu).

Under the QUERY menu, select THIN followed by REVERSE SELECTION. This window will now include only the unmarked solutions — those with the 'text collection' sense.

You will see that the solutions in this window contain instances of both 'corpuses' and 'corpora', whereas the solutions in the other window only contain instances of 'corpora'.

Results   The plural 'corpuses' occurs only in the 'text collection' sense in the BNC. While the numbers involved are too small to draw reliable conclusions, it is nonetheless interesting that the dictionaries cited offer no information on this point.

2.3   Discussion and suggestions for further work

2.3.1   *Phrase Query or Word Query?*

We have so far seen two different ways of formulating a query. While in many cases either procedure can be used, note that only PHRASE QUERY allows you to:

- make a query *case-sensitive* (for instance to include or exclude proper names: see 1.3.2 on page 61, 10.2.4 on page 184);
- search the *text headers* as well as the texts (for instance to include occurrences of keywords, or of a particular author or publisher name);
- search for multi–word phrases (see 4.2.1 on page 87);
- search for orthographic words which are not treated as L-words in the word index (e.g. 'polloi', which only appears in the index under 'hoi polloi'; 'don't' or 'gonna', which are listed under the clitics 'do', 'n't', 'gon' and 'na'; etc.);
- specify punctuation in the query (see 10.2.7 on page 189).

Only WORD QUERY, on the other hand, allows you to:

- generate a list of words matching a pattern from which to make selections (see 2.2.1 on page 64, 8.2.1 on page 147);
- include multiple selections in a query (see 2.2.3 on page 66);
- consult the index to see whether a word occurs in the corpus and with what frequency;
- consult the index to see whether a phrase or clitic is treated as a single L-word.

These last two options are illustrated in the problems in the next section.

2.3.2   *Some similar problems*

The dispersion of different forms   In the task above, we only examined one solution from each text, assuming that no text would use both of the plurals of 'corpus'. Is this in fact the case? Are publishers always consistent? *Carry out a* WORD QUERY *for 'corpuses', then thin the solutions to* ONE PER TEXT *and note their number. Then carry out a second query for 'corpora'. You can either download one solution per text, or simply read off the number of texts containing solutions from the Too many solutions dialogue box.*

The sum of the two numbers is 18 — whereas the number of texts found in the query in 2.2.3 on page 66 was only 17. So there is in fact one text in the corpus where both plural forms are used. You can find out which one it is by comparing the text identifier codes in the two sets of solutions. If you look at the bibliographic data for this text using the SOURCE *option, you can also discover its publisher.*

Strong and weak verb forms   Some English verbs have both strong and weak past tense or past participle forms, which may not be used with the same frequency. In the one million word LOB corpus of British English from the early 1960s, for instance, the strong form 'dreamt' occurs only once, whereas the weak form 'dreamed' occurs 14 times (Hofland & Johansson 1982). Does the BNC confirm that 'dreamt' is less common than 'dreamed'? What about 'knelt' and 'kneeled'? *These instances of strong and weak forms are chosen deliberately. In contrast with 'burned/burnt', say, 'dreamed' and 'dreamt' and 'kneeled' and 'knelt' have clearly distinct pronunciations, so their frequencies should not be influenced by the spelling preferences of the transcribers of the spoken BNC texts. They are also only used as verbs, unlike 'burned' and 'burnt', which may have different relative frequencies as verbs and as adjectives.*

If you use WORD QUERY *to look them up in the word index, you will find substantial differences in the relative frequencies of both 'dreamed' and 'dreamt' (776:284) and 'kneeled' and 'knelt' (24:546). Being derived from a far larger corpus, these figures probably provide a more reliable estimate of relative frequency than those derived from LOB. The LOB figures are unfortunately too small to warrant hypotheses as to whether the relative frequencies of 'dreamed' and 'dreamt' have changed since the 1960s.*

A topical reference: 'annus horribilis'   In her 1992 Christmas speech, Queen Elizabeth referred to that year as an 'annus horribilis', punning on the Latin expression 'annus mirabilis'. Look up both of these expressions in the corpus, and find out which is more frequent, and what the uses of each refer to. *If you look up the string* annus *using* WORD QUERY, *you will find that 'annus', 'annus horribilis' and 'annus mirabilis' are all present in the word index, with a combined total of 45 occurrences. As you will discover, there are good reasons to include all three forms in the query, which you can do either by selecting all of them, or just 'annus'. Download all the solutions, then use the* THIN *option to remove those which are irrelevant.*

'Annus horribilis' (including associated misspelled variants) is the more common form, but with a much narrower range of reference — virtually always alluding to the Queen's speech, and very often in quotation marks. This illustrates how frequency may be affected by the topicality of a particular event at the moment when the corpus texts were created, and may or may not reflect wider trends in the use of the language.

3 When is ajar not a door?

3.1 The problem: words and their company

3.1.1 *Collocation*

The playground riddle "When is a door not a door? — When it's a jar" plays on
the fact that the word 'ajar' is closely associated with the word 'door' in English.
Intuitively, we would therefore expect 'ajar' to co-occur with 'door' in texts,
or *collocate* with it, with greater than chance frequency (see 1.3.3 on page 13).
However, not only doors can be ajar. *OED2* defines this sense of the word as
follows:

```
Of a door or window: On the turn, slightly opened.
[...]
1708 Swift Abol. Chr. Wks. 1755 II. i. 90 Opening
a few wickets, and leaving them at jar.
1786 Beckford Vathek (1868) 92 With a large door
in it standing ajar.
1815 Scott Ld. of Isles v. iii, But the dim lattice
is ajar.
```

The examples here indicate some other possible referents. They also indicate
that 'ajar' may occur either as a complement of *copular* verbs such as 'be'
and 'stand' ('the door stood ajar'), or of *complex transitive* verbs such as 'leave'
('he left the door ajar'). They provide no information, on the other hand,
concerning possible adverbial modifiers indicating, for example, degree (does
one say 'fractionally ajar'?). Nor do they indicate possible metaphorical uses.
And there is no information concerning the relative frequency of alternative
referents.

OED2 also gives a second sense of 'ajar':

```
In a jarring state, out of harmony, at odds.
1860 Hawthorne Marble Farm (1879) I. xiii. 129 Any
accident.. that puts an individual ajar with
the world.
1877 H. Martineau Autobiog. I. 83 My temper was
so thoroughly ajar.
```

This sense would seem to be distinguished from the first by having different
collocates — we would probably not speak of 'putting' a door ajar, or of a door
being 'thoroughly' ajar.

This task looks at 'ajar' in the corpus to see:

- in which of these two senses 'ajar' is mainly used;
- what things tend to be 'ajar';
- in what verb complement structures 'ajar' appears;
- what adverbs modify 'ajar'.

3.1.2 Highlighted features
This task shows you:

- how to investigate collocates and their frequencies using the COLLOCATION option;
- how to highlight collocates adjacent to the query focus using the SORT option;
- how to PRINT solutions in one-per-line (KWIC) format;
- how to use the PATTERN option in WORD QUERY to look up a particular word-form in the index.

It assumes you already know how to:

- adjust the default display settings using the View Preferences option (see 1.2.8 on page 54);
- carry out a Phrase Query (see 1.2.5 on page 51) and a Word Query (see 2.2.2 on page 65);
- adjust downloading procedure in the Too many solutions dialogue box (see 2.2.3 on page 66);
- align displayed solutions (see 2.2.3 on page 68).

3.1.3 Before you start
Log on to SARA and wait for the *Sara-BNC* window to be displayed (see 1.2.2 on page 49). Using the PREFERENCES option under the VIEW menu, set the default settings as follows:

MAX DOWNLOAD LENGTH	400 characters
MAX DOWNLOADS	200
FORMAT	Plain
SCOPE	Paragraph
VIEW: QUERY and ANNOTATION	checked
CONCORDANCE	checked
BROWSER: SHOW TAGS	unchecked

3.2   Procedure

3.2.1   *Using the Collocation option*

The COLLOCATION option allows you to find out exactly how often a particular word occurs in a set of solutions within a given number of words on either side of the query focus.

First, let us find all the occurrences of 'ajar' in the corpus.

(1)   **Click on the WORD QUERY button to display the Word Query dialogue box.**

(2)   **Type in the string** ajar **and click on LOOKUP.**

(3)   **Click on 'ajar' in the matching words display to select it, then click on OK to send the query to the server.**

(4)   **Wait for the solutions to be displayed in the *Query1* window.** There are 133 occurrences of 'ajar', so it may take some time to download them all.

(5)   **Scroll through the concordance display to look at the solutions.** You will see that 'door' occurs in a large number of them.

Now let us find out just how often 'door' appears as a collocate.

(6)   **From the QUERY menu, select COLLOCATION.** The Collocation dialogue box will be displayed. The box initially shows:

- the name of the current query (*Query 1*);

- the number of hits on which collocation frequencies will be calculated. *Where all the solutions to the query have not been downloaded, the USE DOWNLOADED HITS ONLY option will be available (see 3.2.4 on page 82);*

- an empty COLLOCATE window, where you can type or paste in words to find out how often they collocate with the query focus;

- the collocation SPAN, i.e. the maximum number of words from the focus within which an occurrence is to be counted as a collocation.

(7)   **Click in the COLLOCATE window and type in** door. *The collocate must be a single L-word which is included in the Sara word index, a single punctuation symbol, or an SGML element (entered between angle brackets). Phrases or patterns will return zero scores.*

(8)   **Click on the CALCULATE button (or press ENTER).** The word 'door' will appear listed beneath the COLLOCATE window. The numbers in the display indicate:

- the *collocation frequency*, i.e. the number of times the collocate appears within the selected span in the solutions (25);

- the *collocation ratio*, i.e. the ratio of the collocation frequency to the number of solutions (0.19 = 19%).

Assuming that 'ajar' always follows its referent (we do not say 'an ajar door'), this means that almost one in five 'ajar's is immediately preceded by the word 'door' (as in 'he left the door ajar'). *Particularly frequent collocates (especially function words such as 'the', 'of', 'that' etc.) may occur more than once within the span in a particular solution. In such cases the collocation ratio may be greater than 1.00. Any such cases of upwards collocation (Sinclair 1991) will be displayed in the highlight colour.*

Changing the collocation span   A glance at the solutions shows that 'door' may also appear several words before 'ajar'. To include cases where 'door' is a non-adjacent collocate, you must increase the span within which collocation is calculated.

Click in the SPAN box and change the value to 3, then click on the CALCULATE button. You will see that the numbers for 'door' have changed to 71 and 0.53. In other words over half the solutions for 'ajar' have 'door' as a collocate within a span of 3 words on each side of the focus. *The collocation span may be varied up to a maximum of 9, i.e. 9 words to each side of the first word of the query focus. Span is calculated in L-words (see 2.2.1 on page 64); punctuation symbols also count as words. The default span value is 1, i.e. one word to either side of the first word of the query focus.*

While tending to increase collocation frequency, increasing the span decreases the probability that this frequency indicates a strong association between the collocate and the focus, since it makes it more likely that these occur in different clauses, sentences or even paragraphs dealing with different topics. For instance, were you to use a span of 7 or more to calculate occurrences of 'OED2' as a collocate of 'next' in this sentence, you would also include the 'OED2' from the first sentence of the next section.

Investigating other potential collocates   The *OED2* entry (see 3.1.1 on page 74) suggests that nouns which are semantically similar to 'door' may also collocate with 'ajar'. You can investigate these by calculating the collocation frequencies of words which you have observed in the solutions or expect to be present in them.

Click in the COLLOCATE window and type window. **Then click in the SPAN box and set the value to 9, so as to maximize collocation frequency.** You will see that the collocate list now contains both 'door' and 'window', in alphabetical order. Notice that the collocation frequency and ratio for 'door' have been recalculated for the new span. 'Window' collocates very much less frequently with 'ajar' than 'door' does: only 5 times, or in a ratio of

0.04, as opposed to 108 times (ratio 0.81) for 'door'. *You will also notice that the collocate 'door' is now displayed in a different colour. This is because its collocation ratio is close to being that of an upward collocate (between 0.80 and 1.0).*

Printing collocation data   So far we have only considered the singular forms 'door' and 'window'. From the point of view of understanding the semantic categories which can be 'ajar', it may also be relevant to check the collocation frequencies of the plural forms.

⑪   **Type** windows **in the collocate window, and reduce the span to 3. Then click on the CALCULATE button.** 'Windows' collocates only once with 'ajar' in this span; the collocation frequency of 'window' is reduced to 4.

⑫   **Now type the form** doors **and click on CALCULATE.** 'Doors' occurs 5 times in this span.

At the end of this task, we shall compare the collocation frequencies of 'door' and 'window' to see whether they differ significantly. To obtain a record of these numbers, let us print the current contents of the Collocation dialogue box.

⑬   **Click on the PRINT button.**   The Windows Print dialogue box will be displayed.

⑭   **Check that the printer indicated is available, and click on OK to print.** *In the current release of the software, this is the only way of saving the results of a collocation analysis.*

3.2.2   Investigating collocates using the Sort option

Other words which come into mind as possible collocates of 'ajar' are degree adverbs such as 'a little', and copular verbs such as 'be', 'stand', etc. As the COLLOCATION option only allows you to investigate specific words, you will probably need to return to the concordance display in order to identify further words which may recur as collocates.

One way to highlight such words is to use the SORT option. When solutions to a query are first downloaded, they are displayed in the order in which they appear in the corpus. Using SORT enables you to re-order solutions, grouping those which have similar patterns.

⑮   **Click on CLOSE to leave the Collocation dialogue box and return to the concordance display.** *Closing the Collocation dialogue box does not delete its contents: re-selecting COLLOCATION will return you to the previous display.*

⑯   **Select SORT from the QUERY menu to display the Sort dialogue box.** *SORT is only available from a solution display in Line mode.*

The SORT option allows you to specify two sets of criteria, or *keys*, by which downloaded solutions are to be sorted. For each key you can choose:

DIRECTION whether to sort the solutions by the:

> **LEFT** the words which precede the query focus;
>
> **CENTRE** the query focus itself (this is relevant where the query is satisfied by a range of different forms, as in the 'corpora/corpuses' example in the last task: see 2.2.2 on page 65);
>
> **RIGHT** the words which follow the query focus.

ORDER whether to display the sorted solutions in:

> **ASCENDING order** (A-Z, so that 'antelope' precedes 'zebra');
>
> **DESCENDING order** (Z-A, so that 'zebra' precedes 'antelope').

SPAN the number of words to consider in sorting. The maximum span is 5 words. With this span, when sorting by the LEFT, Sara will discriminate between solutions which have the same four words preceding the focus, but the fifth preceding word is different.

The default values for both Primary and Secondary keys are for left sorting, in ascending order, with a span of one word — meaning that solutions will be ordered alphabetically by the word immediately to the left of the query focus. The Secondary key is used where the Primary key does not discriminate between solutions. *The COLLATING options in the Sort dialogue box are fully described in 1.6.2 on page 217. They determine the alphabet which will be used in sorting. ASCII orders words orthographically using the ASCII character sequence, roughly corresponding to A-Z followed by a-z. IGNORE CASE (the default collating order) instead treats upper and lower case letters as identical. IGNORE ACCENTS uses the ASCII sequence, but treats accented and unaccented letters as identical. POS orders words according to their part-of-speech codes rather than their orthographic form; this option is only available when solutions are displayed in POS format (see 7.2.4 on page 137).*

In the current query, using the default sort and collating values will mean that 'door ajar' will precede 'window ajar', but that 'a door ajar' and 'the door ajar' will not be distinguished. Solutions in which particular words recur directly preceding 'ajar' will also be grouped together.

Click on the SORT button and wait for SARA to display the sorted concordance.

Check that the solutions are aligned by the left of the query focus, clicking on the ALIGN button if necessary (see 2.2.3 on page 68).

(19)   **Use the scroll bar to scroll through the solutions.** You will see that the solutions where 'door' directly precedes 'ajar' now form a clearly visible group. You should also see some other groups of solutions where the same word recurs prior to 'ajar' — for instance 'slightly ajar' and 'left ajar'.

Collocate positions   Many collocates have fixed positions, for instance immediately before or after the word they collocate with. While we have seen that the distance between 'door' and 'ajar' varies, the positions of other collocates of 'ajar' may be fixed. For instance, do 'slightly' and 'left' always directly precede 'ajar'? Used together, the SORT and COLLOCATION options can provide answers to such questions.

(20)   **Count the number of occurrences of 'slightly ajar' in the sorted solutions display.**

(21)   **Select COLLOCATION from the QUERY menu to re-display the Collocation dialogue box.**

(22)   **Find the collocation frequency of 'slightly' in a span of 1, then of 3, 5, and 7 words.** The collocation frequency is 15 in each case. This is also the same as the number of 'slightly ajar's. 'Slightly' thus appears to have a fixed position as a collocate of 'ajar', directly preceding it.

(23)   **Click on CLOSE to return to the solutions display.**

(24)   **Repeat the previous four steps for 'left', increasing the span progressively from 1 to 7 words.** You will find that it may occur at any point within a span of 5 words from 'ajar'.

Phrasal collocates   Sorting also provides a useful heuristic to identify phrases, rather than just single words, which collocate with a particular query focus. For instance, in some of the solutions where 'door' precedes 'ajar', 'door ajar' forms part of a larger recurrent phrase.

(25)   **Select SORT from the QUERY menu.** The SORT dialogue box will be displayed, showing the selections of the last sort performed.

(26)   **Change the Primary key span to 3, then click on SORT.** The solutions will be re-sorted, grouping those where the same three words precede 'ajar'.

(27)   **Scroll through the solutions, and make a list of cases where three or more share the same two or more words preceding 'ajar'.** Your list should include 'leave the door ajar', 'the Gates of Heaven Ajar', 'a little ajar', 'a door stood ajar', 'it was ajar', etc.

(28)   **Using the COLLOCATION option, vary the span to see if any of the words in these sequences, such as 'gates' and 'little', always occur in the same position.** You will find that 'little' only occurs as the first word to the left of 'ajar'.

Click on CLOSE to close the Collocation dialogue box. *As well as using* SORT *to highlight collocations where the query focus forms part of a recurrent phrase, you can also highlight cases where the query focus forms part of a recurrent sequence of word classes, or colligations (Sinclair 1991), by sorting solutions with* POS *rather than* ASCII *or* IGNORE CASE *collating (see 7.2.4 on page 137).*

3.2.3 Printing solutions

Other senses of 'ajar' Is the second sense of 'ajar' provided by *OED2*, that of 'out of harmony', present in these solutions?

Rather than scrolling through the sorted solutions, looking for instances which might have this meaning, you may find it easier to work with a printout.

Click on the PRINT button on the toolbar (or select PRINT from the FILE menu). The Print dialogue box will be displayed, showing your currently selected Windows printer.

If your printer supports landscape orientation, but this is not currently selected, click on SETUP to display the Windows PRINT SETUP dialogue box. *You can also access* PRINT SETUP *at any time from the* FILE *menu.*

Click on the LANDSCAPE orientation radio button, then on OK to return to the Print dialogue box. *Landscape orientation allows a larger context to be printed for each solution.*

Click on OK to begin printing. The solutions in the window will be printed as a one-per-line (KWIC) concordance, corresponding to Line display mode in the format currently selected. The corresponding text identifier and sentence number for each solution will be printed at the beginning of each line. *You can get a rough idea of the appearance of a printout with the current settings by selecting* PRINT PREVIEW *from the* FILE *menu.*

Now examine the solutions.

Mark any solutions which look as if they may involve the 'out of harmony' sense of 'ajar'. If you do not have a printout, double-click on them in the Line display. You can safely ignore those where 'ajar' is preceded by 'door', 'left', 'slightly', 'stood', etc.

Check any candidates by switching to Page display mode to see a wider context. You will see there are no solutions where 'ajar' is used with the 'out of harmony' sense, unless you count it to be implied in the following: "The court accepted that the minister would not be expected to hear such representations as if he were a judge. The minister would not be expected to approach the matter with an empty mind, but his mind should, in the words, of the court, at least be ajar."

3.2.4   Investigating collocations without downloading: are men as hand-some as women are beautiful?

In looking at collocates of 'ajar', we were able to download all the solutions and study these individually. For queries which have large numbers of solutions, it may be impractical to download all of them, but it is still possible to use SARA to calculate the frequencies of particular collocates in all the solutions.

Taking the corpus as a whole, the collocates of the words 'women' and 'men' seem likely to differ. For instance, we might expect the former to be 'beautiful', but the latter to be 'handsome'. In this section we look to see if the BNC confirms this stereotype.

(36)   **Click on the PHRASE QUERY button to open the Phrase Query dialogue box.**

(37)   **Type in the string men and click on OK to send the query to the server.** The Too many solutions dialogue box will be displayed, showing that there are 38,892 solutions.

To investigate the frequencies of particular collocates in these solutions, it is only necessary to download one of them.

(38)   **Change the DOWNLOAD HITS number to 1, then click on OK.** Only the first solution in the corpus will be downloaded.

(39)   **Select COLLOCATION from the QUERY menu.** The Collocation dialogue box will be displayed, showing the number of hits for the query as 1.

(40)   **Uncheck the USE DOWNLOADED HITS ONLY box.** The number of hits indicated will change to the total number of solutions that were found to this query, i.e. 38,892.

(41)   **Type the string beautiful in the collocate window and click on the CALCULATE button (or press ENTER).** The collocation frequency and ratio will be shown.

(42)   **Now enter the string handsome in the collocate window and repeat the operation.** You will see that men appear more frequently handsome than beautiful in the corpus.

(43)   **Increase the span to 3, then 5, then 7 words.** You will notice that at a span of 5 words, 'beautiful' becomes a more common collocate than 'handsome'. While 'beautiful' is less closely associated with 'men' than is 'handsome', it is a much more common word overall.

(44)   **Repeat the procedure for 'women'.** You will see that 'handsome' is much less common as a collocate than 'beautiful'. Again, notice that increasing the span for which collocations are calculated has a proportionally greater effect on the more weakly associated collocate: for 'women' the proportion of 'beautiful'

to 'handsome' is, with a span of 1, 70:2; with a span of 5, 105:10; with a span of 9, 134:22.

The numbers of occurrences of 'women' and 'men' in the corpus are very similar, but there are clear differences in their collocates, men being more rarely beautiful and women more rarely handsome.

3.3   Discussion and suggestions for further work

3.3.1   *The significance of collocations*

By using the COLLOCATION option, we have seen that things ajar are generally doors, but also occasionally windows and gates (and even minds and lips!), which are, are left, or stand slightly or a little ajar; that men are rarely beautiful and women rarely handsome. To assess the significance of these results, however, we must consider both the collocation ratios of these words with the query focus, and their relative frequencies in the corpus overall. Fairly frequent recurrence of a relatively rare word as a collocate is likely to be of greater significance than the very frequent recurrence of a very common word, such as 'the' or 'of'. Thus, while we have seen there are very many more beautiful women than there are handsome ones in the corpus (70:2 with a span of 1), we cannot judge whether the former is a stronger association without taking into consideration the fact that 'handsome' is a much less common word in English.

You can get a rough idea of the relative significance of the collocation ratios of two words in a particular set of solutions by comparing these with their z-scores (see 2.2.1 on page 64). For instance, the collocation ratios of 'door' and 'window' with 'ajar', for a span of 3 words, were 0.53 and 0.03 respectively (see 3.2.1 on page 77). Now use WORD QUERY to find out their z-scores.

Click on the WORD QUERY button on the toolbar.

In the Word Query dialogue box, type in the string door and check the PATTERN box before clicking on LOOKUP. If the PATTERN box is checked, only the word which precisely matches the string 'door' will be listed, rather than all the words which begin with those characters.

Select 'door' in the matching words list and read off its z-score. 'door' has a z-score of 2.2725 in the corpus.

Do the same for 'window'. 'window' has a z-score of 0.9408.

Divide the collocation ratio for each word by its z-score. 'door' has a much stronger collocational link with 'ajar' than 'window' does (0.238 vs 0.032).

Corpus linguistics has developed a variety of methods for assessing collocational significance. The best known is probably the *mutual information* score (Church & Hanks 1990), which compares the frequency of co-occurrence of two words in a given span with their predicted frequency of co–occurrence, i.e. that which would be expected were these words each randomly distributed in the corpus. Mutual information can be calculated using the following formula (Stubbs 1995):

```
I = log2 ((f(n,c) x N)/(f(n) x f(c))
```

where `f(n,c)` is the collocation frequency, `f(n)` is the frequency of the node word (the query focus), `f(c)` is the frequency of the collocate, and `N` is the number of words in the corpus.

For instance, using WORD QUERY to look up the overall frequencies in the corpus, the mutual information scores for 'men' and 'handsome', and for 'women' and 'beautiful' in a span of 3 can be calculated as follows:

'handsome/men'

- f(n,c) = 23 (the collocational frequency of 'handsome' with 'men' in a span of 3: see 3.2.4 on page 82);
- f(n) = 1683 (the overall frequency of 'handsome');
- f(c) = 38,892 (the overall frequency of 'men');
- N = 100,000,000 (the approximate total number of words in the BNC);
- I = log2 ((23 x 100,000,000)/(1683 x 36,892)) = log2 (35.1) = 5.13.

'beautiful/women'

- f(n,c) = 92 (the collocational frequency of 'beautiful' with 'women' in a span of 3: see 3.2.4 on page 82);
- f(n) = 8670 (the overall frequency of 'beautiful');
- f(c) = 39,916 (the overall frequency of 'women');
- N = 100,000,000 (the approximate total number of words in the BNC);
- I = log2 ((92 x 100,000,000)/(8670 x 39,916)) = log2 (26.6) = 4.75.

It thus emerges that 'handsome' and 'men' have a marginally higher mutual information score than 'beautiful' and 'women'. Church and Hanks (1990) suggest that for a span of 3 words on either side of the focus, a mutual information score greater than 3 may indicate a significant collocational link. The formula should not however be relied on where the collocates are relatively infrequent — as a rule of thumb, where the product of their individual frequencies is less than the size of the corpus. For this reason, in the case just examined it would have been more prudent to also include collocations of 'beautiful' and 'handsome' with the singular forms 'man' and 'woman' before making the calculation.

3.3.2 Some similar problems

Time immemorial How often does 'immemorial' have 'time' as a collocate, and is this always in the phrase 'time immemorial'? *Use* WORD QUERY *to download all 81 occurrences of 'immemorial' in the corpus. Calculate the collocation ratio of 'time' with a span of 1, and then increase the span to see if the collocation ratio also increases. (As collocation span is calculated on either side of the query focus, you should also sort all the solutions by the first word to the right in order to make sure that there are no cases where 'time' follows rather than precedes 'immemorial'.)*

'Time' collocates with 'immemorial' 45 times within a span of 1, so this is quite the most common use of the latter word. Increasing the span to 9 only increases the collocation frequency by 1 (to 46), suggesting that the position of 'time' as a collocate is fixed.

Wild things Which are more commonly wild in the corpus: animals or flowers? *As there are over 5000 occurrences of 'wild', you should download the minimum number of solutions, and uncheck the* USE DOWNLOADED HITS ONLY *box.*

'Flowers' and 'animals' collocate with 'wild' with almost identical frequency in a span of 1, but at wider spans, 'animals' becomes the more frequent, reflecting its higher z-score. The singular 'animal' is more frequent than the singular 'flower' at all spans, but both are far less common than the plural forms.

The Clapham omnibus How frequently do 'Clapham' and 'omnibus' occur in collocation? What longer phrasal collocates appear in the solutions? *In order to examine phrasal collocates, you will have to download all the solutions. As Sara can take a long time to download and sort, you should generally aim to keep numbers as low as possible. If you first use* WORD QUERY *to look up the frequencies of both 'clapham' and 'omnibus', you can then send the query for the less frequent form, downloading all the solutions and then calculating the collocation frequency of the other. Sorting the solutions using the 5 words to the left as Primary key, and the 5 words to the right as Secondary key will group, inter alia, occurrences of the phrase 'the man on the Clapham omnibus'.*

Mad hatters What proportion of BNC hatters are mad? *Carry out one* WORD QUERY *for 'hatter' and another for 'hatters', and see if their collocation ratios with 'mad' are different. You should use a span of several words if you are to include cases of 'mad as (a) hatter(s)' as well as 'mad hatter(s)': varying the span from 1 to 4 should provide an indication of the relative frequencies of these two forms.*

There are only two cases where 'hatters' has 'mad' as a collocate, and both of them appear to be misprints of 'hatter's'. The singular 'hatter', on the other hand, has 'mad' as a collocate from 28 to 44 percent of the time, according to the span selected. There thus appears to be a strong collocational link for the singular form: for a span of 3 there are 26 occurrences, with a mutual information score of over 13 (see 3.3.1 on page 83). And this is excluding the two cases misprinted as 'hatters' (not to mention a further 'loopy' one).

4   A query too far

4.1   The problem: variation in phrases

4.1.1   A first example: 'the horse's mouth'

Many idiomatic phrases occur in environments which, while less fixed in form than the phrase itself, vary relatively little. Consider 'a stone's throw'. You may 'live within a stone's throw', but perhaps not 'go a stone's throw from here'; you may live 'a stone's throw away', but probably not 'a stone's throw round the corner'. Accounts of idioms in dictionaries rarely describe such limitations, giving at most a few examples of environments they consider typical. The *Cambridge International* and *Collins COBUILD* dictionaries, for instance, illustrate the phrase 'from the horse's mouth' with the examples "hear something from the horse's mouth" and "straight from the horse's mouth". These examples suggest that 'hear' and 'straight' are frequent *collocates* of 'from the horse's mouth' (the *Longman Dictionary of Contemporary English* in fact lists the expression as 'straight from the horse's mouth'). This task examines the BNC to find out what parts of the phrase appear to be fixed, and the range of the environments in which it occurs.

4.1.2   A second example: 'a bridge too far'

Even relatively fixed parts of an idiomatic phrase can occasionally be varied, often for ironic or humorous effect. A headline in *The Guardian* in July 1995 referred to a Bosnian peace conference as 'a fudge too far'. Native speakers of English will recognize this as a punning variant of 'a bridge too far', playing on the latter idiom's meaning of an overambitious objective. 'A bridge too far' is absent from the dictionaries mentioned, and even were it present, we would probably not expect to find variants like 'fudge' illustrated. The second part of this task uses the BNC to investigate the range of such variants.

4.1.3   Highlighted features

This task shows you:

- how to look for occurrences of a phrase using PHRASE QUERY;
- how to look for variant forms of a phrase using the ANYWORD wildcard character;
- how to look for alternative forms of a phrase using the QUERY BUILDER;
- how to edit queries for re-use using the EDIT option on the QUERY menu;
- how to sort solutions to highlight variant forms and environments using PRIMARY and SECONDARY keys.

It assumes you already know how to:

- adjust default settings using the View Preferences option (see 1.2.8 on page 54);
- find occurrences of a word using Phrase Query and Word Query (see 1.2.5 on page 51, 2.2.1 on page 64);
- look up the frequency of a word in the SARA index using the Word Query Pattern option (see 3.3.1 on page 83);
- adjust downloading procedure in the Too many solutions dialogue box (see 2.2.3 on page 66);
- mark and thin solutions (see 2.2.4 on page 68);
- sort solutions using a Primary key (see 3.2.2 on page 78).

4.1.4 Before you start

Log on to SARA and wait for the *SARA-bnc* window to be displayed. Using the VIEW menu PREFERENCES option, set the default settings as follows:

MAX DOWNLOAD LENGTH	400 characters
MAX DOWNLOADS	50
FORMAT	Plain
SCOPE	Automatic
VIEW: QUERY and ANNOTATION	checked
CONCORDANCE	checked
BROWSER: SHOW TAGS	unchecked

4.2 Procedure

4.2.1 Looking for phrases using Phrase Query

To investigate variation in the form and environment of a phrase, we must decide which features of the phrase to treat as fixed, and which as potentially variable. All the dictionaries cited in 4.1.1 on the facing page treat 'from the horse's mouth' as a fixed sequence. Should we therefore design the query to look for occurrences of 'from the horse's mouth', 'the horse's mouth', 'the horse's', or 'the X's mouth'? The first of these options will reduce the risk of spurious solutions, but at the cost of excluding all variation within the sequence. The third and fourth options will capture such variation, but risk finding many spurious solutions which have nothing to do with the idiom, such as 'the horse's bridle' or 'the patient's mouth'. In this example, we shall start from the most restrictive option (maximizing *precision*), and then progressively relax it so as to increase *recall*.

Formulating the Phrase Query   You have already seen how to use PHRASE QUERY to look for a word in the corpus (see 1.2.5 on page 51). As its name suggests, Phrase Query also accepts a sequence of words as input. Any number of words may be given, but the query cannot exceed 200 characters in total length.

(1) **Click on the PHRASE QUERY button to display the Phrase Query dialogue box.**

(2) **Type in the string** from the horse's mouth

(3) **Click on OK (or press ENTER) and wait for SARA to download the solutions in the *Query1* window.** There are 9 solutions.

(4) **Look through these solutions to check that they all involve metaphorical uses of the phrase, rather than literal references to veterinary dentistry.** *Assuming you have checked* QUERY *in the* VIEW PREFERENCES *option (see 4.1.4 on the preceding page), you will also see the text of the query displayed in CQL (Corpus Query Language) format. It reads:* 'from the horse\'s mouth'. *The backslash symbol indicates that the apostrophe following it has a literal, not a parenthetical function.*

If you want to search for occurrences of possessive or other contracted forms (such as 'can't', 'wanna' and 'you'd've'), you must use PHRASE QUERY *rather than* WORD QUERY, *since these forms are not listed in the word index, other than under their component clitics (see 2.2.1 on page 64). You may type such forms into the Phrase Query dialogue box either as one word or else separated by spaces, e.g.* you 'd 've. *A list of contracted forms which are treated as multiple L-words in the BNC is given in the* BNC Users' Reference Guide.

Looking for variants: the Query Edit option   Now let us look for possible variants of 'from the horse's mouth'. Rather than typing in a new query, you may find it easier to modify the current one. You can do this using the EDIT option under the QUERY menu.

First let us remove the word 'from'.

(5) **Select QUERY then EDIT.** You will be returned to the Phrase Query dialogue box, still showing the current query.

(6) **Click on the beginning of the string and use the DELETE key to cancel the word** from.

(7) **Click on OK to send the revised query to the server, and wait for the solutions to be downloaded.** The number of solutions displayed will increase to 20. *Note that these solutions replace the previous ones in the* Query1 *window. If you wish to keep the previous solutions, you should design a new query rather than editing the current one.*

Scroll through the solutions to see what words other than 'from' appear before the query focus, and whether these solutions involve literal or metaphorical uses of 'the horse's mouth'. You should find that as well as several literal uses ('flies enter the horse's mouth'), there are also some new metaphorical ones with prepositions other than 'from', such as 'go to the horse's mouth'.

From these 20 solutions, let us now remove the literal horses, and sort the metaphorical ones according to the words which precede them.

Double-click on the literal solutions to mark them, and use THIN then REVERSE SELECTION to remove them from the list.
Use the SORT option to sort the remaining solutions by the left with a span of 3.

This will group together several phrasal collocates found to the left of 'the horse's mouth' — 'heard it from', 'straight from', and 'go to'. Most of the solutions appear to follow either one of these patterns or a combination of them (such as 'go straight to the horse's mouth').

Looking for further variants The first word in the original phrase, the preposition 'from', thus appears to be variable. Is there any indication in the corpus that the final word of the phrase, 'mouth', may also vary?

Select QUERY then EDIT. You will be returned to the Phrase Query dialogue box.
Click on the beginning of the input string and add the word from **at the beginning, then delete the word** mouth **from the end. Then click on OK to send the query to the server.** 18 solutions will be displayed.

Now see whether any of these solutions involve metaphorical uses.

Sort the solutions by the right with a span of 3, in order to group them according to the words following the query focus. There appear to be no metaphorical uses other than with 'mouth'.

Variants within the phrase: the Anyword wildcard We have so far considered variation on the boundaries of the original phrase: initial prepositions other than 'from', and final parts of the body other than 'mouth'. The results suggest that 'mouth' is fixed, but that 'from' varies. However we have not yet considered whether the central elements of the phrase may also vary. For example, are there any variants of 'horse', such as 'from the cow's mouth'?

You can investigate this issue by formulating a PHRASE QUERY which contains an empty slot in the place of the word 'horse'. The slot is represented by the underline character _. This is an *Anyword* wildcard character, which will match any L-word in the word index.

(14) **Select EDIT from the QUERY menu.** The Phrase Query dialogue box will be displayed.

(15) **Type in the string** the _ 's mouth **(be careful to follow the underline character with a space).** *More than one Anyword character may be used in the same Phrase Query, but the string cannot begin or end with one. The underline must be preceded and followed by a space.*

Searching for the Anyword character is generally faster than searching for a specific but very frequent word. For example, the query stone _ crows *is very much faster than* stone the crows, *because the latter involves processing all of the several million occurrences of 'the' in the corpus. However, in the current example it is not possible to avoid doing this, since 'the' is the first word of the phrase, and an Anyword character can only be used in the middle of a Phrase Query string.*

(16) **Click on OK to send the query to the server.** The Too many solutions dialogue box will eventually be displayed, stating that there are 146 solutions in 116 texts.

Sorting with dual keys   Given the relatively large number of solutions, we will download and sort only a random selection, in order to get an idea whether variants of the idiomatic phrase are at all frequent.

(17) **Click on RANDOM, then on OK to download 50 solutions.**

(18) **Sort the solutions on CENTRE with a span of 2 as Primary key, and on LEFT with a span of 2 as Secondary key.** This will group the solutions according to the variant following 'the' in the query focus, and order the solutions within each group according to the two preceding words. *Dual sort keys are a convenient way of sorting solutions where the form of the query focus varies.*

(19) **Scroll through the solutions to see which words other than 'horse' appear in the query focus, and whether any of them are also used metaphorically.** There appear to be no metaphorical variants of 'horse' among the solutions, suggesting that the sequence 'the horse's mouth' is in fact fixed. *If you choose to download a Random selection, you can always check your findings by selecting Query Edit and repeating the operation to download a different random selection.*

Results   The phrase 'from the horse's mouth' appears to allow variation of its initial preposition, while the rest of the sequence is fixed. This fixed component appears to occur only in a limited range of environments ('straight from', 'heard it from', 'go to', etc.). While these results should be treated with caution given the small number of occurrences of the phrase in the corpus (and hence even smaller numbers of the different environments mentioned), it is worth noting that none of the dictionaries cited provides such detail.

4.2.2 Looking for phrases using Query Builder

We now look at an idiomatic phrase which appears to permit a greater range of variation, 'a bridge too far'. Taking the lead from the *Guardian*'s 'a fudge too far' example, we will look for occurrences of the patterns 'a _ too far' and 'an _ too far'.

With respect to the 'horse's mouth' example, the main difficulty is designing a query to include solutions where the initial article can be either 'a' or 'an'. The only way to do this using PHRASE QUERY would be to reduce the phrase to 'too far'; however this would generate thousands of spurious solutions, allowing anything to precede it. To allow only specific alternatives, we must resort to a more sophisticated query tool, the QUERY BUILDER.

Click on the QUERY BUILDER button on the toolbar. The Query Builder dialogue box will be displayed. *You can also access Query Builder from the FILE menu by selecting NEW QUERY then QUERY BUILDER.*

The Query Builder allows you to construct a complex query whose components are represented by *nodes*. Each query consists of two kinds of nodes: a single *scope node*, and one or more *content nodes*, the latter being joined together by *links*.

The initial dialogue box contains two nodes. The black node on the left is the scope node, and indicates the scope of the query, i.e. the unit or distance within which a solution must be found. The default scope is any one text in the corpus, or *BNC document*, represented by the SGML element <BNCDOC>. *The scope of the query may either be an SGML element, or a span of anything up to 99 words. It can be edited by clicking on it: see 6.2.1 on page 115 and 7.2.2 on page 133.*

The red node on the right is an empty content node, which you must fill in with a part of the query — typically a word, phrase, pattern, or SGML element. Further content nodes can be created by clicking on the branches attached to the first one: vertical branches indicate *AND* links, and horizontal branches *OR* links. Thus, if we fill a first content node with the word 'a', we can link it with a horizontal OR branch to a further node containing the alternative 'an', and then link it with a vertical AND branch to further nodes containing the elements '_ too far'.

Editing the content node Nodes which are displayed in red must be filled in before the query can be sent to the server.

Click on the empty red node. A menu will appear by the box offering EDIT as the sole alternative which is not grayed out.

(22) **Select EDIT.** A submenu will be opened up, listing WORD, PHRASE, POS, PATTERN, SGML and ANY as alternatives.

(23) **Select WORD.** The Word Query dialogue box will be displayed. You can use this box to select a word or list of words to form the content of the current node, in exactly the same way as you used it to formulate Word Queries in 2.2 on page 64. *The options in the Content node menus are fully described in 1.3.7 on page 207. They allow you to DELETE the node, to EDIT its content, or to CLEAR its current content and change its type, as well as to COPY its content to the clipboard, or to PASTE from the clipboard into it. The following types may be selected: Word, Phrase (see 4.2.1 on page 89), POS (see 7.2.1 on page 131), Pattern (see 8.2.2 on page 150), SGML (see 5.2.2 on page 101), and Any (the ANYWORD underline symbol).*

(24) **Type in a, then check the PATTERN box to limit matching to this word.** *You must check the Pattern box here, as otherwise LOOKUP will try to list all the words in the word index which begin with 'a', which would exceed the permitted maximum of 200 (see 2.2.1 on page 64).*

(25) **Click on LOOKUP to display the matching word list.** The word 'a' will be displayed.

(26) **Click on 'a' to select it, then click on OK to insert this selection in the Query Builder node.** You will be returned to the Query Builder dialogue box. You will see that the content node is now black, showing that it is no longer empty. It contains the string "a", which is the CQL representation of this part of the query.

Linking nodes horizontally: OR Let us now create a second content node containing "an" as an alternative to "a".

(27) **Click on the horizontal branch of the 'a' node.** A new red content node will be created at the end of the branch.

(28) **Click on this node and select EDIT then WORD to display the Word Query dialogue box once more.**

(29) **Make sure the PATTERN box is checked, then type in the string an and click on LOOKUP.**

(30) **Click on 'an' in the matching words list to select it, then on OK to insert it in the Query Builder node.** You will be returned to the Query Builder dialogue box. The second content node is now also black, and contains the string "an". The two nodes jointly represent the *disjunction* 'a OR an'.

Linking nodes vertically: AND We now need to add the remaining part of the query, namely '_ too far'.

(31) **Click on the downward vertical branch of the 'a' node.** A new red content node will be added to the branch, and the branch will become a

downwards arrow. The arrow indicates that the link between the two nodes has the value ONE-WAY, i.e. that the content of the second node must follow that of the first, not necessarily directly.

Click on the downward vertical branch of this new node. A further empty red node will be added to the previous one, connected by a further one-way link.

Click in the first red node, and select EDIT then ANY. The Anyword symbol (_) will be placed in the node, showing that the content of this node may be any L-word. The node will remain red, even though it has been filled, but a message will be displayed reminding you that an Anyword symbol must be placed between two NEXT links (see below).

Click in the remaining red node, and select EDIT then PHRASE. The Phrase Query dialogue box will be displayed.

Type in the phrase too far **and click on OK to insert it in the Query Builder node.** You will be returned to the Query Builder dialogue box.

One aspect of the query remains to be specified: how exactly are the various content nodes to be linked? The ONE-WAY links inserted by default mean that the content of the upper node must precede that of the lower, but may be at any distance from it (within the specified scope for the entire query — here, an entire BNC document). As they concern adjacent components of a single phrase, we want the three successive content nodes to be adjacent to one another. So we must change the links between the nodes.

Click on the first One-way link, then on LINK TYPE. The Link type menu will be displayed, offering a choice of NEXT, ONE-WAY, and TWO-WAY.

Click on NEXT. The downward arrow will be replaced by a thick vertical line representing a NEXT link, meaning that the content of the second node must directly follow that of the first.

Click on the second link, and change its value to NEXT in the same way. All the nodes should now be black. If the constructed query is syntactically correct, the message 'Query is OK' will be displayed at the bottom of the box. *Clicking on a link enables you either to change its type, or to insert an additional node. A* NEXT *link, indicated by a thick line, means the content of the lower node directly follows that of the upper node, without any intervening words or punctuation. A* ONE-WAY *link, indicated by a downwards arrow, means that the content of the lower node follows that of the upper node, but is not necessarily adjacent to it (see 5.2.4 on page 105). A* TWO-WAY *link, indicated by a bidirectional arrow, means that the contents of the two nodes may occur in either order, not necessarily adjacently (see 8.2.3 on page 152). The* ANYWORD *symbol can only be used in a node between two* NEXT *links.*

If you INSERT *a node, the link between the upper node and the new one maintains the previous value, while the one between the new node and the lower one is assigned the default value* ONE-WAY. *However, you must ensure that all nodes are joined by links of the same type in the final query. For a full description of links in Query Builder, see 1.3.7 on page 207.*

(39) **Click on OK to send the query to the server.** There are 36 solutions from 32 texts.

Saving the query   The full text of the query will be displayed above the solutions in CQL format.   It should read ("a"|"an")(_)('too far'). Given the work involved in constructing complex queries using Query Builder, it is a good idea to save such queries for future reference. Even if you do not want to repeat exactly the same query, you may want to examine or edit it in order to construct a similar one.

(40) **Select** FILE **then** SAVE **(or click on the** SAVE **button on the toolbar).** Assuming that the solutions are displayed in a window entitled *Query2*, SARA will propose to save the query to your working directory with the name query2.sqy. You are advised to choose a more memorable filename: SARA will add the .sqy extension automatically.

Examining the solutions   First, let us sort the solutions according to the word occupying the variable slot, so as to identify any which do not involve variants of the idiomatic phrase 'a bridge too far'.

(41) **Select** QUERY **then** SORT **to display the Sort dialogue box.**
(42) **Select** CENTRE **with a span of 2 as Primary key.**
(43) **Click on OK to carry out the sort.**

There are two main types of solutions which seem spurious. The first is where the variable is a unit of measure with the literal sense of physical distance ('an inch/a foot/a centimetre/a mile too far'), rather than the metaphorical one of over-ambitiousness. The second is where the noun in the variable slot functions as object rather than as an adverbial quantifier: 'taking a hobby too far', 'drive a man too far', 'relying on a person too far away', etc.

First, thin the solutions to remove these spurious cases.

(44) **Mark all those solutions which do not have the metaphorical sense by double-clicking on them.**
(45) **Select** THIN **and** REVERSE SELECTION **under the** QUERY **menu to remove the marked solutions from the display.**

You should now have about 25 solutions containing 'a bridge too far' or variants of it. Near the top of the list there are two instances where 'a _ too far' occurs in quotation marks (the collating sequence places quotation marks at the beginning of the alphabet). Both are of 'a bridge too far', in the metaphorical sense, confirming that this is the citation form of the phrase. Of the remaining occurrences, several refer to the film or to the historical event behind it, while others pun on the literal sense of 'bridge'. However there are also a number of solutions where other geographical features, physical and even social artifacts are metaphorically invoked with the sense of overambitiousness: 'bomb', 'fair', 'party', 'peak', 'ridge', 'toll', 'treaty'. With the exception of 'treaty', which occurs in a book title mentioned three times, all these forms occur once only in the corpus. This suggests that they are creative rather than conventionalized variants of the basic phrase.

4.3 Discussion and suggestions for further work

4.3.1 Looking for variant phrases

This task has introduced you to a number of ways in which you can look for variant forms of a phrase using SARA.

In PHRASE QUERY or QUERY BUILDER, variants of an element *within* the phrase can be found by using the ANYWORD symbol _ in the relevant slot, while in Query Builder, specific alternatives can also be expressed as alternative content nodes. In either case, the SORT option allows you to group similar solutions.

Variants of the first or last element of the phrase are most easily identified by excluding that element from the query itself, and then sorting the solutions by the words to the left or right of the query focus. Sorting solutions by several words to the left or to the right also highlights recurrent environments in which a phrase is used.

These strategies are appropriate where the phrase can be defined as a fixed sequence of components — as is generally the case with sayings, proverbs and the like. To find variants of phrases where the form and sequencing of components can vary (such as active and passive forms of phrasal verbs: compare 'break ranks' and 'ranks were broken'), you must use more complex query techniques; for some examples, see 8.1.2 on page 144, 8.1.3 on page 145.

4.3.2 Some similar problems

Silver linings When proverbs are cited in English, they are frequently varied or curtailed with respect to their canonical form. Formulate a Phrase Query for 'silver lining', and sort the solutions to see how often it is preceded by 'every cloud has a'. Then compare this with the collocation frequency of 'cloud' within a span of 5, using the COLLOCATION option (see 3.2.1 on page 76). *'Silver lining'* *occurs 53 times in the corpus, and is preceded by 'every cloud has a' in only 7 of these cases. On the other hand 'cloud' occurs as a collocate of 'silver lining' 21 times in a span of 5 (collocation ratio 0.40), showing that variation of the proverb is more common than exact citation.*

To be or not to be   How frequent are quotation and variation of Hamlet's "to be or not to be"? What verbs can replace 'be' in this saying? Is the quotation typically continued with the phrase 'that is the question' or some variant of it? *As in the 'horse's mouth' example (see 4.2.1 on page 87), there is a trade-off to be made between precision (minimizing the number of spurious solutions) and recall (finding all the relevant solutions). The Phrase Query* to _ or not to *finds (after a considerable time) 78 solutions. Note however that this excludes any variant using phrasal verbs, such as 'to give up or not to give up'. To include these in a Phrase Query, you would have to simply use the string* or not to, *which would find very many spurious solutions. (A possible alternative would be to use the* SPAN *scope option in* QUERY BUILDER *to specify that a variable number of words can appear between 'to' and 'or not to': see 8.2.3 on page 150).*

Sort the solutions using CENTRE *with span 2 as Primary key, and* RIGHT *with span 2 as Secondary key. This will group the solutions according to the verbs before and after 'or not to'. Remove any spurious solutions with* THIN. *You will find that you cannot use the* COLLOCATION *option (see 3.2.1 on page 76) to find how often 'question' collocates with 'to be or not to be', because if it appears it will do so more than 9 words after the start of the query focus.*

Dirty looks   The phrase 'give someone a dirty look' would seem to offer numerous possibilities of variation. As well as allowing varying verb tenses, and any number of recipients, it can be pluralized (you can 'give someone dirty looks') and it may be used with other verbs than 'give'. Design a query to find occurrences of 'dirty look(s)', see what verbs occur with it, and whether these are used with both the singular and plural forms. *Use* QUERY BUILDER *to construct a query where a content node containing 'dirty' is joined by a* NEXT *link to alternative nodes containing 'look' or 'looks'. You can specify these three nodes with either* WORD QUERY *or* PHRASE QUERY. *Sort the solutions according to the two words of the focus as Primary key and according to the three words to the left of it as Secondary key.*

As well as people giving (a) dirty look(s), their behaviour can earn them (or it).

And finally. . .   Tired of working on linguistic problems? Try using the BNC as an oracle! Type in the Phrase Query what's for dinner? (including the question mark), and see what suggestions the corpus provides. *To see the answers as well as the questions, which may occur in different utterances or paragraphs, you should select Page mode display and expand the context to the maximum by double-clicking on* *the right mouse button (see 1.2.6 on page 51). You may have to browse extensively in the source text (see 1.2.7 on page 52) to find out what 'curried Geraldo' is, to go with all the broccoli.*

5 Do people ever say 'you can say that again'?

5.1 The problem: comparing types of texts

5.1.1 Spoken and written varieties

The BNC provides a wide range of information on the origin and nature of its component texts. Most of this information is encoded in the <HEADER> to each text, which contains, for example, the bibliographic information displayed using the SOURCE option (see 1.2.7 on page 52). Every text header also includes a *category reference* or <CATREF> element, which categorizes that text according to a series of parameters such as:

- type: whether written, spoken, or written-to-be-spoken (as in the case of drama or broadcasting scripts);
- for written texts: author type (individual, multiple, corporate), author characteristics (age, sex, origin), region of publication, target audience, circulation, cultural level, subject domain, medium (book, periodical, unpublished, etc.);
- for spoken texts: interaction type (monologue or dialogue), speaker characteristics (age, sex, origin, class), region of recording, and, for the non-conversational or *context-governed* texts (see 6.1.2 on page 112), subject domain.

SARA treats these parameters as *attributes* of the <CATREF> element, each of which may have a particular *value*. For instance, a book for children would have the value child for the attribute WRITTEN_AUDIENCE. By searching for instances of <CATREF> elements which have certain attribute values, you can use SARA to find all the texts in the corpus of a certain type. (A list of <CATREF> attribute values is provided in section 5.2.3 on page 103.)

This information can also be used to investigate and compare the use of specific words or phrases in particular text-types. This task asks how far somewhat clichéd expressions which are generally considered to belong to an informal spoken register, actually do occur in real spoken dialogue. The first example inspects instances of 'You can say that again' in the corpus to see in what kinds of texts they appear, and then compares their frequency in real spoken dialogue with that in the imaginary written dialogue of plays, stories and novels. The second instead uses <CATREF> attribute values to compare the use of the phrase 'Good heavens' in spoken and written texts.

5.1.2 Highlighted features

This task shows you:

- how to use the SGML QUERY option to count texts where the <CATREF> element has particular attribute values (for instance those texts written for child audiences in the domain of science);
- how to count numbers of solutions without downloading them, using the MAX DOWNLOADS option as a filter;
- how to look for words or phrases in texts which have particular <CATREF> attribute values using ONE-WAY links in the QUERY BUILDER;
- how to display SGML markup in solutions, using SGML FORMAT under QUERY OPTIONS.

It assumes you already know how to:

- adjust the default download and display settings using the View menu Preferences option (see 1.2.8 on page 54);
- use Word Query and Phrase Query to search for words and phrases (see 2.2.2 on page 65, 4.2.1 on page 87);
- design complex queries with multiple content nodes using the Query Builder (see 4.2.2 on page 91);
- adjust downloading procedure in the Too many solutions dialogue box (see 2.2.3 on page 66).

5.1.3   Before you start
Using the VIEW menu PREFERENCES option, set the SARA defaults as follows:

MAX DOWNLOAD LENGTH	400 characters
MAX DOWNLOADS	10
FORMAT	Plain
SCOPE	Paragraph
VIEW: QUERY and ANNOTATION	checked
CONCORDANCE	checked
BROWSER: SHOW TAGS	unchecked

5.2   Procedure
5.2.1   Identifying text type by using the Source option
The *Longman Dictionary of Contemporary English* lists 'you can say that again' as a spoken phrase, used to indicate complete agreement. But does it in fact occur in real speech? Let us begin by using PHRASE QUERY to find all its occurrences in the corpus.

(1) **Click on the PHRASE QUERY button on the toolbar to display the Phrase Query dialogue box.**

(2) **Type in the string** you can say that again **and click on OK to send the query to the server.** The Too many solutions dialogue box will be displayed, showing that 'you can say that again' occurs 32 times in 26 texts.

(3) **As we are only interested in the kinds of texts in which 'you can say that again' appears, check ONE PER TEXT and then click on the DOWNLOAD ALL button to change the download hits number to 26. Then click on OK to download these solutions.** You will see that the vast majority occur within quotation marks. This suggests that they come from fictional dialogue, since quotation marks are not used in spoken texts in the corpus.

(4) **Select SORT from the QUERY menu and sort the solutions by the Centre with a span of 1 as Primary key, and by the left with a span of 1 as Secondary key.** The solutions in which the focus begins with quotation marks will be grouped near the top of the display.

(5) **Scroll through the remaining solutions, and double-click on those which seem to you to come from actual speech. Then select THIN and SELECTION from the QUERY menu to delete the rest.**

(6) **Using the SOURCE button on the toolbar, check the bibliographic data to see how many of these solutions actually do come from spoken texts.** The bibliographic data displays for written and spoken texts have different formats, the latter including a window showing a list of the participants in the interaction.

(7) **Click on OK to close the Bibliographic data box.**

Only 3 out of the 26 texts in which 'you can say that again' appears are actually spoken ones, while 23 are written. To interpret these figures, however, we need to take into account the relative frequencies of the relevant written and spoken texts in the corpus. We can do this by finding out how often the values of attributes on the <CATREF> element classify the text it heads as spoken dialogue or imaginative writing. While written dialogue is not, of course, found exclusively in imaginative texts, a glance at the solutions would suggest that this is a reasonable approximation in this case.

5.2.2   *Finding text-type frequencies using SGML Query*
The SGML QUERY option allows you to find:

- instances of a particular SGML element;
- instances of a particular SGML element with a particular attribute or attributes having a particular value or values.

Here we shall use it to count the number of texts in a particular category in the corpus. As was explained in 5.1.1 on page 98, we can do this by finding all the instances of <CATREF> elements which have particular attribute values, and counting the number of solutions.

Using the Max downloads option to obtain numerical information
Where we are only interested in finding out the number of solutions to a query, rather than in inspecting them, it is not necessary to download the solutions from the server. Instead, we can simply use the information in the TOO MANY SOLUTIONS dialogue box, which reports the number of solutions found. This dialogue box is displayed when the number of solutions exceeds the number specified for the MAX DOWNLOADS option under VIEW PREFERENCES (see 1.2.8 on page 54). If this number is small (you should have set it to 10 for this task in 5.1.3 on page 99), the Too many solutions dialogue box will appear in response to almost all queries. You can then simply read off the number of solutions from the dialogue box, and click on CANCEL to abort the query without actually downloading any solutions from the server.

Formulating the SGML Query Let us find out how many imaginative written texts there are in the corpus, and how many spoken dialogue ones. A comparison of the numbers of texts in these two categories will provide a rough yardstick against which to evaluate the difference in the frequencies of 'you can say that again'. *Most written texts in the BNC are of roughly similar length (40,000 words) regardless of their type. Spoken texts from the demographically organized part of the corpus are of a similar average length, but with more variability. Spoken texts from the context-governed part of the corpus are on average very much shorter (8,000 words); however only 60% of these involve dialogue. The BNC Users' Reference Guide provides full details of the numbers of texts, sentences and words in the main categories of texts in the corpus: for summary figures, see 2.1.1 on page 31.*

Click on the SGML QUERY button on the toolbar (or select NEW QUERY then SGML from the FILE menu). The SGML dialogue box will be displayed.

Check the SHOW HEADER TAGS box. The dialogue box contains an alphabetical list of all the types of SGML elements used in the BNC. *If the SHOW HEADER TAGS box is not checked, the list will be much shorter, containing only those elements which form part of actual texts, and excluding those which are only found in text headers. As the <CATREF> element appears in text headers, you must use the full list here. This handbook describes some of the most important element types; you will find a complete list in the* BNC Users' Reference Guide.

Scroll through the list until you find the <CATREF> element, and click on it to select it. A brief description of the element will be displayed to the right of the list. The list of attributes for the element will be displayed in the bottom left-hand window.

SARA treats the <CATREF> element as having a large number of possible attributes, whose names indicate whether they are applicable to all, to spoken, or to written texts. They are listed with their values in section 5.2.3 on the facing page.

(11) **Scroll through the list of attributes until you find SPOKEN_TYPE, and click on it to select it.**

(12) **Click on the ADD button to include this attribute in the query.** The ATTRIBUTE dialogue box will be displayed, showing possible values for this attribute.

(13) **Click on the value dialogue to select it, then on OK to insert it in the query.** You will be returned to the SGML dialogue box. Your selected attribute value pair is now displayed in the right-hand window of the box. *Where attributes permit wide ranges of values, you must type in the required value in a modified version of the Attribute dialogue box (see 6.3.2 on page 126, 9.2.4 on page 170, 10.2.3 on page 182 for examples).*

(14) **Click on OK to send the query to the server.** The Too many solutions dialogue box will be displayed, showing the number of solutions to this query. Since there is only one <CATREF> element per text, the number of texts is the same as the number of solutions.

(15) **Make a note of the number of solutions, and click on CANCEL to return to the SGML dialogue box.** The box will still display your previous query, with the <CATREF> element highlighted.

Now find the number of imaginative written texts.

(16) **Scroll through the attribute list till you find the WRITTEN attributes.**

(17) **Click on WRITTEN_DOMAIN to select it, then on the ADD button.** The Attribute dialogue box will be displayed, showing the values for this attribute in the BNC.

(18) **Click on imaginative to select it, then on OK to insert this attribute value pair in the SGML dialogue box.** Your new attribute value selection will be added to the right hand window of the box.

(19) **Remove the previous attribute value selection by clicking on it to select it, then clicking on REMOVE.**

(20) **Click on OK to send the query to the server.** The Too many solutions dialogue box will be displayed, stating that there are 625 solutions in 625 texts.

The proportion of texts in each category containing one or more instances of 'you can say that again' is thus:

imaginative written texts   21/625

spoken dialogue texts   3/654

This suggests that texts with 'you can say that again' are more frequent in the 'imaginative written' category, though the figures are too small for reliable generalization.

5.2.3   Displaying SGML markup in solutions

To see how <CATREF> attributes appear in the BNC, you may like to look at some examples containing the written_domain="imaginative" attribute value pair.

1) **In the Too many solutions dialogue box, click on OK to download the first 10 solutions.**

If you look at the solutions, you will find that the <CATREF> element is not displayed. The query focus is represented only by a vertical red line. This is because we have set the default display as PLAIN (see 5.1.3 on page 99), which only shows the words and punctuation in the text. To display SGML markup, such as <CATREF> elements, you must choose a different display format.

2) **Select OPTIONS under the QUERY menu.** The QUERY OPTIONS dialogue box will be displayed.

3) **Select SGML as format, then click on OK and wait for the solutions to be re-displayed.** You will now see the solutions with their complete SGML markup, shown as tags enclosed in angle brackets. The <CATREF> element is highlighted as the query focus in each concordance line. *The QUERY OPTIONS dialogue box allows you to change the display values of the current query with respect to the defaults selected under VIEW PREFERENCES. The options available are identical to those listed under FORMAT and SCOPE in the User preferences dialogue box under VIEW PREFERENCES (see 1.2.8 on page 54), except that the Query Options dialogue box also allows you to edit the CUSTOM display format using the CONFIGURE option (see 9.2.2 on page 165 for an example).*

Assuming you checked the QUERY box under VIEW PREFERENCES, the *Query Text* will be displayed above the solutions. This shows the text of the query in CQL (Corpus Query Language) format: <catRef target=wriDom1>.

If you look at any solution to this query in SGML format, you will see that the
<CATREF> start-tag actually contains a long string of codes. Each of these
codes is made up of a sequence of letters and a number. The letters are used
to indicate such features as the text availability (allAva), its type (allTy), its
target audience (allAud), its cultural level (wriLev), its domain (wriDom), etc.,
while the number indicates a value for this attribute. For example, wriDom1
represents the first of the WRITTEN_DOMAIN values ('imaginative'). A complete
list of the <CATREF> codes used in the corpus is given in 2.2 on page 234.
These codes are translated into more comprehensible attributes and values by the
SARA software, to make selection easier. *The following table shows the translations
of these codes into attributes, and the values which can be selected for them in the Attribute
dialogue box. Each attribute can also take a value indicating 'information not available'.*

Attribute	Values
ALL_AVAILABILITY	*free; restricted (to various areas)*
ALL_TYPE	*spoken demographic; spoken context-governed; written books and periodicals; written-to-be-spoken; written miscellaneous; spoken; written; unclassified*
SPOKEN_AGE	*(of demographic respondent) under 15; 15-24; 25-34; 35-44; 45-59; 60 or over*
SPOKEN_CLASS	*(of demographic respondent) AB; C1; C2; DE*
SPOKEN_DOMAIN	*(context-governed) educational/informative; business; public/institutional; leisure*
SPOKEN_REGION	*south; midlands; north*
SPOKEN_SEX	*(of demographic respondent) male; female*
SPOKEN_TYPE	*monologue; dialogue*
WRITTEN_AGE	*(of author) under 15; 15-24; 25-34; 35-44; 45-59; 60 or over*
WRITTEN_AUDIENCE	*child; teenage; adult; any*
WRITTEN_DOMAIN	*imaginative; natural and pure sciences; applied sciences; social science; world affairs; commerce and finance; arts; belief and thought; leisure*
WRITTEN_DOMICILE	*(of author) country or region*
WRITTEN_GENDER	*(of target audience) male; female; mixed; unknown*
WRITTEN_LEVEL	*(of circulation) low; medium; high*
WRITTEN_MEDIUM	*book; periodical; misc published; misc unpublished; to-be-spoken*
WRITTEN_PLACE	*(of publication) country or region*
WRITTEN_PUBSTATUS	*published; unpublished*

continued on next page

Attribute	Values
WRITTEN_SAMPLE	*whole text; beginning sample; middle sample; end sample; composite*
WRITTEN_SELECTION	*selective; random*
WRITTEN_SEX	*(of author) male; female; mixed; unknown*
WRITTEN_STATUS	*(of reception) low; medium; high*
WRITTEN_TIME	*1960-1974; 1975-1993*
WRITTEN_TYPE	*(of author) corporate; multiple; sole; unknown*

5.2.4   Searching in specific text-types: 'good heavens' in real and imagined speech

The QUERY BUILDER option allows you to combine not only searches for different words or phrases (see 4.2.2 on page 91), but also different query types. Thus you can join the SGML Query formulated in the last section with a Word or Phrase Query, so as to find all the cases where a word or phrase occurs in texts which have a particular <CATREF> attribute value or values.

Like 'you can say that again', the expression 'good heavens' seems more typical of imagined than of real contemporary speech. As you can discover by using PHRASE QUERY, it occurs 140 times in the corpus, making it too frequent to simply inspect the solutions and their sources with any comfort. We can instead use the QUERY BUILDER to restrict the search to occurrences in imaginative written texts, and then to occurrences in spoken dialogue texts, before comparing their frequencies.

'Good heavens' in imaginative written texts: joining different query types   Let us begin by designing a query to find the frequency of 'good heavens' in texts which fall into the imaginative written category.

Click on the QUERY BUILDER button to display the Query Builder dialogue box.

Click in the content node (displayed in red), and select EDIT then SGML. The SGML dialogue box will be displayed.

Scroll through the list of elements and click on <CATREF> to select it.

Scroll through the attribute list and select WRITTEN_DOMAIN.

Click on the ADD button to display the Attribute dialogue box.

Select imaginative, **then click on OK to insert it in the SGML Query.**

Click on OK to return to the Query Builder. The content node will now contain the specification <catRef target=wriDom1>. The angle brackets indicate that this part of the query regards an SGML element.

(31) **Click on the downwards branch to add a new empty node to the query.**

(32) **Click in this new node and select EDIT then PHRASE.** The Phrase Query dialogue box will be displayed.

(33) **Type in the string 'good heavens' and click on OK to insert it in the Query Builder node.** You will see that the second content node now contains the string `'good heavens'`, representing this Phrase Query.

We now need to consider the relationship between these two nodes, and the scope within which the two nodes must be satisfied. At the moment, they are joined by a downwards arrow, representing the link value ONE-WAY, meaning that the content of the second node follows that of the first within the scope of the query, not necessarily directly (see 4.2.2 on page 91). The scope of the query is any <BNCDOC> element. For this query, both these default values are correct. The <CATREF> element always occurs in the text header, and this precedes the text, in which the phrase 'good heavens' can occur at any point. The scope must contain both the text header and the text: the only element to do so is <BNCDOC>.

(34) **Check that the 'Query is OK' message is displayed at the bottom of the box, and click on OK to send the query to the server.** The Too many solutions dialogue box will be displayed.

(35) **Read off the number of solutions and the number of texts in which they occur.** There are 90 solutions in 64 texts.

(36) **Change the DOWNLOAD HITS number to 30 and download a random set of the solutions.** You will see that the vast majority are in quotation marks, confirming that they come from fictional dialogue. *Note that the query focus is the phrase 'good heavens': in Query Builder the query focus is always the final content node, or the final group of nodes where these are joined by NEXT links.*

'Good heavens' in spoken dialogue: using Query Edit   Let us now look at the use of 'good heavens' in spoken dialogue. The easiest way to do this is to edit the current query, specifying `spoken_type="dialogue"` instead of `written_domain="imaginative"`.

(37) **Select EDIT under the QUERY menu.** You will be returned to the Query Builder. This will still show the previous query.

(38) **Click on the <CATREF> content node and select EDIT.** The SGML dialogue box will be displayed, showing your previous <CATREF> attribute value selection.

(39) **Click on REMOVE ALL to remove the previous attribute value selection.**

Select SPOKEN_TYPE **from the attribute list.**

Click on the ADD **button to display the Attribute dialogue box.**

Select dialogue **from the value list, then click on OK.** You will see that the right hand window of the box now shows the attribute value pair spoken_type="dialogue".

Click on OK to insert this SGML Query in the Query Builder node. The node will now contain the string <catRef target=spoLog2>. spoLog2 *corresponds to the second defined value for the* SPOKEN_TYPE *attribute, that of dialogue; see 2.2 on page 234.*

Check that the 'Query is OK' message is displayed, then click on OK to send the query to the server.

Read off the number of solutions and the number of texts from the TOO MANY SOLUTIONS **dialogue box.** There are 32 solutions in 20 texts.

Click on the DOWNLOAD ALL **radio button, then on OK, to download all the solutions.**

5.2.5 *Comparing frequencies in different text-types*

We now know that there are only 32 occurrences of 'good heavens' in 20 spoken dialogue texts, while there are 90 in 64 imaginative written texts.

To compare the relative frequency of 'good heavens' in each of the above text categories, however, we need to choose an appropriate unit for comparison. One possibility is to compare numbers of occurrences per text for each text-type, as we did in 5.2.2 on page 100. Given the variability of the length of texts in the corpus, however, a more satisfactory way may be to compare numbers of occurrences per million words or per million sentences.

The *BNC Users' Reference Guide* lists the numbers of words and sentences for the main text categories in the corpus. These are also summarized in 2.1.1 on page 28 of this Handbook. Figures for the categories of interest here are as follows:

imaginative written 1,580,771 sentences, 19,664,309 words. The 90 occurrences of 'good heavens' in this text type are thus equivalent to 56.9 per million sentences, or 4.6 per million words.

spoken dialogue 888,535 sentences, 7,760,753 words. The 32 occurrences of 'good heavens' in this text type are thus equivalent to 36.0 per million sentences, or 4.1 per million words.

By both criteria, 'good heavens' is rather more common in imaginative written texts than it is in actual speech. This difference is the more striking because written dialogue forms only a small part of most imaginative written texts. However, for the same reason it makes little sense to test the difference

statistically. *If data for the category you are interested in are not provided in the* BNC
Users' Reference Guide, *you can always find out the number of sentences in a particular
text category using the Query Builder. If you place a* <CATREF> *specification in a first
content node, and a* <S> *(sentence) element in a second content node, and join the two
nodes with a* ONE-WAY *link, the query will eventually find all the sentences in texts
matching the* <CATREF> *specification, and you can read off their number from the* TOO
MANY SOLUTIONS *dialogue box. You cannot count words in this way, because SARA
does not allow you to formulate SGML queries using the* <W> *(word) element.*

5.3   Discussion and suggestions for further work

5.3.1   Investigating other explanations: combining attributes

There are a number of other possible explanations which come to mind for
the difference in the frequency of 'good heavens' in these two text types. One
is historical change: the written component of the BNC is, on average, rather
older than the spoken component. While all the spoken texts in the corpus were
collected after 1990, you may have noticed that the list of <CATREF> attributes
(see 5.2.3 on page 103) includes WRITTEN_TIME, which has 1960-1974
and 1975-1993 as values. It is thus possible that use of 'good heavens' is
concentrated in the older written texts, since when it has progressively been
falling into disuse. For the same reason, it is possible that in spoken dialogue,
'good heavens' is only used in texts involving older speakers.

We can check to see whether time and age are relevant variables by designing
further queries using the <CATREF> element, and comparing the number
of occurrences of 'good heavens' with the number of sentences in each case.
To do this, you need to repeat the procedure used in the last section, this
time designing queries where multiple attribute values are specified for the
<CATREF> element, for instance wriDom1 (i.e. 'written domain: imaginative')
and wriTim1 (i.e. 'written time: 1960-1974').

(47)   **Start a new query using QUERY BUILDER, and click on the empty
content node.**

(48)   **Select EDIT then SGML.**

(49)   **In the SGML dialogue box, select <CATREF> from the list of elements
and WRITTEN_DOMAIN from the list of attributes, then click on ADD
to display the Attribute dialogue box.**

(50)   **Select imaginative from the list of values, and click on OK to insert
the attribute value pair in the SGML dialogue box.**

(51)   **Now select WRITTEN_TIME from the attribute list, and click on ADD
to re-display the Attribute dialogue box.**

Select 1960-74 from the list of values, and click on OK to add this attribute value pair to the query.

Click on OK to return to the Query Builder. You will see that the node now lists two attribute value pairs for the <CATREF> element.

Create a second content node below the first containing the Phrase Query 'good heavens', and join the two nodes with a ONE-WAY link.

Check that the 'Query is OK' message is displayed, and click on OK to send the query to the server.

Wait for the solutions to be downloaded and read off their number from the box on the status bar. This corresponds to the number of occurrences of 'good heavens' in older written imaginative texts.

Select QUERY then EDIT. You will be returned to the Query Builder.

Click on the bottom content node and select CLEAR then SGML. *You must use the CLEAR option here, since the EDIT option only allows you to change the content of the query specified for the node, not its query type.*

Select the <S> element and click on OK to insert it in the Query Builder node.

Click on OK to send the query to the server.

Read off the number of solutions from the Too many solutions dialogue box. This corresponds to the number of sentences in older written imaginative texts.

If you now calculate the frequency of 'good heavens' per million sentences in this text category, you will find that it is rather greater than the frequency for all imaginative written texts which we calculated in 5.2.5 on page 107, suggesting that there may be a historical decline in its use.

To assess the impact of speaker age, edit the <CATREF> node to include values for both the SPOKEN_TYPE and SPOKEN_AGE attributes. The latter indicates the age of the respondent who recorded the text in question. If you design a query to look for occurrences of 'good heavens' with different values for this attribute, you will find that there are only two occurrences in dialogue where the respondent's age is under 35. This suggests that 'good heavens' may be a feature of speech involving older people. *While the <CATREF> element only indicates the age of the respondent (the person who recorded the dialogue), the next task will show you how to find out the age (and sex, class, dialect, education, etc.) of the speaker of a particular utterance (see 6.2 on page 115), and hence how often 'good heavens' is used by speakers from particular age groups (see 6.2.4 on page 123).*

5.3.2   Some similar problems

Talking about politics   At the time the tapes for the spoken component of the BNC were recorded, John Major was first Chancellor of the Exchequer, and then Prime Minister, and Neil Kinnock the Leader of the Opposition. Which of the two men is more frequently mentioned in spoken dialogue? Are they referred to in similar terms? *Use the* QUERY BUILDER *to find all the occurrences of 'Major'. Join an SGML Query for the* <CATREF> *element where the* SPOKEN_TYPE *attribute has the value* dialogue *to a Phrase Query for 'Major', unchecking* IGNORE CASE *in the Phrase Query dialogue box in order to make the search for 'Major' case-sensitive. Download all the solutions, and sort them according to the 2 words to the left in order to check that they do in fact refer to John Major rather than Major Barbara. Mark and thin any spurious solutions, then scroll through the remaining ones to identify adjectives used to describe Major. Then do a similar query for 'Kinnock'.*

There are many more references to Major (over 120 as compared to 35), who is variously described as 'bloody', 'blooming', 'bumbling', while Kinnock is referred to as 'a funny' and 'a daft Welsh git'. Notwithstanding this complimentary tone, both are almost always referred to as 'Mr' or with their first name.

Spoken bodies and written ones   In their *Comprehensive grammar of the English language*, Quirk *et al* (1985: 6.4) state that pronominal forms with 'one' ('someone', 'anyone', etc.) are more commonly used than forms with 'body', citing frequencies in the LOB and Brown corpora of written English in the 1960s. Is this claim borne out by the BNC? And is it also true of spoken English? Compare the frequencies of 'everyone' and 'everybody' in the spoken and in the written texts of the BNC. Which of the two forms is more frequent in the category of 'written-to-be-spoken' texts? *Use the* QUERY BUILDER *to join an SGML Query for the text-type to a Word or Phrase Query for 'everyone' or 'everybody'. As we are only interested in numbers here, you can abort the query from the Too many solutions dialogue box without downloading the solutions: pressing* CANCEL *will then return you to the Query Builder, where you can edit the query to change the word or text-type. You can access the category* WRITTEN-TO-BE-SPOKEN *using either the* ALL_TYPE *or the* WRITTEN_MEDIUM *attribute on the* <CATREF> *element.*

The following tables show the actual frequencies found for these two words in the BNC. First, within the 3209 written texts, totalling 89,740,544 words:

form	occurrences	per text	per million words
everybody	3317	1.03	40.0
everyone	12110	3.77	134.9

For the same two terms, within the 915 spoken texts, totalling 10,365,464 words:

form	occurrences	per text	per million words
everybody	2767	3.02	266.9
everyone	1227	1.34	118.4

These figures make it very clear that the two forms are differently distributed in speech and in writing. While there are too few written-to-be-spoken texts to permit confident generalization, the difference in the frequencies of the two forms parallels that of writing rather than of speech ('everybody' 25; 'everyone' 213).

Talking metric   Since the early 1970s, Britain has in theory been 'going metric', with a gradual changeover to international standards of weights and measures. What evidence is there in the BNC that people now actually talk about 'metres' rather than 'yards', about 'litres' rather than 'pints', or about 'grams' (or 'grammes') rather than 'ounces'?

Compare the frequencies of some imperial and metric measurement terms in spoken dialogue (<CATREF> attribute value `spoken_type="dialogue"`) and in written texts which have a high level of circulation (<CATREF> attribute value `written_level="high"`). *You should include the singular and plural form of the measurement term as alternative nodes in each query (see 4.2.2 on page 91). Note that it would be impossible to do this query sensibly for the measures 'foot' or 'pound', given the many other uses of these words.*

The only case where a metric measure is more frequent than its imperial equivalent is 'gram', which is more frequent than 'ounce' in spoken dialogue. Even here, however, it occurs in fewer texts. You might also like to compare the relative frequencies of these words in spoken texts involving respondents from different age groups.

6 Do men say mauve?

6.1 The problem: investigating sociolinguistic variables

6.1.1 Comparing categories of speakers

In a much-cited book, *Language and woman's place*, Robin Lakoff (1975) argues that men and women differ in their use of many linguistic features. Women, she claims, make use of a wider colour vocabulary, with terms like 'mauve', 'lavender', or 'beige' rarely being used by men; and of different evaluative words, such as 'adorable', 'charming', 'sweet' and 'lovely'. Such sociolinguistic hypotheses readily lend themselves to testing against corpus data. For instance Stenström (1992) compares men and women's use of expletives in the London-Lund spoken corpus, finding that women use proportionally more expletives from a 'heaven' group ('heavens', 'gosh', 'blimey' etc.), while men make greater use of a 'hell' group ('bastard', 'damn' and 'devil'). The BNC provides information as to the age, sex, social and regional provenance of speakers and writers as attributes on a range of SGML elements, which can be used in queries to investigate language use in relation to these variables. *Note that not all this information may be available for every written text, or for every utterance in speech. You can however always find out how many texts and utterances have attributes of any one type, and compare this with the total number of texts and utterances in the corpus (see 6.2.1 on page 115).*

As a first example, this task asks whether female speakers in the corpus use 'mauve' (a relatively rare word) more often than males. It looks at all the occurrences of 'mauve' in spoken utterances, inspecting them to see if they are produced by male or female speakers.

As a second example, it considers whether female speakers use the much commoner word 'lovely' more than males. In this case we shall design separate queries to count the number of utterances containing this word produced by each category of speaker.

Lastly, it returns to a case discussed in the previous task, to see whether use of the expression 'good heavens' is the prerogative of any particular speaker age-group.

6.1.2 Components of BNC texts

Each text document in the BNC, or <BNCDOC>, has the same hierarchic structure, composed of SGML *elements*. At the highest level, each *written text* document contains a <HEADER> element, containing information about the text, and a <TEXT> element, containing the text itself. The header contains the <CATREF> element discussed in the previous task (see 5.1.1 on page 98), along with a series of other elements containing bibliographic information and the like.

The structure of the <TEXT> element reflects the organization of the text itself. Thus at the highest level, it may contain <DIV1> elements, each representing a chapter of a book, an act of a play, an article from a periodical, etc. These may in turn contain <DIV2> elements representing sections or scenes, which may in their turn contain <DIV3> elements representing sub-sections, etc. These are further divided into paragraphs (<P> elements). Portions of written texts which have particular functions, such as headings, lists, quotations, speeches and stage directions, notes, captions, etc., are also marked up in particular ways.

In *spoken text* documents, the <HEADER> element also contains details concerning the setting and the participants, and is followed by an <STEXT> element, containing a transcript of the original tape recordings. Each spoken text from the *demographic* component of the corpus consists of all the conversations recorded by a particular respondent, and is divided into <DIV> elements, each of which corresponds to a single conversation. Each <DIV> element is in turn divided into a series of <U> (utterance) elements corresponding to turns of the various speakers. Spoken texts from the *context-governed* component of the corpus consist of public speech events of various kinds, ranging from phone-ins and meetings to sermons and classroom interaction. They may be dialogue, in which case they consist of a series of <U> elements, or monologue, in which case they consist of a single <U> element. In either case, various paralinguistic features are also identified (see 7.1.2 on page 129, 9.2 on page 163).

At the lower end of the hierarchy, paragraphs and utterances alike consist of sentences (<S> elements), while sentences contain L-words and punctuation (<W> and <C> elements).

All of these features are indicated in the same way in the BNC, using *start-* and *end-tags* placed at the beginning and end of each element. The tags contain the name of the element, placed between angle brackets: in the case of end-tags, the name is preceded by a solidus. Thus the tags <TEXT> and </TEXT> indicate the beginning and end of a written text, <U> and </U> indicate the start and end of a spoken utterance, and so on. As well as allowing you to design queries to find the start or end of a particular element (see 9.3.2 on page 177), these tags enable you to restrict queries so that solutions are found only where they occur within the *scope* of an element, i.e. between a start- and end-tag of that element-type. In this way you can search for only those occurrences of a feature which appear within headings, quotations, speeches, spoken utterances, etc. *The smallest elements of text structure (<S>, <W> and <C> elements) do not have end-tags, since the ending of any sentence is implied by the beginning of the next sentence, just as the ending of any word or punctuation element is implied by the beginning of the next instance of one of these categories.*

All the elements composing the text may have *attributes* of various kinds, which are specified following the element name in the start-tag, along with their *values*. For instance, all <s> (sentence) elements have an N attribute, whose value is the number of that sentence within the text in question. This is the number which is displayed on the status bar at the bottom of the solutions window, and might be represented in the corpus by the tag <s n=123>. All spoken utterances are similarly numbered, and also have a WHO attribute, whose value is a code identifying the speaker. *The easiest way to appreciate the internal structuring of texts in the BNC is to use the Browser display with the SHOW TAGS option checked. This can be accessed via the SOURCE option (see 1.2.7 on page 52), and shows a high-level SGML representation of the entire text from which the current solution is taken. Clicking on the + sign preceding any element in the display shows its components at the next level, enabling you to progressively expand the representation until you reach the lowest level.*

This task shows you how to count the number of utterances which are produced by a particular speaker or category of speaker, by using the SGML Query option to find occurrences of <U> elements whose WHO attributes have particular values. It then shows you how to to restrict other queries to particular classes of speaker by specifying <U> elements with particular WHO attribute values as the query scope.

6.1.3 Highlighted features
This task shows you:

- how to search for words or phrases occurring in particular SGML elements with particular attribute values using the Query Builder SGML SCOPE option;
- how to use CUSTOM display format to show utterance or paragraph boundaries and speaker codes;
- how to identify the characteristics of speakers of particular utterances using the SOURCE option;
- how to search for particular collections of speaker- or author-types by combining multiple attributes and values in an SGML QUERY.

It assumes you already know how to:

- adjust the default download and display settings using the View Preferences option (see 1.2.8 on page 54);
- use the Word Query, Phrase Query, and SGML Query options (see 2.2.1 on page 64, 4.2.1 on page 88, 5.2.2 on page 100);

- design complex queries using Query Builder (see 4.2.2 on page 91, 5.2.4 on page 105);
- adjust downloading procedure using the Too many solutions dialogue box (see 2.2.3 on page 66);
- count the occurrences of particular elements and attribute configurations using the Too many solutions filter (see 2.2.3 on page 66, 5.2.2 on page 100);
- modify queries using the Query Edit option (see 4.2.1 on page 88);
- save and re-open queries (see 2.2.5 on page 70, 4.2.2 on page 94).

6.1.4   Before you start

Using the VIEW menu PREFERENCES option, set the SARA defaults as follows:

MAX DOWNLOAD LENGTH	2000 characters
MAX DOWNLOADS	5
FORMAT	Plain
SCOPE	Automatic
VIEW: QUERY and ANNOTATION	checked
CONCORDANCE	checked
BROWSER: SHOW TAGS	unchecked

6.2   Procedure

6.2.1   Searching in spoken utterances

Let us first design a query to find all the occurrences of 'mauve' in spoken utterances.

Click on the QUERY BUILDER button on the toolbar. The Query Builder will be displayed.

Click in the red content node and select EDIT then WORD to display the Word Query dialogue box.

Type in the string mauve, **then check the PATTERN box and click on LOOKUP.** The word 'mauve' will be displayed in the matching words list.

Select 'mauve' from the matching words list, then click on OK to insert it in the Query Builder node. You will be returned to the Query Builder, where the content node now contains the string "mauve". *The double quotation marks indicate that this is a Word Query.*

Click in the scope node (displayed in black).   This currently contains the default value <BNCDOC>, meaning a complete BNC document.

(6)   **Select SGML.** The SGML dialogue box will be displayed.

(7)   **Scroll through the list of elements and click on <U> to select it.** As <U> is an element which occurs within texts rather than text headers, there is no need for SHOW HEADER TAGS to be checked.

(8)   **Click on OK to insert it in the Query Builder scope node.** You will be returned to the Query Builder, where the scope node now contains the string <u>, indicating that the entire content of the query must be found within the scope of a single spoken utterance.

(9)   **Check that the 'Query is OK' message is displayed, then click on OK to send the query to the server.** The Too many solutions dialogue box will be displayed, stating that there are 14 solutions in 11 texts.

(10)   **Click on the DOWNLOAD ALL button, then on OK to download all the solutions.**

6.2.2   Using Custom display format

We now want to find out the sex of the speaker in each of these solutions. At first glance, many solutions may make little sense. This is because they come from spoken dialogue, but do not show where one utterance ends and another begins. While PLAIN display format (selected as default in 6.1.4 on the preceding page) shows only the words and punctuation of the text, CUSTOM display format additionally shows selected SGML elements and attribute values. It is particularly useful for viewing solutions from spoken texts. We shall now select this format, using the Query Options command (see 5.2.3 on page 103).

(11)   **Select OPTIONS from the QUERY menu.** The Query Options dialogue box will be displayed.

(12)   **Click on CUSTOM to select it, then click on OK.** You will have to wait while the solutions are downloaded from the server once more, with the additional information required for this display format. *You can select Custom as the default display format using the* VIEW PREFERENCES *option (see 1.2.8 on page 55). You can also design your own custom display to visualize such features as truncations, pauses, gaps, overlaps, voice quality and vocal and non-vocal events by using the* CONFIGURE *option in the Query Options dialogue box (see 9.2.2 on page 165).*

Custom format operates differently in Line and Page display modes. Assuming you are using the default version of Custom format and are in Line display mode, you will see that the solutions now contain vertical lines. These indicate paragraph or utterance boundaries.

(13)   **Use the arrow buttons to select the last solution, then click on the CONCORDANCE button on the toolbar to switch to Page display mode.**

You will see that the display shows each utterance beginning on a new line, preceded by a speaker identification code between curly brackets. Each speaker has a unique identification code, even those whose identity is unknown. The code PS000 is used for an unidentifiable speaker. *In written texts, the default Custom format for Page mode displays shows the start of each paragraph indented on a new line. To exploit its ability to display utterance and paragraph boundaries fully, Custom format should be used selecting* MAXIMUM *scope with a high* MAX DOWNLOAD LENGTH *under* VIEW PREFERENCES *(see 1.2.8 on page 56).*

Make a note of the speaker identification code for the utterance containing the query focus in this solution.

Click on the SOURCE **button on the toolbar (or select** SOURCE **from the** QUERY **menu).** The Bibliographic data box will be displayed, showing the data for the source of the current solution. The lower window lists the participants in this text, giving their speaker identification code, name, sex, class, age, profession and relationship to the other speakers, where these are known.

Note down the sex of the speaker with this identification code, then click on OK to return to the solutions display.

Use the left arrow button on the toolbar or the PGUP **key to page through the remaining solutions, looking up the sex of the speaker who says 'mauve' in each case.** If the amount of context displayed is insufficient to show the beginning of the utterance with the speaker identification code, you can always double-click on the right mouse button to expand the context, or, if this is still insufficient, use the BROWSE option (see 1.2.7 on page 52).

In 11 cases, the speaker is identified as female; in 2 as a male; in one case, the speaker's sex is unknown. While these numbers are too small for reliable inferences, they suggest that 'mauve' may be more common in women's speech than in men's.

6.2.3 Comparing frequencies for different types of speaker: male and female 'lovely'

Let us now examine a case where the word is sufficiently frequent to allow a statistical comparison in terms of speaker sex. To adopt a chi-squared test, for instance, the observed and expected frequencies for each category should both be greater than 5. As you can discover by looking up the word index with Word Query, 'lovely' occurs a total of 6278 times in the corpus as a whole, so it seems almost certain to meet this requirement. To find whether it is more frequently used in utterances by male or female speakers, we shall find out:

- the number of utterances containing 'lovely' produced by male speakers;
- the number of utterances containing 'lovely' produced by female speakers;

- the total number of utterances produced by male speakers;
- the total number of utterances produced by female speakers.

With this information we can carry out a chi-squared test to compare the observed and expected frequencies of utterances containing 'lovely' for each speaker-type, and assess the significance of any difference. *Another way of comparing male and female use of 'lovely' might be to calculate the total number of occurrences of 'lovely', and compare that with the total number of words produced. However the current release of SARA does not allow you to count the number of words produced by a particular speaker or speaker-type, only the number of sentences or utterances.*

Counting SGML elements with particular attribute values Let us start by counting the total numbers of utterances by male and female speakers in the spoken texts of the corpus. The last task showed you how to use the SGML Query option to count occurrences of a <CATREF> element with particular attribute values (see 5.2.2 on page 101). Here we shall use a similar procedure to count occurrences of the <U> (utterance) element with particular attribute values.

(18) **Click on the SGML QUERY button on the toolbar (or select NEW QUERY then SGML from the FILE menu).** The SGML dialogue box will be displayed.

(19) **Scroll through the list of elements and click on <U> to select it.** The list of attributes for the <U> element will be displayed in the bottom left hand window of the box.

(20) **Scroll through the attributes list and click on WHO.SEX to select it, then on the ADD button.** The Attribute dialogue box will be displayed, showing the list of values for the WHO.SEX attribute.

(21) **Click on m to select male speakers, then on OK to insert this attribute value pair in the SGML Query.**

Other attributes whose values can be specified to find utterances by particular types of speaker include the following: they do not apply to any <U> element for which the speaker is unknown.

Attribute	Meaning	Values
WHO.AGE	*speaker's age*	*0 (under 15); 1 (15-24); 2 (25-34); 3 (35-44); 4 (45-59); 5 (60 or over); X (unknown)*
WHO.DIALECT	*speaker's dialect*	*(see 2.4 on page 239 for values)*

continued on next page

Attribute	Meaning	Values
WHO.EDUC	speaker's level of education	still in education; -14; 15-16; 17-18; 19+; unknown
WHO.FLANG	speaker's first language	(see 2.4 on page 239 for values)
WHO.RESP	speaker who recorded the text	identifier of respondent (only for utterances produced by other participants)
WHO.ROLE	speaker's role in recording	respondent; other
WHO.SEX	speaker's sex	m; f; u (unknown)
WHO.SOC	speaker's social class	AB; C1; C2; DE; UU (unknown)

Click on OK to send the query to the server.

Read off the number of solutions from the TOO MANY SOLUTIONS dialogue box. This corresponds to the number of utterances produced by male speakers.

If you are interested in examining gender as a variable, this number is a useful piece of general information, so it is a good idea to save this query for future reference.

Click on OK to download the first 5 solutions. You cannot save a query without downloading at least some solutions.

Click on the SAVE button on the toolbar (or select SAVE from the FILE menu). Choose a suitable mnemonic as a name, such as USEX_M, then click on OK to save the query.

Now find out the number of utterances produced by female speakers.

Select EDIT from the QUERY menu. You will be returned to the SGML dialogue box showing the previous query.

In the list of attributes, click on the WHO.SEX attribute to select it, then on ADD. The Attribute dialogue box will be displayed.

Click on f to select female, then on OK to insert this attribute value pair in the query. The previous selection for the same attribute will be removed automatically.

Click on OK to send the query to the server.

(30) **Wait to read off the number of solutions from the TOO MANY SOLUTIONS dialogue box.** This corresponds to the number of utterances produced by female speakers.

(31) **Click on OK to download the first 5 solutions.**

(32) **Select SAVE AS from the FILE menu, and save the query with a new mnemonic, such as** USEX_F. *If you edit a saved query, then want to save the edited version under a different name, you must use the* SAVE AS *option under the* FILE *menu: using the* SAVE *button on the toolbar will automatically overwrite the saved version.*

You should also find out the total number of utterances in the corpus, in order to check what proportion of the utterances in the corpus are in fact categorized as by male or female speakers. You can do this by simply removing the attribute value specification from the query.

(33) **Select EDIT from the QUERY menu to return to the SGML dialogue box.**

(34) **Click on REMOVE ALL.**

(35) **Click on OK to send the query to the server.**

(36) **Wait to read off the number of solutions from the TOO MANY SOLUTIONS dialogue box.** This corresponds to the total number of utterances in the corpus.

(37) **Click on OK to download the first 5 solutions, then select SAVE AS from the FILE menu.**

(38) **Save the query with a suitable mnemonic, such as** UALL.

You should now have the following numbers:

- female utterances: 307,539
- male utterances: 304,278
- total utterances: 753,395

As you can see, the BNC contains similar numbers of utterances by male and female speakers. The difference between the total for female and male utterances (611,817), and the grand total gives the number of utterances for which either no speaker has been identified, or the speaker's sex is unknown (141,578).

Searching in elements with particular attribute values   We now want to find out how often 'lovely' appears in male and female speech. To do this we must first limit the scope of a query for the word 'lovely' to utterances produced by a particular speaker-type.

(39) **Click on the QUERY BUILDER button on the toolbar to display the Query Builder.**

Click in the scope node and select SGML. The SGML dialogue box will be displayed.

Using the same procedure as in the last section, select the <u> element and the attribute value pair who.sex=f.

Click on OK. You will see that the node now contains the string

```
<person ID=_0 sex="f">#<u who=_0>
```

meaning an utterance by a female speaker. *The complexity of the query syntax here is due to the fact that strictly speaking, <u> elements in the BNC do not have all the attributes and values listed in the SGML and Attribute dialogue boxes, but merely a* WHO *attribute whose value is a speaker identification code. SARA interprets choices from the lists displayed for the <u> element in the SGML and Attribute dialogue boxes by matching this speaker identification code against the information given in the corresponding* <PERSON> *element in the text header.*

Now specify the content node, namely the word 'lovely'.

Click in the red content node, and select EDIT then WORD. The Word Query dialogue box will be displayed.

Check the PATTERN box and type in the string lovely, **then click on LOOKUP.**

Click on 'lovely' in the matching words list to select it, then on OK to insert it in the Query Builder node. The content node should now contain the string "lovely".

Check that the 'Query is OK' message is displayed, and click on OK to send the query to the server.

Read off the total number of solutions from the Too many solutions dialogue box. This corresponds to the number of 'lovely's produced by female speakers.

Now find out the number of 'lovely's produced by male speakers.

Click on CANCEL to abort the query. You will be returned to the Query Builder dialogue box.

Click in the scope node and select SGML. The SGML dialogue box will be displayed.

Select the <u> element, then select the value m **for the** WHO.SEX **attribute.**

Click on OK to insert this query in the scope node.

Click on OK to send the revised query to the server.

53   **Read off the total number of solutions from the Too many solutions dialogue box.** This corresponds to the number of 'lovely's produced by male speakers.

54   **Click on CANCEL to return to the Query Builder.**

We have so far counted the numbers of occurrences of 'lovely' in utterances by male and female speakers respectively. These may not however be the same as the numbers of utterances containing the word 'lovely', since it is possible that in some utterances the word 'lovely' is used more than once. To calculate the number of utterances with 'lovely', we must count the number of times there are two occurrences of 'lovely' within a single utterance, and subtract this figure from the totals we obtained above.

55   **Click on the downward branch of the `"lovely"` content node to create a second node.**

56   **Click in the new node and select EDIT then WORD.**

57   **Type in the string `lovely` and click on LOOKUP.**

58   **Select 'lovely' from the list of matching words and click on OK to insert the query in the Query Builder node.** The two nodes are connected with a ONE-WAY link, meaning that the second occurrence of 'lovely' follows the first at any distance within the specified scope, i.e. a single utterance.

59   **Check that the 'Query is OK' message is displayed, and click on OK to send the query to the server.**

60   **Read off the number of solutions from the Too many solutions dialogue box, then click on CANCEL to return to the Query Builder.** There are 42 solutions, corresponding to the number of repetitions of 'lovely' within male utterances.

Now find the number of times there are two occurrences of 'lovely' in female utterances, by changing the scope of the query.

61   **Click in the scope node and select SGML.** The SGML dialogue box will be displayed.

62   **Select the value `f` for the WHO.SEX attribute on the `<U>` element.**

63   **Click on OK to insert the query in the scope node, then click on OK to send the query to the server.**

64   **Read off the number of solutions from the Too many solutions dialogue box.** There are 83 repetitions of 'lovely' within female utterances.

65   **Click on OK to download the first five solutions.**

Results The numbers of occurrences of 'lovely' and of repetitions of 'lovely' in male and female utterances respectively are thus:

- female speakers: 1439, of which 83 are repetitions
- male speakers: 716, of which 42 are repetitions

This means that the numbers of utterances containing 'lovely' are respectively 1356 and 674. If, for each type of speaker, you divide the number of utterances containing 'lovely' by the total number of utterances, you can then compare their frequencies per 1000 utterances. These are:

- female speakers: (1356/307,539) x 1000 = 4.4
- male speakers: (674/304,278) x 1000 = 2.2

With the same data, you can also perform a chi-squared test of significance for the absolute frequencies. Given the combined number of utterances and the combined number of utterances containing 'lovely', the expected frequencies of utterances with 'lovely' for women and men would respectively be 1020 and 1010, in comparison with the observed frequencies of 1356 and 674. This difference is significant, corresponding to a probability of $p < .0001$ for one degree of freedom, and it therefore seems plausible to claim that women do use the word 'lovely' more frequently than men.

6.2.4 Investigating other sociolinguistic variables: age and 'good heavens'

The last query looked at the hypothesis that women use the word 'lovely' more than men. Such questions may also be posed concerning other sociolinguistic variables encoded as utterance attributes.

Take the expression 'good heavens'. In the last task, we found that this was more common in written than in spoken dialogue, and, in the latter, more common in data collected by older respondents (see 5.2.4 on page 105). Can we also link its use to any particular age-group of speakers?

Using the Query Builder, first design a query to find all the occurrences of this phrase in spoken utterances.

Click on the QUERY BUILDER button on the toolbar. The Query Builder dialogue box will be displayed.

Click in the scope node and select SGML.

In the SGML dialogue box, select <U> from the list of elements.

Click on OK to insert it in the Query Builder node.

Click in the content node and select EDIT then PHRASE to display the Phrase Query dialogue box.

(71) **Type in the string** good heavens **and click on OK to insert the query in the Query Builder node.**

(72) **Check that the 'Query is OK' message is displayed, then click on OK to send the query to the server.**

(73) **Note the number of solutions and texts from the Too Many Solutions dialogue box, and then download the first ten, checking the ONE PER TEXT option.**

(74) **Select OPTIONS from the QUERY menu.** The Query Options dialogue box will be displayed.

(75) **Click on CUSTOM to select it, then on OK.**

(76) **When downloading is complete, click on the CONCORDANCE button on the toolbar to select Page display mode.**

(77) **Make a note of the speaker identification code for the first solution, then click on the SOURCE button on the toolbar.** The Bibliographic data box will be displayed, showing the data for the current solution.

(78) **Make a note of the sex and age of the speaker with that code, then click on OK to return to the solutions display.**

(79) **Use the right arrow button on the toolbar to page through the remaining solutions, looking up the details of the speaker who says 'good heavens' in each case.**

(80) **Do you notice any features shared by many of these speakers?** While roughly equal numbers of speakers of each sex seem to use 'good heavens', they tend to be relatively old — most of them over 40.

Testing the hypothesis: alternative attribute values   The hypothesis just formulated was derived from the first ten solutions. Let us now see exactly how often 'good heavens' is used by older and by younger speakers, searching first for all occurrences in utterances by speakers over 45, then for all those in utterances by speakers under 35.

(81) **Select QUERY then EDIT to return to the Query Builder dialogue box, showing the previous query.**

(82) **Click in the scope node and select SGML. Select the <U> element and the attribute WHO.AGE, then click on ADD.** The Attribute dialogue box will be displayed, showing values for the WHO.AGE attribute. *Values for age are listed in bands (0 = under 15, 1 = 15-24, 2 = 25-34, 3 = 35-44, 4 = 45-59, 5 = 60 or over, unknown). You can combine two or more bands in a single query by co-selecting them.*

(83) **Holding down the CTRL key, click on the value 4 (45-59), then on the value 5 (60+) to select them, then click on OK.** The selection will

be displayed in the right hand window of the SGML dialogue box, with the alternative values for the attribute shown as a disjunction separated by a vertical bar.

Click on OK to insert this scope in the Query Builder node.

Check that the 'Query is OK' message is displayed, and click on OK to send the query to the server.

Read off the number of solutions from the Too many solutions dialogue box, then click on CANCEL to return to the Query Builder.

Now re-edit the query to consider the under-35 age group (age-band values 0, 1 and 2), and read off the number of solutions. You will find that out of the 33 occurrences of 'good heavens' in spoken utterances, 20 occur in utterances produced by speakers aged 45 or over, whereas only 6 are in utterances by speakers aged under 35.

Click on CANCEL once to return to the Query Builder, and once more to return to the previous solutions display.

As in the case of 'lovely', we can interpret these figures by comparing the numbers of utterances containing 'good heavens' with the total numbers of utterances produced by speakers over 45 and under 35 respectively. As you can find out by designing appropriate queries and drinking large amounts of coffee while waiting for the results, the spoken component of the BNC contains 210,666 utterances produced by speakers over 45, and 232,476 utterances produced by speakers under 35. Since the total numbers of utterances are similar for each of the two groups, the expected frequencies of 'good heavens' are also similar (13). *Comparison of the two groups is also simplified by the fact that there are no cases where 'good heavens' occurs twice in the same utterance.*

6.3   Discussion and suggestions for further work

6.3.1   Sociolinguistic variables in spoken and written texts

The design of queries concerning categories of speakers in spoken texts and categories of authors in written texts requires different approaches. In spoken texts, the relevant unit of analysis is the individual utterance or <u> element, each of which is associated with a particular speaker. In this task you have seen how to restrict queries to particular categories of speakers by restricting their scope to <u> elements with specific attribute values. In written texts, on the other hand, the relevant unit is generally the entire text. As we saw in the previous task (see 5.1.1 on page 98), authorship is not indicated as an attribute value on the <TEXT> element, but in the text header, as an attribute value on the <CATREF> element. Since the latter element does not contain the text itself, this means that you cannot specify authorship as a scope restriction.

Instead, to find cases where a particular feature is produced by a particular category of author, you must follow a procedure analogous to that described in the previous task (see 5.2.4 on page 105):

- design a first content node containing an SGML query for the value of the AUTHOR attribute on the <CATREF> element;
- join this with a ONE-WAY link to a second content node containing a query for the desired text feature;
- use the default scope of <BNCDOC> (the only element to contain both the text header and the text: see 6.1.2 on page 112).

Restricting the scope of a query to the <U> element limits the search to spoken texts for the reason that utterances only occur within spoken texts in the BNC. Other scope selections have similar effects: <P> elements (paragraphs) only occur within written texts, and <SP> elements (speeches) only occur within written-to-be-spoken texts. Numbered divisions (<DIV1>, <DIV2> etc.) occur only in written texts, while unnumbered divisions (<DIV>) occur only in spoken ones. You can find out what type(s) of text an element occurs in by clicking on its name in the list of elements in the SGML dialogue box (see 5.2.2 on page 100).

Using any of these structural elements to restrict the scope of a search to a particular text-type will also of course exclude any portions of the text which are not contained within them. For instance, if you restrict the scope of a search to <P> or <SP>, you will also exclude headings, captions, stage directions, lists and notes, since these do not generally appear within paragraphs or speeches. Moreover, any scope restriction based on text elements will necessarily exclude elements contained within the text header, such as <CATREF> elements and attributes. This means, for example, that Query Builder does not allow you to combine a restriction of scope to female utterances with a restriction of text-type to spoken monologue, nor in general to limit queries to particular elements occurring in texts of particular types, such as headlines in periodicals, stage directions in plays, or recipes by male and female cooks. The next task shows how you can overcome this difficulty using a CQL QUERY (see 7.2.3 on page 135).

6.3.2   Some similar problems

Ruddy   When the spoken component of the BNC was collected, the compilers noticed that the expletive 'ruddy' seemed to be predominantly used by older speakers (Rundell 1995). What proportion of the spoken occurrences of 'ruddy' are in fact by speakers over the age of 45? Are similar proportions also found for authors of written texts? *Use QUERY BUILDER to restrict the scope of a Word*

Query for 'ruddy' to utterances whose speakers are aged over and under 45, following the procedure adopted for 'good heavens' (see 6.2.4 on page 123). Count the numbers of occurrences, then carry out SGML queries to find the total number of utterances produced by speakers in these age-bands.

While SARA allows you to treat speaker age as an attribute of utterances (see 6.2.4 on page 123), author age is only indicated as an attribute of the <CATREF> element in the text header (see 5.2.2 on page 101). Consequently, to find figures for written texts you should use the Query Builder default scope of <BNCDOC>, then join an SGML Query for the <CATREF> attribute values written_age=45-59 *and* written_age=60+ *to a Word Query for* ruddy *with a One-way link.*

There are 204 occurrences of 'ruddy' in the corpus, 78 of them in speech. In no case is 'ruddy' repeated within a single utterance. 57 of these occurrences are produced by speakers over 45, and only 11 by speakers under 45, even though there are 50% more utterances by the younger group. Most written occurrences of 'ruddy' are in texts which are unclassified for author age. There are only 7 occurrences produced by authors over 45 as opposed to 14 by authors under 45: numbers of texts in the corpus produced by each age group are equal. However, a glance at these occurrences suggests that 'ruddy' is used mainly in the sense of 'red' in writing, e.g. 'a ruddy complexion', rather than as an expletive, as it is in speech.

Foreign speakers   A potentially weak point of the methodology in this task is that frequencies in utterances by different categories of speakers have been compared without considering the number of speakers in each category. While for variables such as sex and age, numbers of speakers in each category are predictably large enough to even out the effects of individual styles, this may not be the case when categories have few members. For instance, the WHO.FLANG and WHO.DIALECT attributes have values indicating the first language and the dialect of the speaker (for a list of languages and dialects, see 2.4 on page 239). For some of these values, there may only be a single speaker in the BNC. Design queries to find out how many speakers in the BNC have French as their first language, and how many of their utterances are contained in the corpus. *To find the number of speakers, use an SGML QUERY to count occurrences of the <PERSON> element with the attribute value pair* flang=FR-FRA, *which indicates French-from-France. You will have to type the value* FR-FRA *(in upper case) in the Attribute dialogue box. Then edit the query to count occurrences of the <U> element where the* WHO.FLANG *attribute has the value* FR-FRA.

There are only three French speakers from France in the BNC (2 women and 1 man), who produce a total of 873 utterances. Clearly this is too few to allow any reliable inferences about the characteristics of utterances produced by French speakers.

Class consciousness   Where known, the social class of speakers in the BNC is indicated by the value of the WHO.SOC attribute on utterance elements. However, due to the way the corpus was collected, for spoken demographic texts this information is only reliable for the social class of the respondents who made the recordings. Bearing this in mind, does the corpus provide any evidence of class differences in ways of speaking about the establishment and its institutions, such as universities? *Use Query Builder to design queries to find occurrences of the forms 'university' and 'universities' in the utterances of speakers who are indicated as respondents (i.e. whose* WHO.ROLE *attribute has the value* resp*) and as upper-middle class (i.e. whose* WHO.SOC *attribute has the value* AB*). Then design a similar query for respondents from lower class (*DE*) backgrounds. Note the numbers of solutions in each case, and download them using* CUSTOM *display format.*

Frequencies of the words 'university' and 'universities' are similar for respondents in the two social groups. It is however interesting that many of the references in the 'DE' group occur in explanations of why the recordings are being made, suggesting that the data collection procedure may be a source of bias here.

7 'Madonna hits album' — did it hit back?

7.1 The problem: linguistic ambiguity

7.1.1 The English of headlines

The newspaper headline in the title to this task is mildly amusing insofar as it is syntactically and semantically ambiguous. On one reading, 'hits' is a plural noun; on another, it is a singular verb in the present tense. As a verb, it may have its literal sense of physical aggression, or the metaphorical meaning of criticism. While the most likely reading is perhaps the noun one — an album of Madonna's hits — the fact that the phrase comes from a newspaper headline, where present tense verbs are frequent (Bell 1991), underlines the ambiguity, suggesting the alternative interpretation of 'hits' as a verb.

How justified is such an interpretation? This task examines the word 'hits' in the BNC, to see whether it is generally used in headlines as a verb or a noun, and whether it is used literally as well as metaphorically — as the joke would seem to require.

7.1.2 Particular parts of speech, particular portions of texts

There are three main problems to be faced in carrying out the task:

- how to find occurrences of a word as a particular part-of-speech (in the case of 'hits', as a singular verb rather than as a plural noun);
- how to restrict a query to particular portions of texts, such as headlines;
- how to further restrict a query to particular portions of particular text-types, such as headlines in newspapers and periodicals.

As you will have noticed when examining solutions in SGML format (see 5.2.3 on page 103) and when browsing texts using the SHOW TAGS option (see 1.2.7 on page 52), every L-word in the BNC is tagged as a <w> element with a *Part-of-speech* or *POS code*. Assigned by the probabilistic CLAWS program (see 2.1.2 on page 34), this code indicates whether the word is a noun (common or proper, singular or plural), a verb (in its root, '-s', '-ing', past, or past participle form), an adjective, a determiner, a conjunction, etc. SARA enables you to use these POS codes to:

- restrict queries to cases where a word is tagged with a particular POS code, or one of a series of such codes, using the POS QUERY option;
- display solutions with different parts-of-speech in different colours, using the POS FORMAT display option;
- sort solutions by their POS codes rather than by their orthographic form, using the POS CODE collating option.

The POS codes used in the BNC are listed in 2.1 on page 230, as well as in the HELP *file.*

As we saw in the last task, structural components of texts such as sections, paragraphs, utterances, sentences, etc. are indicated as SGML elements in the BNC (see 6.1.2 on page 112). In the QUERY BUILDER, these can be used to restrict the scope of a query to occurrences within a particular type of component (see 6.2.3 on page 117). Specialized components such as headings, captions, quotations, notes, etc. are similarly marked, so that by restricting the scope of a query to <HEAD> elements, for example, you can find all the occurrences in headings of a particular word or phrase.

The Query Builder does not permit you to restrict a query to a particular text-type as well as to a particular type of component. To do this you must instead use a CQL QUERY.

7.1.3 Highlighted features
This task shows you:

- how to copy a string from the Word Query dialogue box to a different dialogue box using the COPY option;
- how to use the POS QUERY option to search for a word as a particular part of speech;
- how to use the QUERY BUILDER to restrict the scope of a query to particular components of texts;
- how to use the POS FORMAT option to display different parts of speech in different colours;
- how to sort solutions according to part-of-speech values using POS CODE collating;
- how to use a CQL QUERY to restrict a query to particular portions of particular text-types by combining SCOPE and <CATREF> specifications.

It assumes you already know how to:

- adjust default settings using the View menu Preferences option (see 1.2.8 on page 54);
- carry out a Word Query (see 2.2.1 on page 64);
- carry out an SGML Query (see 5.2.2 on page 100);
- use the Query Builder to join queries and restrict query scope (see 4.2.2 on page 91, 5.2.4 on page 105, 6.2.3 on page 117);
- adjust downloading procedure in the Too many solutions dialogue box (see 2.2.3 on page 66);

- sort solutions using Primary and Secondary keys (see 3.2.2 on page 78, 4.2.1 on page 89);
- mark and thin selected solutions (see 2.2.4 on page 68).

7.1.4 *Before you start*

Using the VIEW menu PREFERENCES option, set the default settings as follows:

MAX DOWNLOAD LENGTH	400 characters
MAX DOWNLOADS	10
FORMAT	Plain
SCOPE	Paragraph
VIEW: QUERY and ANNOTATION	checked
CONCORDANCE	checked
BROWSER: SHOW TAGS	unchecked

7.2   Procedure

7.2.1   *Searching for particular parts-of-speech with POS Query: 'hits' as a verb*

SARA's POS QUERY option enables you to search for an L-word with a particular POS code or codes. This is particularly useful where the word is a frequent one, and can act as more than one part of speech, since searching only for a particular part-of-speech value will reduce the total number of solutions and may increase overall precision.

Let us begin by looking up the frequency of 'hits' in the word index.

Click on the WORD QUERY button on the toolbar, and type the string hits **in the dialogue box.**

Check the PATTERN box so as to search the index for this word only, then click on LOOKUP.

Select 'hits' from the matching words list. You will see that 'hits' occurs 1319 times in the corpus.

Let us now find out the frequency of 'hits' as a verb.

Click on COPY to copy the string hits **to the clipboard, then click on CANCEL to leave Word Query.** *Using the* COPY *option in Word Query saves you from having to retype the string if you decide to switch to another query type. Note that it copies the input string, not selections from the matching words list.*

(5) **Click on the POS QUERY button on the toolbar (or select NEW QUERY and POS from the FILE menu).** The POS Query dialogue box will be displayed.

(6) **Click in the L-WORD window, and press SHIFT+INSERT to paste in the string** hits **from the clipboard.** *Only those words which appear in the word index (L-words: see 2.2.1 on page 64) can be used in a POS Query. To find out what L-words start with a particular string of letters, or match a particular pattern, you must first look them up in the index using Word Query (see 2.2.1 on page 64, 8.2.1 on page 147).*

(7) **Click in the PART-OF-SPEECH window (or press TAB).** The POS codes used with the word 'hits' will be displayed, in alphabetical order. These are: NN2, NN2-VVZ, and VVZ, .

(8) **Click on the** NN2 **code.** An explanation of the code will appear to the right of the window.

(9) **Do the same for the** VVZ **and** NN2-VVZ **codes.** The latter is an ambiguous *portmanteau code*, meaning that CLAWS was unable to decide whether a NN2 or VVZ code should be assigned — i.e. whether 'hits' was a plural noun or a singular present-tense verb. *Portmanteau codes list the two most probable parts of speech for the L-word in question. They are used for some 5% of words in the corpus. The two alternatives are given in alphabetical order.*

(10) **Click on** VVZ **to select it, then on OK to send the query to the server.** The Too many solutions dialogue box will be displayed, stating that there are 404 cases where 'hits' has a VVZ code.

While much smaller than the total frequency of 'hits', 404 is still a very large number of solutions to have to deal with. Moreover, we do not know how many other instances of 'hits' as a verb may lurk among the cases with portmanteau NN2-VVZ codes. If the emphasis is on recall (finding all the relevant solutions), rather than precision (minimizing the number of spurious solutions: see 1.3.1 on page 60, 4.2.1 on page 87, 4.3.2 on page 96), you should always include relevant portmanteau instances in POS queries. We should certainly check how many occurrences of 'hits' have portmanteau codes before drawing conclusions as to its frequency as a verb.

(11) **Click on CANCEL to return to the POS Query dialogue box.** The list of POS codes for 'hits' should still be displayed.

(12) **Holding down the CTRL key, click on** NN2-VVZ **and on** VVZ **to select both.** Holding down CTRL when clicking in the POS code display box allows you to select multiple codes.

Click on OK to send the revised query to the server. The Too many solutions dialogue box will be displayed, telling you that 780 cases of 'hits' have now been found.

This is almost double the previous number, showing that there are a great many cases where the coding of 'hits' is uncertain. It means you should undoubtedly include portmanteau instances in a query aiming to examine occurrences of 'hits' as a verb. You will then have to inspect the solutions and use the THIN option to delete those occurrences with portmanteau codes where 'hits' is in fact a noun (see 7.2.4 on page 137).

Inspecting 780 solutions would be no joke, however, so let us first further restrict the query to those cases of 'hits' as VVZ or NN2-VVZ which occur in portions of texts marked as headings.

Click on CANCEL in the Too many solutions dialogue box to abort the query. You will be returned to the POS Query dialogue box.

Click on CANCEL to return to the main *SARA-bnc* window.

7.2.2 Searching within particular portions of texts with Query Builder

Specifying the content node   First, let us transfer the POS Query for 'hits' to a Query Builder content node.

Click on the QUERY BUILDER button on the toolbar (or select NEW QUERY and QUERY BUILDER from the FILE menu). The Query Builder will be displayed.

Click in the empty content node and select EDIT, then POS. The POS Query dialogue box will be displayed.

Click in the L-word window, then press SHIFT+INSERT to paste in the string hits **from the clipboard.**

Click in the Part-of-speech window (or press TAB) to display the POS codes associated with 'hits'.

Holding down the CTRL key, click on VVZ and NN2-VVZ to select them, then click on OK to insert this query into the Query Builder node. This component of the query is displayed in the node as:

```
"hits"=VVZ|"hits"=NN2-VVZ
```

In CQL, POS specifications are represented by double quotes round the L-word, followed by an equals sign and the POS code. The vertical bar represents the disjunction between the alternative values.

Specifying the scope node   We now need to add the requirement that
'hits' should fall inside a heading. While this will potentially include not only
headlines from newspapers and periodicals, but also chapter and section titles
in other written text-types, it should significantly reduce the overall number of
solutions.

To do this we must change the scope of the query. The default value shown
in the scope node on the left of the Query Builder, <BNCDOC>, implies that
the content of the query may occur anywhere in the text or text header. We
shall change this to <HEAD>, i.e. those portions of text marked as headings.
*Other elements which can be used to restrict the scope of queries to particular portions of
texts include <STAGE> (stage direction), <POEM> (verse), <CAPTION> (of a table or
figure), <ITEM> (in a list), <SALUTE> (in a letter). As seen in the last task, you can
also use structural elements such as <S> (sentence), <U> (utterance), <P> (paragraph)
or <SP> (speech) to restrict scope in the same way (see 6.2.1 on page 115).*

(21)   **Click on the scope node and select SGML.** The SGML dialogue box will
be displayed.

(22)   **Make sure that the SHOW HEADER TAGS box is unchecked.** This reduces
the length of the list of elements in the display, excluding those which only
appear in text headers.

(23)   **Scroll through the list of elements and click on <HEAD> to select it.**
The list of attributes for the <HEAD> element will be displayed. *You should not
confuse <HEADER> elements, which contain information about entire texts, and precede
the text itself, with <HEAD> elements, which indicate headings within texts.*

(24)   **Click on TYPE, then on the ADD button.** The Attribute dialogue box
will be displayed, showing the list of values for the TYPE attribute. *These include*
main *(the main heading to a chapter, article, or section),* sub *(a sub-heading following
a main heading),* byline *(a byline, typically giving the name of the author or source),
and* unspec *(type unspecified).*

(25)   **Click on** main, **then on OK to select this attribute value pair.** You will
be returned to the SGML dialogue box.

(26)   **Click on OK to insert this selection into the Query Builder scope node.**
The scope is displayed as <head type="main">.

(27)   **Check that the 'Query is OK' message is displayed, then click on OK
to send the query to the server.** The Too many solutions dialogue box will
be displayed, showing that there are 98 solutions in 58 texts.

Since the query did not specify the text-type in which the verb 'hits' should
occur, it is now advisable to check whether these solutions generally come from
headings in newspapers and periodicals or from other text-types. We can get

some idea by looking at a sample of the 58 texts from which the solutions are taken.

Change the DOWNLOAD HITS number to 20, select ONE PER TEXT, and click on the RANDOM button. Then click on OK to send the query to the server.

Scroll through the solutions, clicking on the SOURCE button on the toolbar to find where each comes from. Nearly all the solutions appear to come from newspapers and periodicals. This is also evident from the fact that many are followed by a byline giving the name of the author — a feature typical of headlines in periodicals.

While it would be convenient to formally restrict this query to periodicals — not least so as to further reduce the number of solutions — we cannot do this using the Query Builder. This is because the scope restriction in the Query Builder applies to the entire content of the query, so that restricting the scope to <HEAD> elements within the text excludes the text header where the <CATREF> element specifying the text-type is located (see 5.2.2 on page 101).

In the current version of SARA, the only way to get round this problem is to formulate the query directly in the corpus query language, using the CQL QUERY option. This requires you to write the full text of the query yourself without the aid of the Query Builder.

To formulate a CQL Query, you must first find out exactly how the various components of the query and their links need to be represented. You can do this by carefully examining the texts of other queries you have designed using the Query Builder.

7.2.3 Searching within particular portions of particular text-types with CQL Query

Provided that you checked the QUERY option in the display preferences under the VIEW menu (see 7.1.4 on page 131), you will see the text of the current query displayed above the solutions in the *Query1* window. It should read:

```
((("hits"=VVZ|"hits"=NN2-VVZ))/<head type="main">)
```

This query matches any occurrence of 'hits' which has been given a POS code of either VVZ or NN2-VVZ, provided that it occurs within the scope of a <HEAD> element whose TYPE attribute has the value main. In order to further restrict this query to periodicals, we now need to discover how to represent a restriction to this text-type in CQL, and how to join such a restriction to the rest of the query.

(30)   **Click on the QUERY BUILDER button on the toolbar to display a new Query Builder window.**

(31)   **Click in the content node and select EDIT then SGML.** The SGML dialogue box will be displayed.

(32)   **Check the SHOW HEADER TAGS box.** The <CATREF> element, which appears in the text header, will now be included in the list of elements.

(33)   **Select <CATREF> from the list of elements.** The list of attributes for <CATREF> will be displayed.

(34)   **Select WRITTEN_MEDIUM, then click on the ADD button.** The Attribute dialogue box will be displayed, showing the list of values for the WRITTEN_MEDIUM attribute.

(35)   **Select** Periodical **and click on OK to return to the SGML dialogue box.**

(36)   **Click on OK to insert this component of the query in the Query Builder node.** You will see this component is displayed as:

```
<catRef target=wriMed2>
```

wriMed2 *is the code for periodicals, the second of the categories of written media in the BNC. For a full list, see 2.2 on page 234.*

We now need to find out how to represent the link between this component and the rest of a query. We can do so by completing the current query with a search for any word that occurs in written periodicals.

(37)   **Click on the downward branch of the content node to add a second node to the query.**

(38)   **Click on the new node, and select EDIT then PHRASE.** The Phrase Query dialogue box will be displayed.

(39)   **Type in** dummy, **and click on OK to insert it in the Query Builder node.**

The link between the two nodes currently has the default value ONE-WAY, displayed as a downward arrow, meaning that the <CATREF> node precedes the 'dummy' node. This is correct (see 5.2.4 on page 105).

(40)   **Check that the 'Query is OK' message is displayed and click on OK to send the query to the server.** The Too many solutions dialogue box will be displayed.

(41)   **Click on OK to download the first 10 solutions.** The query text will be displayed above the solutions in the *Query2* window. It should read: (<catRef target=wriMed2>)*("dummy")

The One-way link between the two components of the query is represented by a star. Each of the two components is enclosed in parentheses.

Formulating the CQL Query   You should now be able to formulate the text of a CQL Query which combines the desired text-type and scope restrictions. It should read:

```
(<catRef target=wriMed2>) *
(("hits"=VVZ|"hits"=NN2-VVZ)
/ <head type="main">)
```

Click on the CQL QUERY button on the toolbar (or select NEW QUERY and CQL from the FILE menu). The CQL dialogue box will be displayed.

Type in the text of the query *exactly* as above, taking special care over case and parentheses. Spaces around the * and / operators are not significant. The text will automatically wrap round to the next line as you type it.

Click on OK to send the query to the server. The Too many solutions dialogue box will be displayed, stating that there are 77 solutions in 44 texts.

These numbers are only a little smaller than those for the earlier query (*Query1*), which did not include a <CATREF> restriction (see 7.2.2 on page 134). This confirms that most of the occurrences of 'hits' in headings in the corpus do indeed come from periodicals (77/98).

Download all the solutions. The solutions should be displayed in the *Query3* window.

7.2.4   Displaying and sorting part-of-speech codes

Since we have included cases where 'hits' has the portmanteau code NN2-VVZ in the query, in some of the solutions 'hits' may be a noun rather than a verb. We therefore need to inspect all the solutions where 'hits' has a portmanteau code in order to delete these cases. We can do this by displaying the solutions in POS format and then using the POS CODE collating option to sort them according to their part-of-speech codes.

Select OPTIONS from the QUERY menu. The Query Options dialogue box will be displayed.

Select POS format, then click on OK, and wait while SARA downloads the part-of-speech information from the server. The solutions will be re-displayed, using different colours for different parts of speech.

The query focus (the word 'hits') may not always appear in the same colour. Unless you have radically modified the default colour scheme (see 1.7.4 on page 227), cases of 'hits' with a VVZ code will be in a different colour from those with a portmanteau NN2-VVZ code. First, check to make sure this is the case.

(48) **Position the mouse on the word 'hits' in the first solution, and hold down the right mouse button.** The POS code for this word will be displayed.

(49) **Release the button, and go through the solutions until you find one where 'hits' is displayed in a different colour.** Repeating the above procedure, you will find it has a different POS code. *In a POS format display, positioning the mouse on any word on the screen and holding down the right mouse button will display its POS code.*

We now want to remove any solutions where 'hits' has a NN2-VVZ portmanteau code but is in fact a plural noun. We shall first sort the solutions by the POS code for 'hits', so as to group those with portmanteau codes.

(50) **Select SORT from the QUERY menu.**

(51) **Select CENTRE as Primary key with a span of 1.**

(52) **Select POS CODE collating.**

(53) **Click on OK to perform the sort.** As the sorting of POS codes is alphabetical, solutions where 'hits' is coded as NN2-VVZ will be grouped before those where it is coded as VVZ. In each group, the word 'hits' should be displayed in a different colour. *You can only use POS code collating in a POS format display.*

(54) **Scroll through the NN2-VVZ group of solutions, and mark those where 'hits' is in fact a noun by double-clicking on them (or pressing the space bar).** The solutions with nouns are virtually all cases where 'hits' has the meaning of 'successes', as in 'Beatles hits', 'video hits', etc.

(55) **Select THIN then REVERSE SELECTION from the QUERY menu to delete the marked solutions.** The solutions should now only contain instances where 'hits' is a verb. You can see how many of these there are by looking at the number on the status bar.

7.2.5 *Re-using the text of one query in another: 'hits' as a noun*

Having determined the frequency of 'hits' as a verb in periodical headings, it is relatively straightforward to compare it with the frequency of 'hits' as a noun. If we design a new query to find the frequency of 'hits' in periodical headings regardless of part of speech, subtracting the number of verbs from this latter figure will give us the number of nouns.

The easiest way to produce this new CQL query is to copy the text of the previous version to the clipboard, and then edit it.

(56) **Select EDIT from the QUERY menu to return to the CQL query.** The query text will be displayed in reverse video, showing that it is selected.

Press CTRL+INSERT to copy the query text to the clipboard. *Only the Word Query dialogue box has a dedicated* COPY *button (see 7.2.1 on page 131). To copy query text from a Phrase Query, Pattern Query or CQL dialogue box, you must select it and then use the Windows* CTRL+INSERT *command.*

Click on CANCEL to return to the solutions display, then click on the CQL QUERY button on the toolbar. A new CQL dialogue box will be displayed.

Press SHIFT+INSERT to copy the text of the previous query into the dialogue box.

Delete the POS code specifications. The query should now read:

```
(<catRef target=wriMed2>)
*  (("hits")/<head type="main">)
```

Click on OK to send the query to the server. The Too many solutions dialogue box will be displayed, stating that there are 100 solutions. This suggests that the vast majority of occurrences of 'hits' in periodical headings are in fact verbs. You can if you want verify this by displaying the solutions in POS format and sorting them by the focus using POS code collating, then examining those tagged as nouns.

7.2.6   *Investigating colligations using POS collating*

Literal and metaphorical uses   Let us now see what sorts of things hit and are hit in the headlines where 'hits' is a verb, i.e. whether there are literal as well as metaphorical uses. When the word is being used in the literal sense, there will typically be a noun both before and after it, so we can make these cases somewhat easier to find simply by sorting the solutions according to the parts-of-speech of the words to the left and to the right. This will highlight grammatical patterns, or *colligations*, which typically precede and follow the query focus.

Download the first 10 solutions, then use the WINDOW menu to return to the window of solutions where 'hits' is a verb (*Query3*).
Re-sort these solutions using the two words to the right of the focus as Primary key, with POS CODE collating. The solutions will be grouped according to the codes of the two words following 'hits'.

This grouping highlights many phrasal and prepositional verb forms, such as 'hits back' and 'hits at'. There are also a number of verb-adverb-preposition combinations, like 'hits back at', 'hits out at/over', etc. All these seem metaphorical. We also find a range of metaphorical uses indicating increase or decline: 'hits high', 'hits record', 'hits target', 'hits the roof', 'hits rock bottom', 'hits buffers' etc. In the group where a noun immediately follows 'hits', we find a wide range of affected people, companies, places and objects, but only "Train hits getaway van" and "Baby hurt as firework hits her on head" stand out as clearly literal. When you enlarge the context, the mysterious "Blunt instrument hits Oslo" turns out to be a pun on the name of a sportsman whose team beat Oslo's.

Now let us see what precedes 'hits'.

(64) **Re-sort the solutions using the two words to the left of the focus as Primary key, again with POS CODE collating.** The solutions will be grouped according to the part-of-speech sequence preceding the verb 'hits' — typically including some noun as its subject.

Many preceding nouns denote violent catastrophes ('attack', 'blast', 'blaze', 'blow', 'bombshell', 'hurricane'), and negative economic and political events ('letdown', 'confusion', 'scandal', 'gloom', 'crisis'). All of these involve metaphorical uses of 'hits'. Where names of people, companies and institutions occur, they are generally followed by a phrasal or prepositional verb form — again, as we have seen, metaphorical. In no case do we find an animate agent acting as the subject of 'hits' in a literal sense.

Results   There is thus little evidence in the corpus to warrant a literal reading of 'hits' as a verb in the headline 'Madonna hits album'. While considerably more frequent as a verb than as a noun, the verb 'hits' seems overwhelmingly metaphorical in headings, and where literal, not to refer to deliberate human action. A literal reading would seem to depend on the application of a 'person-hits-object' schema which is probably associated with other types or components of texts.

7.3   Discussion and suggestions for further work

7.3.1   Using part-of-speech codes

You may have noticed that even after eliminating spurious solutions to the query involving portmanteau codes, there still remain a few solutions where 'hits' is clearly a noun — but is coded unambiguously as a verb! CLAWS, like all automatic part-of-speech tagging programs, is less than 100 percent accurate, so any POS QUERY or sort with POS CODE collating is likely to involve some errors. One useful indication of the probable accuracy of the tagging of a particular word as a given part of speech is the relative frequency with which portmanteau tags have been assigned: generally speaking, the smaller the number of cases with a given portmanteau code as compared to the number which are assigned unambiguously to one or other of the categories in the portmanteau, the more reliable the tagging of the word. Thus in the case of 'hits', we found a very high proportion of occurrences with portmanteau tags, a fact reflected in the number of tagging errors encountered.

SARA does not allow you to formulate queries in terms of parts of speech without specifying the words in question. If you are interested (say) in finding cases where an adverb precedes a modal verb and a pronominal subject, as in 'Nor could I', you cannot simply look for this sequence of POS codes. The only way to find particular part-of-speech sequences is as colligations: you must specify a word, word-POS pair, pattern, or phrase (with disjunctions as necessary, such as nor|neither), and then sort the solutions to this query according to the POS codes of the surrounding words. In this manner those solutions which match the desired pattern of codes can be grouped, and the remainder removed by thinning. The main difficulty with this procedure is that the number of solutions initially downloaded may be very large in comparison with the number which match the desired colligational pattern.

7.3.2 Some similar problems

'Blasts' A verb which appears to be used in headlines with a similar metaphorical meaning to 'hits' is 'blasts'. How frequent is it, and does it also occur in headlines as other parts of speech? Is it ever used literally? *Use the QUERY BUILDER to design a query which looks for occurrences of 'blasts' which have VVZ codes, in <HEAD> elements whose TYPE attribute has the value main. Then edit the query to look for occurrences which have other POS codes.*

There are 20 occurrences of 'blasts' coded as a verb, nearly all of them metaphorical. In the second version of the query, if you download all 16 solutions and display them using POS format, you will see that there are only two unambiguous noun uses, which stand out in a different colour. All the cases with portmanteau codes appear to be verbs. The most frequent verb use is in the phrasal form 'blasts back'.

Whose 'Whom'? The use of 'whom' is often considered formal, particularly where it is preceded by a preposition. How frequently does 'whom' appear in informal conversation, as represented by the spoken demographic component of the BNC? Which prepositions usually precede it? And how do these figures compare with its use in the spoken context-governed component of the corpus, which contains more 'public' speech (see 6.1.2 on page 112)? *Use QUERY BUILDER to search for occurrences of 'whom' where the <CATREF> ALL_TYPE attribute has the value spoken_demographic. Then design a second query where it has the value spoken_context-governed. In both cases, use POS CODE collating to sort the solutions according to the first word to the left of the query focus, in order to group those where 'whom' is preceded by PRF (the code for 'of') or PRP (other prepositions). Mark the solutions in these groups and delete the remainder using the THIN SELECTION option. Then re-sort, again according to the first word on the left,* *but this time using* IGNORE CASE *collating. This will group the solutions according to the orthographic form of the preceding preposition.*

There are only 21 occurrences of 'whom' in the spoken demographic component of the BNC, in 10 of which 'whom' is preceded by a preposition ('from', 'of', 'to', or 'with'). In the similarly-sized context-governed component, on the other hand, there are 250 occurrences: the most common prepositions appear to be the same.

Exit 'exeunt'   Are the words 'exit' and 'exeunt' still used in stage directions in contemporary English? *Rather than the number of occurrences of 'exit' and 'exeunt' in stage directions, a better indicator of their use might be the proportion of texts containing stage directions in which they appear. You can calculate this by first performing an* SGML QUERY *to find occurrences of the* <STAGE> *element (see 5.2.2 on page 100) and reading off the number of texts containing solutions, and then using* QUERY BUILDER *to find occurrences where 'exit' or 'exeunt' appear within the scope of a* <STAGE> *element, again reading off the number of texts.*

This question is too specialized to be answered using the BNC. There are only 9 texts which include <STAGE> *elements, and only 2 occurrences of 'exit' or 'exeunt' in such elements, both of them in the same text. These numbers are clearly far too small to permit reliable inferences.*

8 Springing surprises on the armchair linguist

8.1 The problem: intuitions about grammar

8.1.1 Participant roles and syntactic variants

In discussing the role of corpora in aiding those 'armchair linguists' who work with intuitive judgements, Fillmore (1992) argues that corpora cannot fully replace native-speaker intuitions about a language. No corpus can exhaustively indicate what is and is not grammatical. However large, it will not attest every form which is correct, and will indeed attest many forms which are incorrect in the terms of any descriptive grammar (Aarts 1991). Moreover, corpus data may not provide appropriate instances to illustrate every kind of grammatical distinction. Noting that dictionaries do not distinguish between 'running risks' and 'taking' them, Fillmore argues that unlike 'running a risk', 'taking a risk' seems to imply that harm may occur as a result of deliberate action by the subject. Thus, the second of the following sentences seems unacceptable because a car cannot take deliberate action, as it is not a volitional subject:

- A car parked here runs the risk of getting dented.
- *A car parked here takes the risk of getting dented.

Looking at corpus examples, however, Fillmore found no cases where 'run' could not apparently be substituted by 'take', or vice-versa. Nor did he find examples which contradicted his proposed generalization, i.e. where 'take' did not have a volitional subject. The use of corpora, he argues, still leaves a place for invented examples in order to highlight such distinctions.

Fillmore's examples concern the semantic restrictions on the kinds of participants that can be associated with 'take a risk'. Restrictions on the use of such expressions may also be syntactic. Discussing the phrase 'bear love', Bolinger (1976: 9) argues that "it is normal to have 'bear' in a relative clause in an expression like 'the love that I bear them' [. . .]. A declarative or interrogative is all right with a negation or implied negation: 'I bear them no love'. But a simple straightforward affirmative declaration is out of the question: '*I bear them love'." Again, corpora may not provide clear evidence to support these intuitions. What is intuitively 'normal' may nonetheless be too rare to be adequately documented in a corpus, and what is 'out of the question' may on occasion be found in creative (or linguistics) texts.

Evidence from corpora may nonetheless help armchair linguists to refine their hypotheses. What occurs in the corpus must be accounted for in some way; the absence of what does not occur is at any rate matter for reflection. This task uses the BNC to look at limits on the use of the expression 'spring a surprise', seeing what sorts of participants it involves, and what syntactic forms it takes. Questions to be asked include:

- Does 'spring a surprise' require an animate agent as subject, or can an event also spring a surprise ('The rain sprang a surprise on us')?

- What sort of syntactic variation is possible? Do we find plurals ('spring surprises'), passives ('a surprise was sprung'), continuous forms ('he was springing a surprise'), definite uses ('they sprang the surprise on him after lunch'), nominalizations ('the springing of surprises' or 'a springer of surprises')?

- In what collocations does it occur? For instance, what modifiers are used with 'surprise' (e.g. 'he sprang a big surprise', 'springer of an unexpected surprise')?

To look at these questions poses two main problems in the design of appropriate queries:

- how to include inflections and other derivates of a base or root form, such as variants in number, tense, aspect, mood, and voice, etc., nominal forms derived from a verb, verbal forms derived from a noun or adjective, etc.;

- how to include variants of phrases where components appear in different orders, or at different distances from each other.

8.1.2   Inflections and derived forms

While English morphology has fewer inflections than most other European languages, there are still a significant number to be considered. Most nouns have two different forms, a singular and a plural, or four if singular and plural possessives are included (SARA counts possessives as two *L-words*: see 2.2.1 on page 64). Adjectives and adverbs may have a comparative and a superlative in addition to their base form, while regular verbs have an '-s' form for the third person singular present, an '-ing' participle, and an '-ed' form used in the past tense and as past participle. Many irregular verbs also have distinct forms for past tense and past participle. In the case of 'spring a surprise', alongside the base forms 'spring' and 'surprise', we need to consider the inflected forms 'springs', 'springing', 'sprang', 'sprung', and 'surprises'.

English also uses affixation to derive other words from a base form. Thus adverbs, nouns and verbs may be derived from adjectives ('softly', 'softness', and 'soften' from 'soft'), nouns and adjectives from verbs ('proof', 'proven', 'provenly', 'provable', 'provably' from 'prove'), etc. When examining possible variants, we may also want to take such derived forms into consideration — for instance, is 'springer of surprises' found in the corpus?

We have already seen two ways in which SARA allows you to include a range of alternative forms in a single query. The LOOKUP facility in WORD QUERY provides an alphabetical list of all the words in the corpus which begin with the same string of characters: thus typing in 'limit' generates a list including 'limitation', 'limitations', 'limited', 'limitedly', 'limiting', 'limits', etc. From this list you can select those items you wish to include in the query (see 2.2.1 on page 64). This approach is not always adequate, however. Looking up words beginning with the letters 'go' is hardly the way to list forms derived from the verb 'go': it will include an enormous number of spurious items (from 'goad' to 'gout' via 'Gotham'), and it will not include 'went'.

One way to avoid this difficulty is to specify each of the forms required as an alternative node in QUERY BUILDER, using OR links (as we did for 'a' and 'an' in the phrase 'a/an _ too far': see 4.2.2 on page 92). A more economical alternative is to specify a *pattern* which matches only the required forms. Thus in the case of 'go', we can reduce the number of spurious matches by specifying that if there is a third character following the letters 'go', it must be either an 'e' ('goes', 'goer', 'goers'), an 'i' ('going', 'goings'), or an 'n' ('gone'). 'Goad' and 'gout' will now be excluded. We will still have 'Goebbels' and 'Goethe' to contend with, but these too might be eliminated by specifying that any fourth character must be 'e', 'n', 'r' or 's'.

SARA allows you to create queries using patterns in two ways. You can use the PATTERN option under WORD QUERY to create a list of words which match the pattern, or else you can use the PATTERN QUERY option to include a pattern in the query directly. In this task we shall use Word Query in order to design and test particular pattern specifications, and then apply them using the Pattern Query option.

8.1.3 Variation in order and distance

In the case of a phrase such as 'spring a surprise', we need to consider not only possible inflected and derived forms of its components, but also variations in their order and distance. Syntactic variants might involve modifiers ('spring an unpleasant surprise'), passives ('a surprise was sprung on them'), or relative constructions ('the surprise he sprang on them'). To include these we must design a query where forms of 'spring' and 'surprise' may occur in either order, and at a variable distance from each other.

QUERY BUILDER allows you to search for different orderings of the components of complex queries by using a TWO-WAY link-type, and to vary the distance between them by using the SPAN scope option.

8.1.4   Highlighted features

This task shows you:

- how to list words which match a specified pattern using the PATTERN option in WORD QUERY;
- how to find occurrences of words which match specified patterns using PATTERN QUERY;
- how to combine query components in any order using TWO-WAY links between nodes in Query Builder;
- how to restrict the scope of a query to a maximum number of words using the SPAN scope option in Query Builder;
- how to save solutions to a file using the LISTING option.

It assumes you already know how to:

- adjust default settings (see 1.2.8 on page 54);
- carry out a Word Query look up (see 2.2.1 on page 64);
- design complex queries using Query Builder (see 4.2.2 on page 91, 5.2.4 on page 105, 6.2.3 on page 117, 7.2.2 on page 133);
- adjust downloading procedure in the Too many solutions dialogue box (see 2.2.3 on page 66);
- sort and thin solutions (see 3.2.2 on page 78, 2.2.4 on page 68);
- calculate collocates (see 3.2.1 on page 76);
- save queries (see 2.2.5 on page 70).

8.1.5   Before you start

Using the VIEW menu PREFERENCES option, set the defaults as follows:

MAX DOWNLOAD LENGTH	500 characters
MAX DOWNLOADS	10
FORMAT	Plain
SCOPE	Paragraph
VIEW: QUERY and ANNOTATION	checked
CONCORDANCE	checked
BROWSER: SHOW TAGS	unchecked

8.2 Procedure

8.2.1 Designing patterns using Word Query: forms of 'spring'

To investigate the use of 'spring a surprise', what inflections and derived forms must be considered? The only inflected form of the noun 'surprise' which seems relevant is the plural, with its '-s' suffix. Inflections of the verb 'spring', on the other hand, include not only the suffixed forms 'springs' and 'springing', but also those with a changed stem, namely 'sprang' and 'sprung'.

If you are familiar with Unix *regular expressions*, you will understand how a pattern can easily be constructed to match all these forms. If you are not, you will need to learn only a small amount of their syntax in order to understand how to construct patterns using SARA.

The easiest way to master the syntax of regular expressions is through WORD QUERY. If you check the PATTERN option in the dialogue box, Word Query allows you to type in a pattern and obtain a list of the words in the word index that match that pattern. This provides a good way of testing a pattern and of seeing what the effect is before you apply it.

We will begin by using Word Query to create a pattern which matches the base, inflected and derived forms of 'spring'. If you are already familiar with the syntax of regular expressions you may prefer to go directly to 8.2.2 on page 150.

Click on the WORD QUERY button, then check the PATTERN option in the dialogue box. *Checking the Pattern option indicates that the input string is to be interpreted as a pattern rather than as a normal character sequence.*

Type in the string spring **and click on LOOKUP.** Where the pattern is a string of letters without variables, there can be at most one word in the word index that will match it — in this case, the word 'spring'.

Any character: the dot symbol A *variable* in a regular expression is part of a pattern which can match more than one letter. For instance, to include the forms 'sprang' and 'sprung' as well as 'spring', we can use a pattern which will match any one character in place of the vowel 'i'.

Change the input string to spr.ng *The dot variable matches any single character at all, vowel or consonant.*

Click on LOOKUP. The list of matching words now contains all the six-letter words in the word index which have 's p r n g' as their first, second, third, fifth and sixth characters respectively. This includes 'sprang', 'spring', 'sprung', but also 'spreng' and 'sprong' — remember that the index includes proper names, acronyms, foreign words, printing and spelling errors.

Alternation in pattern components: square brackets To exclude the forms 'spreng' and 'sprong' from this list, you can either:

- specify that the second character must be 'a', 'i', or 'u';
- specify that the second character must not be 'e' or 'o'.

We demonstrate both methods.

(5)   **Change the input string to** spr[aiu]ng **and click on** LOOKUP. The list of matching words now includes only 'sprang', 'spring' and 'sprung'. *Square brackets indicate that any one of the characters listed between them must match for the pattern to be successful.*

(6)   **Change the input string to** spr[^eo]ng **and click on** LOOKUP. The list of matching words should be unchanged. *A carat symbol (^) immediately following the opening square bracket indicates that any character other than those listed between the brackets must match for the pattern to be successful.*

Whether it is more appropriate to list permitted or excluded alternatives will depend on which is more accurate and/or easy to formulate. In this case there is little difference, so for the moment let us stick to the list of exclusions just constructed.

Repetition of pattern components: the ? and * characters   The list of matching words now includes the base and irregular inflected forms of the verb 'spring'. It does not yet include the regular inflected forms, i.e. with the suffixes '-s' and '-ing'.

(7)   **Change the input string to** spr[^eo]ng.* **by adding a dot and a star.** *A character followed by a star matches any number of occurrences of that character (including zero). Thus AB* matches 'A', 'AB', 'ABB' etc. The dot character followed by a star (.*) matches any number of any characters (including zero). This sequence should not be used as the first component of a pattern.*

(8)   **Click on** LOOKUP. The list of matching words is now much longer, and clearly includes many spurious items, from 'spranger' and 'spring-cleaning' to 'springsteen' and 'spryngabedde'. The final .* sequence clearly allows too many matches.

(9)   **Change the input string to** spr[^eo]ng.? *A character followed by a question mark matches one or zero occurrences of that character. Thus the dot character followed by a question mark matches one or zero occurrences of any character.*

(10)   **Click on** LOOKUP. The list of matching words is now shorter, being limited to six-and seven-letter words, but it still includes 'spring-' and 'springy' as well as 'springs'.

(11)   **Change the input string to** spr[^eo]ngs? **and click on** LOOKUP. By substituting the dot with an 's' followed by a question mark, you have stated that any seventh letter must be 's', and the list of matching words now includes only

'springs' in addition to the previous six-letter forms. The list still however lacks the '-ing' inflection.

Change the input string to `spr[^eo]ngs?i?n?g?` **and click on LOOKUP.** This pattern allows each of the characters 's i n g' to appear after the base stem, provided that they occur in that order, and the matching words list now includes all the inflections of the verb 'spring'. It still however excludes other derived forms, notably 'springer' and 'springers'.

Change the input string to `spr[^eo]nge?r?s?i?n?g?` **and click on LOOKUP.** The list of matching words now includes 'springer' and 'springers', but has also introduced 'spranger' and 'springen'. *You can also use the question mark to include prefixed or infixed forms in a pattern. For instance,* `u?n?necessary` *will match both 'necessary' and 'unnecessary';* `orienta?t?ed` *will match both 'oriented' and 'orientated'.*

A question worth asking at this point is whether it is really necessary for the pattern to exclude all spurious matches.

Click on 'spranger', then on 'springen', to find out their respective frequencies in the corpus. 'Springen' occurs only once in the BNC, so even if it were included in the solutions to a query, it would be easy to identify and eliminate it using the SORT and THIN options (see 3.2.2 on page 78, 2.2.3 on page 66). 'Spranger', however, occurs ten times, so it might be better to make the effort to exclude it from the pattern. The problem is how to do so without excluding other similar forms, such as 'springer' and 'springers'.

Alternative patterns: the vertical bar symbol We can exclude 'spranger' but not 'springer' by only allowing `[iu]` as variants for the base vowel in our pattern, specifying 'sprang' as a separate alternative.

Change the input string to `spr(ang|[iu]nge?r?s?i?n?g?)` **and click on LOOKUP.** The matching words list now includes only the forms 'sprang', 'spring', 'springen', 'springer', 'springers', 'springing', 'springs', and 'sprung'. In the next section we will use this pattern to include variants of 'spring' in a PATTERN QUERY. *The | symbol indicates a disjunction, i.e. words in the list must match either the pattern preceding the | or that following it. The parentheses indicate the part of the string for which alternatives are given. The | symbol is particularly useful where there is one form (in this case 'sprang') which radically differs from the others to be included, as is often the case with the past tense form of irregular verbs.*

To avoid having to retype the pattern you have so painstakingly designed, click on COPY to copy the input string to the clipboard for later re-use, then on CANCEL to close the Word Query dialogue box.

8.2.2 Using Pattern Query

Let us now construct a PATTERN QUERY which will include these inflected and derived forms of the verb 'spring'.

Why not just use WORD QUERY, selecting all the relevant forms from the word index as alternatives? The main reason is economic: Word Query allows you to include multiple selections from the index in a single query (see 2.2.2 on page 65), but if too many are chosen, the server may not be able to handle them all. The Pattern Query option, on the other hand, sends the server a pattern which is treated as a single alternative regardless of the number of words which match it. It thus makes fewer demands on resources. This is particularly important where, as in this task, you want to design a complex query involving more than one pattern. *Note that Pattern Queries are very much slower where they include disjunctions at the start of the pattern. For this reason you should always use a pattern like* spr(ang|ing) *rather than* sprang|spring.

Other procedures which may overload the server are multiple OR disjunctions in QUERY BUILDER *(see 4.2.2 on page 92), and multiple selections from the POS list using* POS QUERY *(see 7.2.1 on page 131).*

(17) **Click on the PATTERN QUERY button on the toolbar (or select PATTERN under NEW QUERY from the FILE menu).** The Pattern Query dialogue box will be displayed.

(18) **Press SHIFT+INSERT to paste the pattern you designed in the last section from the clipboard.** The clipboard should still contain the required string: spr(ang|[iu]nge?r?s?i?n?g?). Type it in, if it does not. The text of the query will wrap automatically at the end of the line.

(19) **Click on OK to send the query to the server.** The Too many solutions dialogue box will be displayed.

(20) **Click on OK to download the first 10 solutions.** You will see that these already include two instances of the phrase 'spring a surprise'.

8.2.3 Varying order and distance between nodes in Query Builder

We are now in a position to build a complex query combining the pattern for forms of 'spring' with one for forms of 'surprise'. We need to design a query which:

- finds cases where 'spring' and 'surprise' co-occur, including inflected and derived forms of either word (for instance 'springer of surprises');
- finds cases where the two forms are not adjacent ('spring a big surprise' as well as 'springing surprises');
- finds cases where these forms appear in either order (both 'spring a surprise' and 'the surprise he sprang').

Using the QUERY BUILDER, you can satisfy these requirements by specifying two patterns as content nodes, to be joined in either order, and restricting the scope of the query to a small number of words.

Specifying the content nodes   First, let us create the two content nodes in the query, one corresponding to forms of 'spring', and one to forms of 'surprise'.

Click on the QUERY BUILDER button on the toolbar to display the Query Builder.
Click on the downward branch of the empty content node to create a second content node.

In the first node, we need to provide a pattern which will include inflections and derived forms of the base form 'spring'.

Click on the first node, and select EDIT then PATTERN. The Pattern Query dialogue box will be displayed.
Press SHIFT+INSERT to paste the pattern you designed in the last section from the clipboard. The clipboard should still contain the required string: [spr(ang|[iu]nge?r?s?i?n?g?). Type it in, if it does not.
Click on OK to return to the Query Builder. You will see that the pattern has been inserted in the first content node. The curly brackets surrounding the string indicate that it is to be interpreted as a pattern.

We now need to design a Pattern Query for the second node, corresponding to forms of 'surprise'. As a regular noun, this may have the forms 'surprise' and 'surprises'. To make sure that the pattern is correct, we will again use Word Query to design and test it before copying it to the Pattern Query. You can do this without leaving the Query Builder.

Click in the second node and select EDIT then WORD to display the Word Query dialogue box.
Type in the string surprises? **and click on LOOKUP, making sure that the PATTERN box is checked.** You will see that the matching words list includes only the desired forms.
Click on COPY to copy this pattern to the clipboard, then on CANCEL to return to the Query Builder.
Click in the second content node again, this time selecting EDIT then PATTERN.
Paste the pattern from the clipboard into the Pattern Query dialogue box using SHIFT+INSERT.
Click on OK to insert this component in the Query Builder node.

Linking the content nodes   We now need to specify the link-type between the two content nodes. The downward arrow joining the nodes indicates that this currently has the default value of ONE-WAY, meaning that the 'surprise' pattern follows the 'spring' pattern. As we also want to find cases where these nodes occur in the opposite order, we must change the link-type to TWO-WAY.

(32) **Click on the link between the two nodes and select LINK TYPE then TWO-WAY.** The link between the two nodes will be displayed as a two-way arrow, indicating that the contents of the nodes in question may occur in either order, and not necessarily adjacently (see 4.2.2 on page 92).

Scoping the query   Lastly, we need to specify the scope of the query — the limit within which all the content nodes must occur. The default scope (<BNCDOC>) requires only that 'spring' and 'surprise' be present in the same BNC document, which is clearly excessive.

In selecting a scope we need to find a balance between, on the one hand, maximizing *recall* (ensuring that *all* the relevant solutions are found), and on the other hand maximizing *precision* (ensuring that *only* relevant solutions are found). For instance, if we restrict the scope to a single sentence (an <s> element), this will exclude any cases where 'spring' and 'surprise' occur in different sentences, along such lines as 'They were unaware they were in for a surprise. He sprang it on them after lunch.' If, on the other hand, we use a larger element as scope, such as a paragraph (a <P> element), we will increase the risk of spurious solutions — as well as excluding any occurrences in spoken texts, where <P> elements do not occur.

Where it is difficult to identify an appropriate element, you can specify the scope as a number of words, using the Query Builder SPAN option. This allows you to indicate the maximum number of L-words within which all the content nodes must be found.

(33) **Click on the scope node and select SPAN.** The Span dialogue box will be displayed.

(34) **Type in the number 10 and click on OK.** You will see that the scope node now contains the number 10, meaning a span of 10 L-words. *The maximum span permitted is 99 L-words. The default value is 5 L-words.*

(35) **Check to see that the 'Query is OK' message is displayed, then click on OK to send the query to the server.** After a while, the Too many solutions dialogue box will be displayed, telling you that there are 62 solutions.

(36) **Click on the DOWNLOAD ALL button, then on OK to download all the solutions.** *Provided that you checked QUERY in the VIEW PREFERENCES options*

(see 8.1.5 on page 146), the query text will be displayed at the top of the solutions in its CQL form. You will see that:

- *each Pattern Query is surrounded by curly brackets;*
- *the Two-way link is indicated by a sharp sign;*
- *the scope is indicated at the end of the query by a slash followed by the number of words selected as span.*

8.2.4   Checking precision with the Collocation and Sort options

We now need to remove any spurious solutions from the display — i.e. which do not contain some form of the phrase 'spring a surprise'. Ultimately, the only way of doing this is by inspecting the solutions, but you can facilitate the process using the COLLOCATION and SORT options.

You may remember from designing the component of the query relating to forms of 'spring' that this pattern also matched the spurious item 'springen' (see 8.2.1 on page 148). Before going any further, let us make sure that this form is not included among the solutions to the query.

Because the second node in the query, {surprises?}, is highlighted as the query focus (see 8.3.1 on page 157), and its distance from the first node varies, you cannot locate 'springen' by sorting the solutions. You can however find out if it occurs within a span of up to 9 L-words by using the COLLOCATION option under the QUERY menu (see 3.2.1 on page 76). *In the example here, a collocation span of 9 is equivalent to a span of 10 as a scope in Query Builder. This is because SPAN is measured differently in the Collocation option from the way it is measured in the Query Builder. In the Query Builder, a span is the number of L-words within which the entire query must be satisfied; that is, it must include everything from the beginning of the first node to the end of the query focus. Thus, if the query focus is a single word, a span of 2 will include the query focus and one word either to the left or to the right of it. In the Collocation option it is assumed that the query focus will normally be a single L-word, and the span is calculated as the distance of the collocate from the leftmost word of the query focus, not counting the latter. Thus a collocation span of 2 will include the two words to the left and the two words to the right of the leftmost word of the query focus — a total of five words as measured in Query Builder. In the example here, we wish to find occurrences within the 9 L-words which precede the query focus — a span of 9 in Collocation, and one of 10 in Query Builder.*

Select QUERY then COLLOCATION.

Type the string springen **in the COLLOCATE box and set the span to the maximum value of 9 words.**

Click on CALCULATE. The collocation frequency of 'springen' is 0, meaning that this form does not occur as a collocate.

(40) **Click on CLOSE to return to the solutions display.**

Sorting and thinning the solutions   A glance through the solutions suggests
that active forms (where 'spring' precedes 'surprise') are much more frequent
than passive or relative ones (where 'surprise' precedes 'spring'). For this reason
it would seem most appropriate to sort the solutions by the left. This will group
recurrent articles and modifiers preceding forms of 'surprise' (such as 'a' and
'big'), together with the varying forms of 'spring' occurring before the same
article or pre-modifier.

(41) **Click on QUERY then SORT, and specify the Primary key as LEFT
with a span of 5 and IGNORE CASE collating.**

(42) **Click on SORT to sort the solutions.** *Note that when sorting Plain format
displays, span is counted in terms of orthographic (blank-delimited) words rather than
L-words.*

(43) **Scroll through the solutions to identify spurious ones.** You may find a
number of cases where 'spring' refers to the season, or 'springer' to a breed of
dog.

(44) **Double-click on these solutions (or press the space bar) to mark them,
then eliminate them using THIN and REVERSE SELECTION from the
QUERY menu.**

Saving the query   Given the amount of hard work you have dedicated to its
design, it may be a good idea to save this query for future reference.

(45) **Click on the SAVE button on the toolbar (or select SAVE from the
FILE menu), and type in an appropriate mnemonic as the filename.**
The query will automatically be saved with the extension .sqy (see 4.2.2 on
page 94).

8.2.5 Saving solutions with the Listing option

You should now inspect and categorize the remaining solutions. You may find
this easier using a printout. Printing directly using the PRINT button on the
toolbar will provide only one line of context for each solution (see 3.2.3 on
page 81), which may not be enough to see both 'spring' and 'surprise'. It may
therefore be better to save the solutions with a larger context and then print
them using another application. The LISTING option under the QUERY menu
allows you to save the solutions to a query together with the full downloaded
context. You can then retrieve the Listing file into a word processor, or SGML-
aware browser, and edit or print it.

Select QUERY then LISTING. The Listing SAVE As dialogue box will be displayed, proposing the current window title as filename, with an .sgm extension. *SARA automatically assigns* .sgm *extensions to Listing files.*

Click on OK to save the solutions. You will be returned to the solutions display. *Listing files save solutions in the currently displayed order, with the currently selected format and scope (see 1.2.8 on page 55, 5.2.3 on page 103).* PLAIN *format listings consist only of the words and punctuation.* POS *and* SGML *format listings show all SGML markup, with the angle brackets of the original SGML tags replaced by square brackets.* CUSTOM *format listings follow the indications in the Custom* linefmt.txt *file, which you can edit using the* CONFIGURE *option (see 9.2.2 on page 165).*

Remember that you can also save individual solutions by copying them to the clipboard using the COPY *option (see 1.2.7 on page 54). Copying to the clipboard only preserves Plain, Custom, or SGML format, however:* POS *format is converted to Plain.*

Without exiting from SARA, switch to a word processor, retrieve your .sgm file, and print it.

When you have finished, exit from your word processor and return to SARA.

The following extract from an .sgm listing file (saved from a Plain format display with Paragraph scope) shows the markup inserted in listing files. Each solution is marked up as an SGML <HIT> element, whose attributes specify the text identifier and sentence number displayed on the status bar. The query focus and the text to the left and right of it are indicated by <FOCUS>, <LEFT> and <RIGHT> tags respectively.

```
<hit text=A05 n=386><left>
Glasser orders his events thematically,
while also wanting to tell a story and to
spring <focus>surprises.<right> Charlie's
departure is the first of several, and this
event is succeeded by the announcement of
a further theme when the rabbi's thunderings
pass over the heads of his congregation.
</hit>
```

Study your printout of the solutions (or scroll carefully through the solutions on screen) to see:

- whether there are any more spurious solutions to be deleted;
- whether the subject of 'spring' is always animate;

- how frequently 'surprise' is pre-modified, and whether these modifiers fall into any particular class;
- what sorts of syntactic variants are present, e.g. passive and relative constructions, nominalization with 'springing', 'springer', etc.

Results   Inspecting the solutions shows that:

- There are quite a few spurious solutions. The main reason appears to be the frequency of the noun 'spring', as in "to her great surprise she is asked to the Spring ball". *It would be possible to exclude these occurrences by limiting the Pattern Query and using* POS QUERY *to search for those forms which need to be specified as verbs (see 7.2.1 on page 131). We would thus have three alternative content nodes:*

  ```
  {spr([au]ng|inging)}
  "spring"=VVB|"spring"=VVI
  "springs"=VVZ
  ```

- By no means all the solutions have animate individual or institutional agents as their subjects. Along with Mr Kinnock, Calvin Smith, and a number of racehorses and football teams, we find discussion, bad news, a Scottish burn, the onset of spring, the domestic financial system, and technology can all spring surprises.
- Relatively few instances use an 'on' phrase to specify the victim of the surprise ("we decided to spring a little surprise on two friends"). It is far more common for this participant to be left unspecified.
- 'Spring' most frequently appears in the active singular, with 'surprise' directly preceded by the indefinite article 'a' (21 occurrences). The article is omitted in two cases from newspaper headlines, as is typical in such contexts.
- Pre-modifiers of 'surprise' generally indicate size or pleasantness: 'a little surprise', 'a major surprise', 'maximum surprise', 'a dazzling surprise', 'a This is Your Life surprise', 'a nasty surprise', and 'the cruellest surprise (of all)'. With the plural 'surprises' we find 'some', 'any' and 'many', as well as 'one of the biggest surprises', and 'unpleasant', 'ghastly' and 'delicious' ones.
- 'Surprise' occurs both as a countable and as an uncountable or mass noun, as in 'spring maximum surprise'.
- There are only a few cases where 'surprise' precedes 'spring', all involving post-modifying relative or infinitive structures: "Norwich's victory was a

triumph for the tactical surprise sprung by manager Walker", "a new and exciting field of research which no doubt has many surprises to spring", and "if you've got any more surprises waiting to spring on us, then warn me about them now". There are no simple passives.

- There are no cases with continuous aspect: 'springing' only occurs as a gerund following a preposition.
- There are no cases of nominalization with 'springer' or 'springers'.

With respect to the questions posed at the beginning of the task, there would seem to be plenty of evidence that 'spring a surprise' does not require an animate subject. As far as syntactic restrictions are concerned, there is little evidence of passive or continuous forms, or of nominalized derivates.

8.3   Discussion and suggestions for further work

8.3.1   Using Two-way links

Where a TWO-WAY link is used to join two content nodes in the Query Builder, the query focus always corresponds to the content of the lower node, regardless of the order in which matches for the two nodes appear in the text. This means that according to which of the two nodes is placed above, and which below, different displays of solutions will be provided to otherwise identical queries. When using a Two-way link, you should therefore think carefully which node you wish to be treated as the query focus, and consequently used as a basis for sorting solutions and for calculating collocates.

As well as providing a different query focus, you should also note that inverting the nodes may provide different numbers of solutions where there is more than one match for either node within the scope specified. Roughly, SARA interprets any query involving a one-way or two-way link as "find all the cases matching the lower node where there is also a match for the upper node". This means that if we take as our scope the part of the previous sentence in inverted commas, and design a query with a two-way link where the first node contains the word 'the' and the second one 'node', there will be two solutions, with 'node' as the query focus. If, on the other hand, the two nodes are inverted, there will be three solutions, with 'the' as the focus.

One case where this feature can be useful is in obtaining information from the text headers relative to a group of solutions. For instance, you may want to know what text-types are represented in the solutions to, say, a Phrase Query for 'time immemorial'. This phrase, you may remember, occurs 45 times in the BNC (see 3.3.2 on page 85). You could, of course, use the Browse option to examine the attributes of the <CATREF> element in the header of each text (see 5.2.4 on page 105). However this would be a tedious process. A more practical option is to join the Phrase Query to an SGML query for <CATREF> with a Two-way link.

(51) **Invoke the QUERY BUILDER, and join a first node containing the SGML Query <CATREF> to a second node containing the Phrase Query** time immemorial **with a Two-way link.**

(52) **Leaving the scope as <BNCDOC>, click on OK to send the query to the server.** The Too many solutions dialogue box will be displayed, stating that there are 45 solutions in 40 texts.

(53) **Download one solution per text.** The solutions will be displayed with 'time immemorial' as the query focus.

(54) **Click on the QUERY BUILDER button to start a new query.**

(55) **Design exactly the same query as before, but with the two content nodes inverted.** The upper node should now contain the Phrase Query and the lower node the SGML Query.

(56) **Click on OK to send the query to the server.** The Too many solutions dialogue box will be displayed, stating that there are 40 solutions in 40 texts.

(57) **Download all the solutions, and select SGML under QUERY OPTIONS to display them in SGML format.** The solutions will be displayed with the <CATREF> element highlighted as the query focus.

(58) **Select TILE from the WINDOW menu to display both sets of solutions.** As the solutions in both windows are in the same order, you can see what text-type each of the solutions with 'time immemorial' comes from by examining the corresponding solution in the other window. *As the two queries find different numbers of solutions, it is essential to thin the solutions to the first query to ONE PER TEXT in order to obtain an exact correspondence between the concordance lines in the two displays.*

8.3.2   Some similar problems

Taps   Suppose that, having an interest in plumbing or the interception of telephone calls, you want to find all the occurrences of the word 'tap' and its inflections in the BNC. Use WORD QUERY to design an appropriate pattern. *If you type in the string* tapp?i?n?g?e?d?s?, *you will find that as well as 'tap', 'tapped', 'taps', and 'tapping', the list of matching words includes 'tape', 'taped', 'tapes', 'tapie', 'tapin' and 'taping'. However relevant many of these may be to the activity in question, they are not inflections of the verb 'tap'. The problem is a common one: verbs whose base form ends in a short vowel plus consonant usually double that consonant in their '-ing' and '-ed' inflections. One answer is to specify separate alternatives for the forms with single and double consonants: for instance* tap(s?|p[ie].*)

Spelling babysitting Are forms of 'baby-sit' more commonly hyphenated or unhyphenated in the BNC? *Within* QUERY BUILDER, *design a Pattern Query which includes both hyphenated and unhyphenated forms of 'baby-sit', by placing a ? character after the hyphen. As this query concerns orthography, you should limit it to written texts, by using the* <TEXT> *element as scope.*

Sorting the solutions by the query focus shows that only about a quarter are hyphenated.

Running risks Is there any evidence in the BNC to support Fillmore's hypothesis that, unlike 'running risks', 'taking risks' requires a volitional subject (see 8.1.1 on page 143)? *As in the 'spring a surprise' example, you should use* QUERY BUILDER *to specify patterns for each of two content nodes, with a two-way link, and a limited span as scope, since both 'run'/'take' and 'risk' may be inflected, occurring in either order, and at a variable distance apart. For the patterns with forms of 'run'/'take', you need to provide the forms 'ran'/'took' as separate alternatives (see 8.2.1 on page 147).*

There are 418 occurrences of forms of 'run' and 'risk' within a span of 5 words, and 971 of forms of 'take' and 'risk' within the same span. Examining the first 50 solutions to each query, we find that both are fairly precise, there being relatively few cases not involving the compounds 'take/run risks', such as "Crawl out onto the road and risk getting run over". While the subjects of forms of 'take risks' all appear to be volitional, there are several solutions with forms of 'run risks' that have non-volitional subjects, such as "a meal that didn't run any cholesterol risks"; "things that have run the risk of acquiring the patina of nostalgia"; "the reforms run a very high risk of being set back". There also appear to be differences in the colligational patterns associated with the two sets of forms, the plural 'risks' being more frequent with 'take', and the phrase 'the risk of' with 'run'. This suggests that the choice of verb may be determined by colligational as well as semantic criteria.

Bearing love What evidence is there in the BNC to support Bolinger's claim that the expression 'bear love' is found in negative and relative constructions but not simple declaratives (see 8.1.1 on page 143)? *To exclude people who love bears or bores, you can use* POS QUERY *to specify that 'love' should be a noun.*

Using QUERY BUILDER *to join a Pattern Query matching forms of 'bear' to a POS Query for the noun 'love', in either order and within the scope of an* <s> *(sentence) element, finds 48 solutions. Of these, only 5 seem relevant. While 4 of them occur in relative constructions, along the lines of 'the love they bore him', there is also one example of a simple declarative, "because she bore them so much love", suggesting that Bolinger's claim may not be fully accurate.*

Looking up Is it more common to 'look something up' in a dictionary or to 'consult' one? Which do you do with a corpus? *First design a query to find* *out how often a form of 'look' and a form of 'dictionary' co-occur in a span of 10 words. (You need to specify the pattern* `dictionar[iy]e?s?` *in order to include the plural 'dictionaries'.) Then formulate a second query to include forms of 'consult'. After you have looked at the solutions, edit the two queries to replace the pattern for 'dictionary' with one for 'corpus' (bearing in mind that the latter has both 'corpora' and 'corpuses' as plurals: see 2.1 on page 63).*

There are 79 cases where a form of 'look' co-occurs with a form of 'dictionary' within a span of 10 words, some 50 of them involving the phrasal verb 'look up'. In contrast there are only 8 where a form of 'consult' does. Neither 'look up' nor 'consult' occurs with forms of 'corpus' — so what do you do with one?

Many happy returns   Try looking up your birthday in the corpus, bearing in mind that dates can be written and said in a variety of ways, with the day before or after the month, and with varying distances between them . . .

9   Returning to more serious matters

9.1   The problem: investigating positions in texts

9.1.1   *Meaning and position*

One of the main differences between the salutations 'Hello' and 'Goodbye' is that the former tends to open conversations, while the latter closes them. The word 'yet' generally means something different when it appears at the beginning and at the end of clauses (compare 'Yet I don't miss her' with 'I don't miss her yet'). There are many other words and phrases whose meanings are closely linked with their position within the structural components of a text — the paragraphs, speeches, sentences, or clauses of which it is composed. This task looks at ways in which you can use SARA to examine usage in particular positions. This will involve searches that take account of the beginnings and ends of such units as sentences, utterances, paragraphs, sections, conversations, etc. (for an overview of the units marked up in the BNC see 6.1.2 on page 112).

The task focuses on occurrences of the adverbs 'anyway' and 'anyhow'. Most dictionaries regard these two words as virtually synonymous. With one exception, they both have exactly the same three senses. One of these senses is roughly equivalent to 'besides', a second corresponds to 'nevertheless', whereas a third is generally described in pragmatic terms, as a means of changing or cutting short a topic in speech, for example when returning from a digression to the main point, cutting out minor details, or closing down the conversation. (The exception is that 'anyhow' has an additional specific sense 'in a disorderly manner'.)

One distinctive aspect of the third use described is that almost all the examples provided by dictionaries place 'anyway/anyhow' as the first word in the sentence: "Anyhow, let's forget about that for the moment" (*Oxford Advanced Learners Dictionary*); "Anyway, in the end I didn't wear your jacket" (*Cambridge International Dictionary of English*); "Anyway, I'd better let you have your dinner" (*Collins COBUILD Dictionary*). In this task we begin by checking whether or not this third sense of 'anyway' and 'anyhow' is specific to appearances of the words at the beginning of spoken sentences and whether the two forms are used interchangeably in this position.

9.1.2   *Laughter and topic change*

Speakers frequently digress from the main line of talk when they make a mistake, or see a possibility for teasing or joking. Such shifts of 'footing', as Goffman (1979) calls them, often lead to laughter, leaving participants with the task of then shifting the back to more serious matters. In the second part of this task, we look at some ways in which this is achieved, examining cases where sentence-initial 'anyway' or 'anyhow' are used to change the topic following laughs or laughing speech. In particular, the task investigates whether these words are typically produced by the participant who has just laughed, or by another speaker.

9.1.3 Highlighted features

This task shows you:

- how to design an SGML QUERY to find the beginning or end of the structural units encoded as elements in the BNC;
- how to design an SGML QUERY to find non-verbal and non-vocal events (such as laughs and applause) and features of voice quality (such as laughing and whispering);
- how to display utterance boundaries and speaker codes, overlapping segments, non-verbal and non-vocal events, and other features of spoken texts by configuring the CUSTOM display format;
- how to sort solutions by reference to these features.

It assumes you already know how to:

- adjust default settings (see 1.2.8 on page 54);
- carry out an SGML Query (see 5.2.2 on page 100);
- use the Pattern option in Word Query to find all the forms which match a pattern (see 8.2.1 on page 147);
- design complex queries using the Query Builder (see 4.2.2 on page 91, 5.2.4 on page 105, 6.2.3 on page 117, 7.2.2 on page 133, 8.2.3 on page 150);
- adjust downloading procedure in the Too many solutions dialogue box (see 2.2.3 on page 66);
- sort and thin solutions (see 3.2.2 on page 78, 2.2.4 on page 68);
- save and re-open queries (see 2.2.5 on page 70);
- save listings of solutions (see 8.2.5 on page 154).

9.1.4 Before you start

Using the VIEW PREFERENCES option, set the defaults as follows:

MAX DOWNLOAD LENGTH	1500 characters
MAX DOWNLOADS	25
FORMAT	Custom
SCOPE	Maximum
VIEW: QUERY and ANNOTATION	checked
CONCORDANCE	checked
BROWSER: SHOW TAGS	unchecked

9.2   Procedure

9.2.1   Searching in sentence–initial position: 'anyway' and 'anyhow'

Frequencies in speech   Let us begin by finding out how frequent these two forms are, first in the corpus in general, and then in spoken texts in particular.

Click on the WORD QUERY button on the toolbar, and check the PATTERN option in the dialogue box.

Type in any(how|way) **and click on LOOKUP.** The matching words list will contain the two forms 'anyhow' and 'anyway'.

Click on 'anyhow' to find out its frequency in the corpus, then do the same for 'anyway'. You will see that 'anyway' is about 25 times more frequent than 'anyhow' (12,232 as opposed to 471 instances).

Copy the input string to the clipboard, then click on CANCEL to close the dialogue box.

If you look up the frequency of a word using Word Query, you can only find its total frequency in the entire corpus. To find its frequency in a subset of the corpus, you must use QUERY BUILDER to restrict the scope of your query (see 5.2.4 on page 105).

Click on the QUERY BUILDER button on the toolbar. The Query Builder will be displayed.

Click in the scope node, then select SGML. The SGML dialogue box will be displayed.

Check that the SHOW HEADER TAGS box is unchecked, then scroll through the element list and select <STEXT>.

Click on OK to insert this selection in the Query Builder scope node.

Click in the content node, and select EDIT then WORD. The Word Query dialogue box will be displayed.

Check the PATTERN box and paste in the string any(how|way) **from the clipboard, then click on LOOKUP.**

Select 'anyway' from the matching words list and click on OK to insert it in the Query Builder node.

Check that the 'Query is OK' message is displayed, then click on OK to send the query to the server. The Too many solutions dialogue box will be displayed, stating that there are 5221 occurrences of 'anyway' in 584 texts.

Now find the frequency of 'anyhow' in spoken texts.

Click on CANCEL to return to the Query Builder.

(14) **Click in the content node and select EDIT.** You will be returned to the Word Query dialogue box, still highlighting your selection of 'anyway' in the matching words list.

(15) **Change the selection to 'anyhow', then click on OK to insert it in the Query Builder node.**

(16) **Click on OK to send the revised query to the server.** The Too many solutions dialogue box will again be displayed, stating that there are 178 occurrences of 'anyhow' in 81 texts.

In speech, the difference in the frequency of the two forms is thus even greater than in writing, with 'anyway' 30 times more frequent than 'anyhow'. Given the size of this difference, it is perhaps surprising that some dictionaries list 'anyway' as a variant of 'anyhow', rather than vice-versa.

Sentence-initial position   Let us now move on to examine occurrences of 'anyway' and 'anyhow' at the beginning of sentences in spoken texts. One obvious way of doing this might be simply to search for cases where 'anyway' or 'anyhow' are capitalised. Although this is technically possible using a PHRASE QUERY (see 10.2.4 on page 184), it cannot be relied on to find all and only sentence-initial occurrences of these words. In the BNC spoken component, the first word of a sentence is not always capitalised, while in the written component, it is common for all the words in headings etc. to be capitalized. We will instead use the SGML tagging in the corpus, which unequivocally identifies the start of every sentence.

(17) **Click on CANCEL to return to the Query Builder.**

(18) **Click on the upward branch of the 'anyhow' content node to create a further node above it.**

(19) **Click in this node, and select EDIT then SGML.**

(20) **In the SGML dialogue box, select the <s> element (which represents a new sentence), then click on OK to insert it in the Query Builder node.** The two nodes are linked by a downwards arrow, indicating the default ONE-WAY value for the link-type. To find only cases where a new sentence tag is *immediately* followed by 'anyhow', we must change the link-type to NEXT.

(21) **Click on the link and select LINK TYPE then NEXT.** The link will be shown as a thick vertical bar.

(22) **Click on OK to send the query to the server.**

(23) **Read off the number of solutions from the Too many solutions dialogue box, then click on CANCEL to return to the Query Builder.**

(24) **Click in the second content node and select EDIT.** You will be returned to the Word Query dialogue box.

Select 'anyway', then click on OK to insert it in the node.

Click on OK to send the revised query to the server, and wait for the new number of solutions to be displayed in the Too many solutions dialogue box. While there are 53 occurrences of sentence-initial 'anyhow' in spoken utterances, from 28 texts, there are 1009 occurrences of sentence-initial 'anyway', from 279 texts.

Roughly half the occurrences in spoken utterances of these forms thus occur in sentence-initial position. The relative proportions of 'anyway' and 'anyhow' are still around 20:1, suggesting that position in the sentence makes little difference to the relative frequency of the two forms.

9.2.2   Customizing the solution display format

We now want to find out if these sentence-initial uses typically mark a change in topic. Let us begin by looking at sentence-initial 'anyway'. Clearly, to examine 1009 solutions individually would take an inordinately long time, so we will limit ourselves to the first 50.

In the Too many solutions dialogue box, change the DOWNLOAD HITS number to 50, click on the INITIAL radio button, then on OK. If you have correctly selected CUSTOM as the default display format (see 9.1.4 on page 162), and have not modified the default configuration, you will see that there is a vertical line before many of the 'anyway's in the solutions display. This line indicates a new utterance (i.e. a change of speaker).

To see whether 'anyway' generally introduces a new topic, we must compare what occurs before and after 'anyway' in these solutions. A written transcript of conversational data can never fully capture the information which was available to the participants, but it will be easier to understand what is going on if you show more of the available contextual information. It may be particularly useful to display:

overlapping speech A plain transcript where one utterance is shown following another hides those cases where speakers talk at the same time, overlapping with each other.

pausing, gaps and unclear speech A plain transcript does not show pauses, which may indicate that the previous topic has exhausted itself or that a section has come to a close. Nor does it show where personal references have been omitted from the transcription, or where portions of the speech were too unclear to transcribe reliably.

non-verbal and non-vocal events A plain transcript does not show non-verbal events, such as laughs, or non-vocal ones, such as applause, which may in fact mark the end of a topic or section of the talk.

All of these features are explicitly tagged in the BNC, along with others. Choosing the CUSTOM display format allows you to specify your own rules for the display of such features.

- **Select QUERY OPTIONS then click on CONFIGURE in the FOR-MAT section.** The LINE (`linefmt.txt`) and PAGE (`pagefmt.txt`) files will be displayed, listing the current rules for custom display when in Line mode and Page mode respectively.

You may now edit these files, changing these rules or adding new ones.

The format of the two files is identical. Each consists of a series of rules, one per line. Each line begins with the name of an SGML element, followed in the simplest case by just a single *replacement string* enclosed in double quotes. For example, if you are currently using the default versions, you will see that the `linefmt.txt` file begins with the rule:

```
p "|"
```

This indicates that in Line mode, the replacement string "|" (vertical bar) is to appear at the beginning of every <P> element, i.e. at the start of each new paragraph.

Since rules can only occupy a single line, a special code is needed to indicate where new lines are required within the replacement string. The convention used is to represent new lines by the sequence \n . The sequence \t can be used similarly to insert a TAB character. For example, you will see that several of the elements in the Page file (<DIV1>, <DIV2>, etc.) have a replacement string consisting of the text "\n" while the <P> element in this file has a replacement string "\n\t". This means that sections will always begin on a new line in Page mode displays, while paragraphs will begin with both a new line and an indent.

Important information about an SGML element occurrence is often represented by its attributes. You can display the value of any SGML attribute by including its name in the rule together with the special symbol %s in the replacement string. For example, towards the bottom of the Page file, you will see a sequence of rules like the following:

```
gap desc "[%s]"
```

This indicates that when a <GAP> element is to be displayed in Page mode, the value of its DESC attribute should be inserted within square brackets. You can mix attribute values with any other text, simply by specifying where each is to appear in the replacement string by a distinct %s symbol. For example, the default Page format file has a rule like this:

```
u who "\n{%s}: "
```

This states that in Custom format the start of each utterance (<u>) should begin on a new line, followed by whatever value its WHO attribute has between curly braces, a colon, and a space. If you want to display more than one attribute value for a given element, you can do so simply by supplying more than one name, and including a %s sequence for each value. For example, the following rule would display both description and duration for every <VOCAL> element:

```
vocal desc dur "[%s for %s seconds]"
```

Finally, you can also supply a second replacement string if you want to specify some additional formatting for the end of an element, for example to output a string at its end. An example of this procedure is given below for the <TRUNC> element.

In the PAGE file, change the pause **and** unclear **lines to read:**

```
pause dur "(.%s)"
unclear "(...)"
```

and add the following lines at the end of the file:

```
ptr "^"
trunc "" "-"
&hellip "..."
```

These changes will affect the Page display as follows:

- each <PAUSE> element will be displayed as a dot followed by its duration, in parentheses (in the BNC, pause duration is only specified where over 5 seconds);
- each <UNCLEAR> element will be displayed as three dots in parentheses;
- each <PTR> element (which in spoken texts indicates the beginning or end of overlapping speech) will be displayed as a carat;
- a dash will be displayed after each <TRUNC> element to indicate that the content of that element is truncated. (Note that an empty string has to be supplied for the start-tag as well.)

• each entity reference representing a horizontal ellipsis will be displayed as three dots. (Ellipses pose a particular display problem in that there is no single Windows character corresponding to their conventional representation as a sequence of three dots.) *In the BNC all characters outside the basic alphabet are displayed as SGML entity references. These take the form of a brief mnemonic preceded by an ampersand (&) and followed by a semi-colon (;). Thus the string* &bquo; *indicates the opening of a quotation, while* &equo; *indicates the end of a quotation. Apart from* …, *SARA converts most other entity references to appropriate screen characters automatically, other than in* SGML FORMAT. *A full list of entity references used in the corpus is included in the* BNC Users' Reference Guide.

(29) **Copy all the lines from** u who "{%s}:   " **onwards to the clipboard, then paste them into the LINE file, replacing the previous rule for <U> in Line mode.** This will provide the same low-level information in Page and Line mode displays.

(30) **Click on OK to save the edited format files.** The formats you have defined will be used for all subsequent displays in Custom format. You will be returned to the Query Options dialogue box.

(31) **Click on OK to return to the solutions display.** The solutions will be re-displayed in your new Custom format, with Maximum scope, as specified in the VIEW PREFERENCES options (see 9.1.4 on page 162). MAXIMUM *scope displays all the complete sentences contained within the* MAX DOWNLOAD LENGTH *specified under* VIEW PREFERENCES *(see 1.2.8 on page 54). If you want to display conversational data in Custom format, you should always use Maximum scope, since this is the only option to provide more than a single utterance as context. You can change the display format and scope for the current query at any time from the Query Options dialogue box (see 5.2.3 on page 103).*

(32) **Click on the CONCORDANCE button on the toolbar to change from Line to Page display mode.** You will now see the current solution displayed as in a playscript, with the code for the speaker given at the beginning of each utterance. This makes it much easier to follow the talk.

(33) **Using the arrow buttons on the toolbar (or the PGDN key), page through the solutions to see what happens before and after 'anyway'.** You will find that in the vast majority of cases, 'anyway' marks a topic shift. You will also see from the carets in the display, representing <PTR> elements, that it often seems to overlap with the end of the preceding utterance.

9.2.3   Sorting and saving solutions in Custom format

We can highlight recurrent patterns in what precedes and follows 'anyway' in these examples by sorting them. In Custom format solutions are sorted as they appear on the screen: that is, if you introduce new characters (for example to indicate utterance boundaries) these will be taken into account as well the actual words of the solutions when sorting.

4) **Click on the CONCORDANCE button to return to Line display mode.**

5) **Select SORT from the QUERY menu, and set the Primary sort key to LEFT with a span of 3 words. Then click on OK to sort the solutions.** If you scroll through the solutions you should see groups where 'anyway' is preceded by an utterance boundary and 'Yeah' or 'Right', that is, following an expression of agreement by another speaker which concludes a previous topic. You may also notice that 'anyway' is often preceded by a laugh by another speaker.

Now let us look at the solutions for sentence-initial 'anyhow'. Since editing the current query would replace the current display of solutions, we shall design a second query in a new window so as to be able to compare the two sets of solutions.

6) **Click on the QUERY BUILDER button on the toolbar to display the Query Builder dialogue box.**

7) **Follow the same procedure as in 9.2.1 on page 163 to insert <STEXT> in the scope node, and <S> in the content node. Then create a second content node below the first, this time specifying the word 'anyhow', and join the nodes with a NEXT link.**

8) **Check that the 'Query is OK' message is displayed, and click on OK to send the query to the server.**

9) **In the Too many solutions dialogue box, click on the DOWNLOAD ALL radio button, then on OK.** The solutions will be displayed in the revised Custom format.

10) **Click on the CONCORDANCE button to display the solutions in Page mode, and page through them using the arrow buttons on the toolbar (or the PGDN key).** You will see that 'anyhow' also generally appears to mark a change of topic.

11) **Switch back to Line display mode and sort the solutions by the left and then by the right, to see what precedes and follows 'anyhow'.**

12) **Use the Window menu to switch between this and the 'anyway' query. Do you notice any differences between the contexts of the two words?** We also find agreement markers before 'anyhow', so in this respect there appears to be no particular difference in the environments of the two words. *You may find it easier to compare these solutions if you print them. Since the PRINT option only allows you to print one line for each solution, and you may need to see a relatively large*

context to identify topic change, you should first use the LISTING *option to save the solutions to a file, which you can then print by switching to a word processor (see 8.2.5 on page 154).*

In sentence-initial position, 'anyhow' and 'anyway' both generally seem to indicate a shift of topic in speech.

9.2.4   *Searching at utterance boundaries: laughs and laughing speech*

One particular use of 'anyway' and 'anyhow' appears to be to shift the topic back to more serious issues following laughter.   A question which arises is whose job this is: is it more usually the producer of the laughter who follows this with 'anyway/anyhow', or is it more often another participant? We can answer this question by seeing what proportion of the occurrences of sentence-initial 'anyway/anyhow' subsequent to laughter follow a change of speaker, occurring at the beginning of an utterance. If 'anyway/anyhow' is produced indiscriminately, both by producers and by recipients of laughter, we would expect it to be utterance-initial in approximately half the cases.

Laughter and topic change   Let us first design a query to find all the cases where sentence-initial 'anyway' or 'anyhow' follows laughter.   We shall work backwards from the final component of the query.

(43) **Click on the QUERY BUILDER button on the toolbar to display the Query Builder.**

(44) **Click in the content node and select EDIT then WORD to display the Word Query dialogue box.**

(45) **Check the PATTERN box, paste in the pattern** any(way|how), **and click on LOOKUP.**

(46) **Select both 'anyhow' and 'anyway' by dragging the mouse or holding down CTRL when clicking on these items in the matching words list.**

(47) **Click on OK to insert this component in the Query Builder node.**

Now add the requirement that 'anyway/anyhow' must be directly preceded by a sentence boundary.

(48) **Click on the upwards branch of the upper content node to add a further node to the query.**

(49) **Change the link type to NEXT.**

(50) **Click in the new content node and select EDIT then SGML to display the SGML dialogue box.**

(51) **Select <s> from the element list, then click on OK to insert this component in the Query Builder node.**

Now add the requirement that the new sentence beginning with 'anyway/anyhow' should be directly preceded by laughter.

In the BNC, laughter is represented in two manners, which we shall consider separately. In the first, most frequent case, it is treated as a *vocal event* occurring between two segments of speech, and is represented using the <VOCAL> element. The DESC attribute for this element is assigned the value laugh. The full representation is thus <vocal desc="laugh">. *Other values of the* DESC *attribute on the* <VOCAL> *element include* cough, sigh, clears throat, *etc.*

Click on the upwards branch of the content node to add a further node to the query.

Change the link type to NEXT.

Click in the new content node and select EDIT then SGML to display the SGML dialogue box.

Select <VOCAL> from the list of elements. The list of attributes for the <VOCAL> element will be displayed.

Select DESC from the list of attributes, then click on ADD to display the Attribute dialogue box. As the possible values for the DESC attribute are not a predetermined set, SARA does not provide a list; you must type in the value you require.

Type in the value laugh **and click on OK to return to the SGML dialogue box.**

Click on OK to insert this component in the query.

Check that the scope node contains the element <BNCDOC>. As <VOCAL> elements only occur in spoken texts in the BNC, it is not necessary to restrict the query explicitly by specifying <STEXT>as scope.

Check that the 'Query is OK' message is displayed and click on OK to send the query to the server. There are 42 solutions.

Click on the DOWNLOAD ALL radio button and download the solutions. You will see that the query focus begins with [laugh] (indicating non-verbal laughter), generally followed by a speaker code and 'anyway'. *Where the bottom node of a query is joined to a previous node or nodes with* NEXT *links, the query focus corresponds to this entire sequence of nodes.*

Thinning the solutions   Even though we joined the various nodes of the query with NEXT links, you may notice that in some solutions, there are features occurring between a laugh and 'anyway/anyhow'. A NEXT link simply means that no *words* may occur between the content of the two nodes in question (see 4.2.2 on page 92). Other elements, however, may intervene. For instance, there might be:

- <UNCLEAR> or <GAP> elements indicating intervening speech which could not be transcribed;
- <PAUSE>, <EVENT> or <VOCAL> elements of significant length (these elements are assigned a DUR (duration) attribute value where they exceed 5 seconds);
- <PTR> elements, indicating that parts of two utterances were spoken simultaneously rather than consecutively.

Most significantly for our purposes, the current query also allows an utterance boundary to occur between a laugh and the sentence beginning with 'anyway/anyhow'. You should therefore inspect the solutions to make sure none of them are spurious in these respects.

First, let us sort the solutions by the query focus. This will help group cases where particular features occur between laughs and 'anyway/anyhow'.

(62) **Select SORT from the QUERY menu, and set the Primary sort key to CENTRE with a span of 4 words. Then click on OK to sort the solutions.**

(63) **Scroll through the solutions looking for any feature displayed between a laugh and 'anyway/anyhow' which is not an indication of a new speaker, and double-click on those cases where this implies that 'anyway/anyhow' does not immediately follow the laughter.**

There are a couple of cases where there is intervening unclear speech, clearly implying a space between laughter and 'anyway', and which should therefore be marked. On the other hand, there are cases where there is an intervening laugh by another participant, or where 'anyway' is preceded by a shift to a laughing voice quality (see 9.2.4 on the next page), which should be maintained. Finally, towards the top of the display you will find cases with intervening <PTR> elements (represented by carets), which indicate overlaps. To assess the implications of these for the sequencing of the talk, they will need to be examined more closely.

Overlaps in spoken dialogue   In spoken dialogue texts in the BNC, <PTR> elements are placed at the beginning and end of those portions of utterances which *overlap* with others, for example where one speaker begins to speak before another has finished. For each of the overlapping segments, the <PTR> elements marking the beginning of overlap have the same value on their T attribute. Similarly, the elements marking the end of overlap also have the same value on this attribute. By comparing the attribute values of the various <PTR> elements, you can thus identify what overlaps with what. As our Custom format display does not show these attribute values, we shall examine the solutions in SGML format.

Delete the solutions you have already marked as spurious using THIN and REVERSE SELECTION under the QUERY menu.

Again under the QUERY menu, select OPTIONS then SGML.

Examine all the solutions where <PTR> elements occur between the <VOCAL> element and 'anyway/anyhow'. These should be grouped at the top of the display.

Double-click on any cases where the overlapping implies that there is a gap between the laughter and 'anyway/anyhow'. In most cases, you will find that the <PTR> elements indicate either that the laughter overlaps with the previous utterance, or that it overlaps with 'anyway' or with further laughter produced prior to it. None of these implies a gap between laughter and 'anyway/anyhow'.

Delete any solutions you have marked using THIN and REVERSE SELECTION from the QUERY menu.

All the remaining solutions to the query should now be cases where 'anyway/anyhow' directly follows laughter, with or without a change of speaker. Scrolling through them, you will see that in the vast majority there is a change of speaker, and that there are no occurrences of 'anyhow'.

Laughing speech and topic change Not all laughter in the BNC is encoded using the <VOCAL> element. Speakers may also utter words while laughing, or speak in a laughing tone. In these cases, laughter is considered to be a feature of the *voice quality* with which a particular piece of speech is produced. Such changes in voice quality are represented by <SHIFT> element, whose NEW attribute describes the quality. The end of the piece of speech with this voice quality is indicated by a second <SHIFT> element, this time without attributes. For example, if the word 'Yeah' is spoken with a laughing voice, the full representation is:

```
<shift new="laughing">Yeah<shift>
```

To find instances of laughing voice quality immediately before 'anyway' or 'anyhow', we must identify cases where the latter is preceded by a <SHIFT> element indicating the end of laughing voice quality. However, the particular type of voice quality is only indicated at the point where it *begins* (by the value of the NEW attribute), not where it ends. Consequently, you cannot formulate a query to find the end of a specific kind of changed voice quality, but only one which will find a return to unmarked voice quality. The solutions to such a query will thus include cases where other voice qualities are involved, and these spurious solutions will have to be identified by inspection and removed by thinning. *Other values of the* NEW *attribute on the* <SHIFT> *element include* reading, shouting, singing, whispering, imitating Italian accent, mimicking baby voice *etc. You can generate a more complete list of such values by designing an* SGML QUERY *to find occurrences of the* <SHIFT> *element, and sorting the solutions in SGML format.*

First, let us save the solutions to the last query, involving non-verbal laughs.

(69) **Select SAVE from the FILE menu, and save the query as** laugh. The window title will change to *LAUGH.SQY.*

(70) **Select EDIT from the QUERY menu to display the Query Builder.**

(71) **Click in the** <vocal desc=laugh> **node and select EDIT to display the SGML Query dialogue box.**

(72) **Select <SHIFT> from the list of elements, and click on OK to insert it into the Query Builder node.**

(73) **Click on OK to send the query to the server.** There are 7 solutions.

We now need to remove any solutions where the shift in voice quality preceding 'anyway/anyhow' does not involve laughing. These will be easier to identify if we view the solutions in Custom format.

(74) **Select OPTIONS from the QUERY menu and display the solutions in CUSTOM format.** Assuming you have adopted the format specified in 9.2.2 on page 165, the <SHIFT> element indicating the end of marked voice quality will appear as a box-shape — actually, an empty pair of square brackets.

(75) **Scroll through the solutions, using the buttons on the horizontal scroll bar to examine the text to the left of the query focus. Note the NEW attribute value on the previous <SHIFT> element indicating the beginning of marked voice quality, which should be displayed between square brackets.** You will find cases of [singing], [screaming] and [whispering] as well as [laughing].

(76) **Mark all the solutions where the marked voice quality prior to the query focus does not involve laughing, then use REVERSE SELECTION from the THIN menu to remove them from the display.**

As in the previous query, we now need to examine the remaining solutions and remove any where other SGML elements between laughing speech and 'anyway/anyhow' indicate that these are not consecutive.

(77) **Select OPTIONS then SGML from the QUERY menu to re-display the solutions in SGML format.** You will see that there is one solution

where laughing speech is followed by a laugh from the same speaker prior to an utterance boundary and 'anyway'. As this instance should already have been included in the previous query as a case of laughter preceding 'anyway/anyhow', we can delete it here.

Mark this solution and remove it from the display using the THIN REVERSE SELECTION option. You will be left with 3 solutions. In all of these, the next sentence following laughing speech begins with 'anyway'. There are no occurrences with 'anyhow'.

Select SAVE AS from the FILE menu and save the query as laughing. You must use SAVE AS rather than SAVE here, in order not to overwrite the previous query (laugh.sqy).

Results Having removed all the spurious solutions, we can now examine both queries to see whether, following laughter or laughing speech, 'anyway/anyhow' is typically produced by the same or by a different speaker. This involves establishing the proportion of solutions in which there is an utterance boundary between laughter or laughing speech and 'anyway/anyhow'. We can do this by sorting them in Custom format. As new utterances are indicated by the speaker code between curly brackets, sorting by the centre (the query focus) will group those cases where shifts in voice quality or laughs are followed by an utterance boundary.

Select OPEN from the FILE menu and re-open the query laugh.sqy **in a new window.**

Download all the solutions, and display them in Custom format.

Sort the solutions by the Centre, with a span of 4.

Scroll through the solutions to see if there are any cases where there is no utterance boundary between laughter and 'anyway/anyhow'. While there are some cases where more than one speaker laughs prior to 'anyway', there are none where laughter is only produced by the same speaker who says 'anyway'.

Use the WINDOW menu to switch to your second query (_LAUGH-ING.SQY_).

Display the solutions in CUSTOM format, and see if there are any of these where 'anyway' is produced by the same speaker as the preceding laughing speech. In contrast with the previous query, in two of the three occurrences there is no intervening utterance boundary, the speaker who laughs going on to produce 'anyway'.

We are now in a position to provide answers to some of the questions posed at the beginning of this section concerning the use of 'anyway' and 'anyhow' following laughter.

As far as their relative frequencies are concerned, if we take the two queries together, there are 43 occurrences of 'anyway' following a laugh or laughing speech, and none of 'anyhow'. However, given the overall proportions of these two forms in speech in the BNC (30:1), we would not have expected to find more than a few occurrences of 'anyhow', and its absence here can hardly be judged significant.

'Anyway' tends to follow laughter by another rather than by the same speaker. There are only two cases where laughter is followed by 'anyway' with no intervening utterance boundary, both involving laughing speech. Since they appear to be exceptions, it may be of interest to look at these two cases in greater detail.

(86) **Click in the *LAUGHING.SQY* window, then click on the CONCOR-DANCE button on the toolbar to change to Page display mode, and examine the two solutions where laughing speech is followed by an 'anyway' from the same speaker.**

You will see that in both these solutions 'anyway' marks a switch from dialogue to monologue. If you look up their sources using the SOURCE option, you will find that both in fact come from television programmes. This provides further support for the hypothesis that after laughter, the job of changing topic with 'anyway' is preferably performed by a different participant from the one who laughed. As often happens in corpus-based work, it is this exception which seems to confirm the rule.

9.3 Discussion and suggestions for further work

9.3.1 Searching near particular positions

We have now confirmed our hypothesis that most sentence-initial occurrences of 'anyway' and 'anyhow' in speech appear to indicate a topic change. We have not however attempted to see if occurrences which are *not* in sentence-initial position can have this function. We can investigate this issue in a number of ways, most simply by formulating a query to search for occurrences of 'anyway/anyhow' as the second word of the sentence in speech.

Using the Query Builder, we can use the ANY option under EDIT to insert a one-word slot between an <s> node and an 'anyway/anyhow' node, within the scope of an <STEXT> element. This shows that the most common words to preface 'anyway/anyhow' are 'and', 'but' and 'so'. In most of these solutions, 'anyway/anyhow' again seems to indicate a topic change. *A wider range of positions can be investigated by using the* SPAN *scope option (see 8.2.3 on page 150). For instance, to find cases where 'anyway' or 'anyhow' occurs within the first four words of a sentence, we can join an SGML Query for <s> to a Pattern Query for* {any(way|how)} *with a One-way link, specifying the scope of the query as a span of 4 words. Such a query will not, however, be restricted to spoken texts: Query Builder will only allow us to define a single scope node, which we have used to specify the span of 4 words. To supply the additional constraint that this must be done within a spoken text, it is necessary to use a* CQL QUERY *(see 7.2.3 on page 135), with a formulation such as the following:*

```
<stext>*((<s>*("anyway"|"anyhow"))/5)
```

This specifies that the scoped part of the query is to be joined to an SGML Query for an <STEXT> *element, where the latter (whose start-tag occurs at the beginning of each spoken text in the corpus) may occur outside the span of 5 words in which the rest of the query is to be solved.*

9.3.2 Some similar problems

And so to bed Prescriptive grammars traditionally deplore the use of sentence-initial 'And' (such as Pepys' "And so to bed"). Design a query to find sentence-initial occurrences of 'And so to' in written texts in the BNC. *Use the* <TEXT> *element to restrict the scope of the query to written texts.*

Bed may be a good place to go at this point, as you will have a long wait for solutions, there being an enormous number of occurrences of 'and', of 'so', and of 'to' in the BNC for SARA to examine, even if there are in fact only 47 solutions where they occur together as a phrase, 4 of them preceding 'bed'.

How are you? Faced with the everyday question 'How are you?', it seems that everybody has to lie for much of the time if they are to get on to other topics of conversation (Sacks 1975, 1992). How do people actually answer this question in the corpus? Design a query to find occurrences of 'how are you?' at the end of a spoken utterance, then select Plain display format and sort the solutions by the right to identify the most frequent answers. *Use* PHRASE QUERY *to specify 'how are you?' (including the question mark) as the content of a first node in the Query Builder. Then attach it with a* NEXT *link to a second node containing a* </u> *end-tag. You can select the end-tag by clicking on the* END *radio button in the SGML dialogue box.*

There are 128 occurrences of utterance-final 'how are you?' in the BNC. Sorting these by the right, you will find that the most frequent responses are '(I'm) fine' and 'All right'/'Alright'. 'Very well' and 'Not too bad' are less common. Negative responses are very rare indeed.

Goodbye When we say 'goodbye', do we mean it? Is that really the end of the conversation? In the BNC, each recorded conversation is treated as a distinct <DIV> element (only used in spoken texts: see 6.1.2 on page 112). Find out how often 'Bye', 'Good-bye' and 'Goodbye' occur within the scope of a <DIV> element. Then, design a query to find out how often they occur near the close of that element, i.e. within (say) the 10 words before a </DIV> end-tag. *While it is easy to find the number of occurrences of these forms within <DIV> elements (1260), it is less straightforward to find how often they occur near the end of such elements. In Query Builder, when two or more content nodes are joined with One- or Two-way links, the query focus corresponds to the bottom node, and the number of solutions is the number of times that this bottom node is found. Thus, if you use a one-way link to join an upper node containing forms of 'goodbye' to a lower node containing a </DIV> end-tag, you will find the number of times a </DIV> tag is preceded by 'goodbye', rather than the number of times that a form of 'goodbye' occurs before a </DIV> tag. So, for example, if someone says 'Goodbye, goodbye' at the end of a conversation, this will only count once.*

There are two ways of getting round this problem.

- *You can place the </DIV> node before the 'Goodbye' node, joining them with a Two-way link. This will count all occurrences of 'Goodbye' whether they immediately precede or follow the end of a conversation; you will then have to run a separate query to find the occurrences immediately following the end of a conversation and subtract them from the total.*

- *You can simply do an SGML query for the </DIV> tag and then use the* COLLOCATION *option to count the number of times a form of 'Goodbye' is found within the required span. Again, however, this will also include occurrences which follow the end of the conversation, which will have to be separately counted and subtracted from the total.*

In either case, counting the number of 'false positives' is easily done: use Query Builder to search for a </DIV> tag followed by a form of 'Goodbye' within the required span using a One-way link.

Only 17% (211/1260) of occurrences of forms of 'goodbye' occur within the last ten words of a <DIV> element in speech. Overall, it appears that saying "Goodbye" in conversation may be anything but final. However, we need to bear in mind that strictly speaking, a </DIV> tag only marks the end of a recording, so in many cases we cannot be sure that this was in fact the end of the conversation.

10   What does 'SARA' mean?

10.1   The problem: studying pragmatic features

10.1.1   How are terms defined?

Rather than a particular language form, this final task investigates a particular pragmatic function of language: the definition of terms. Obviously, there is no way we can design a query or queries to locate all of the ways definitions are provided in the BNC, so we must follow an ad hoc procedure. We will start by examining some contexts where definitions seem likely to be found, in the hope that by progressively accumulating examples, we may find recurrent features which can then be investigated more systematically. The procedure will illustrate how different options and query-types may be used to complement each other in a wider research perspective.

10.1.2   Highlighted features

This task shows you:

- how to classify and retrieve particular solutions from different queries using the BOOKMARK command;
- how to search for solutions in specific texts in the corpus by using the ID attribute on the <BNCDOC> element;
- how to design queries which are case-sensitive, or which include punctuation, using the PHRASE QUERY option;
- how to group solutions according to case using the ASCII collating option;
- how to combine a WORD QUERY and a PHRASE QUERY to find occurrences of compounds which may be written as one word, two words, or with a hyphen;
- how to use the COLLOCATION option as a heuristic to evaluate potential queries.

It assumes you already know how to:

- design Word, Phrase, POS, Pattern, and SGML queries, and combine these using the Query Builder (see 5.2.4 on page 105, 6.2.3 on page 117, 7.2.2 on page 133);
- design CQL queries (see 7.2.3 on page 137);
- copy a selected solution to the Windows clipboard using the Copy option (see 1.2.7 on page 54);
- sort and thin solutions (see 3.2.2 on page 78, 2.2.4 on page 68);
- save and re-open queries (see 2.2.5 on page 70);

- look up collocation frequencies using the Collocation option (see 3.2.1 on page 76);
- browse through individual texts (see 1.2.7 on page 52).

10.1.3 Before you start

Set the following defaults using the VIEW PREFERENCES option:

MAX DOWNLOAD LENGTH	2000 characters
MAX DOWNLOADS	15
FORMAT	Plain
SCOPE	Maximum
VIEW: QUERY and ANNOTATION	unchecked
CONCORDANCE	checked
BROWSER: SHOW TAGS	unchecked

10.2   Procedure

10.2.1   Looking for acronyms with POS Query

Let us start by choosing an easily-recognisable class of expressions which are likely to be defined in texts: acronyms. We shall attempt to make a collection of acronym definitions, arbitrarily beginning with definitions of 'SARA'. Since the BNC was collected some time before the baptism of the SARA described in this handbook, we are hardly likely to find references to an 'SGML Aware Retrieval Application'. However, it is quite probable that the same series of letters will be used as an acronym with other senses in the corpus.

As acronyms are generally proper nouns, we shall use the POS QUERY option (see 7.2.1 on page 131).

(1) **Click on the POS QUERY button on the toolbar.** The POS Query dialogue box will be displayed.

(2) **Type in the string sara, and click in the Part-of-speech display window (or press TAB) to display the POS codes associated with 'sara' in the corpus. Select NP0 (proper noun) and click on OK to send the query to the server.** The Too many solutions dialogue box will be displayed, stating that there are 1266 solutions in 149 texts.

(3) **Check the ONE PER TEXT box and download all the solutions.** It seems reasonable to assume that repeated references to 'sara' in any one text will probably have the same meaning, and that the first one in each text is as likely as any to be flanked by a definition or explanation.

Scroll through the solutions to see if you can find any acronyms. While most of the solutions involve reference to women called Sara, you may notice some cases where 'SARA' is in upper case throughout, suggesting that it may be an acronym.

Let us start by looking at these cases.

Sort the solutions with Centre and span 1 as Primary key, and Right and span 2 as Secondary key, using ASCII collating. ASCII collating distinguishes upper and lower case, and will group solutions where 'SARA' is in upper case throughout at the top of the display. Several of these appear to be acronyms — 'SARA title', 'SARA rules', 'SARA the Severn Auxiliary Rescue Association', and 'super SARA', for example.

Mark these solutions and remove the rest by thinning; then click on the CONCORDANCE button to switch to Page display mode.

Page through the remaining solutions to see which, if any, provide definitions of 'SARA'. Of the cases listed above, only 'SARA, the Severn Auxiliary Rescue Association' is defined in these solutions.

10.2.2   Classifying solutions with bookmarks

The one definition of 'SARA' we have found takes the form of a parenthetical explanation immediately following the acronym, placed between commas. Let us mark and classify it so that we can find it again without difficulty. We can do this using the BOOKMARK option.

Click on the CONCORDANCE button to return to Line display mode.

Select the solution referring to the 'Severn Auxiliary Rescue Association' by clicking on it.

Select BOOKMARK from the EDIT menu. The BOOKMARK NAME dialogue box will be displayed. The name of the current query is shown in the top left of the box: bookmark names are stored together with the name of the query.

Click in the input window at the top of the box and type in a suitable name for this acronym definition, such as ACR, DEF. The name is a mnemonic indicating that the acronym is followed by a comma and the definition. *Unlike Query names, Bookmark names can contain spaces and punctuation, with a total of up to 12 characters. You can if you want give more than one name to a solution, but each name can only refer to one solution in a given query.*

Click on ADD to register the bookmark. The Bookmark name dialogue box disappears.

To check that your bookmark has been registered, select BOOKMARK from the EDIT menu again. You will see that the bookmark name now appears in the lower window of the dialogue box. *The* DELETE *option in the dialogue box allows you to remove a selected bookmark from the list in the lower window.*

(14) **Click on** CANCEL **to close the dialogue box.**

(15) **Save the query as** sara.sqy**.** The bookmark will be saved along with the query.

10.2.3 *Searching in specified texts*

The solutions in the window *SARA.SQY* all come from different texts, and all appear to involve different meanings of 'SARA'. Only some of them include definitions, however. It seems worthwhile to look in each text to see whether the acronym is defined at some other point. To do this, we need to restrict our search to the specific texts identified during the last query.

(16) **Scroll through the solutions in the** *SARA.SQY* **window using the arrow buttons or the cursor keys, and make a note of the text identifier code (displayed on the Status bar) for each of the solutions in which no definition is given.**

(17) **Invoke the** QUERY BUILDER **and insert the POS** QUERY "sara"=NP0 **in the content node.**

(18) **Click on the upward branch of this node to create a new content node.**

(19) **Click in the new node and select** EDIT **then** SGML**.** The SGML dialogue box will be displayed.

(20) **Select** <BNCDOC> **from the list of elements.** The list of attributes for this element will be displayed.

(21) **Select** ID **from the list of attributes, and click on** ADD **to display the Attribute dialogue box.** The text identifier of each document is indicated as a value of the ID attribute on the <BNCDOC> element. It takes the form <bncDoc id=BDXXX>, where 'XXX' corresponds to the text identifier code displayed on the status bar.

(22) **Type in as the value the letters** BD **followed by the first text identifier code (all in upper case).** The first text identifier code should be B7L.

(23) **Click on OK to insert this attribute value pair in the right hand window of the SGML dialogue box.** *You can only type in a single explicit value as the target for an attribute search like this one: patterns or wildcards are not allowed.*

(24) **Click on OK to insert this component in the Query Builder node.** It will be displayed as <bncDoc id="BDB7L">.

(25) **Click on the right-hand branch of this content node to create an alternative content node, then click in the new node and select** EDIT**.**

Select SGML and repeat the previous procedure, specifying the next text identifier code in your list (K5A).

Create a third alternative content node corresponding to the next text in your list (K9E).

Create a fourth alternative content node corresponding to text B75, **the final text in your list.** *If you were looking for all the solutions in only one text, you could specify this text as the scope of the query rather than as a content node.*

Check that the 'Query is OK' message is displayed, and click on OK to send the query to the server. There are 6 solutions.

Save the query using a suitable mnemonic, such as sara2.sqy.

Use the SOURCE option to browse through the text preceding each hit. You will find that one of the things SARA stands for is the 'Scottish Amateur Rowing Association'.

In this example, the acronym 'SARA' is used some way after the full name, and it is assumed that the reader will associate the acronym to the referent without this link being specifically marked. We will treat this as a new category, of implicit definition by anaphora.

Return to the solutions display and bookmark this solution with the name ACR ANA Remember to save the query again in order to keep this new bookmark. *In this text (a collection of newspaper articles from The Scotsman), you may have noticed that the full name precedes what is in fact the second use of 'SARA'. Here we would hardly want to say that the third use of the acronym is explained subsequently, since the explanation appears in a different article. BNC texts from periodicals often consist of more than one text in the usual sense of the word, just as those from the spoken demographic component consist of more than one conversation (see 6.1.2 on page 112). Where such texts are involved, you should carefully consider the implications of selecting One-per-text thinning, or of using One-way or Two-way links to join content nodes in the scope of a single <BNCDOC> element.*

There remain three texts in which 'SARA' appears not to be defined. One is a reference to 'SARA title 111' in text K9E — a specialised report, where it appears to be assumed that readers are already familiar with the acronym. The others are references to 'Super SARA' and 'Super- SARA' in texts B7L and B75. In both these texts, however, you may have noticed that there is also a hyphenated one-word version of the acronym ('Super-SARA'), which is defined as a nuclear reactor safety project. We will return to the problem of dealing with such variants in 10.2.5 on page 186.

10.2.4   Serendipitous searching: varying the query type

Solutions to queries often contain unexpected or curious features, which may or may not be related to the original purpose of the query. It is tempting — and often rewarding — to go off at a tangent to investigate casually-encountered features, following a 'serendipity principle'. For instance, a glance through the solutions in the *SARA2.SQY* window shows that acronyms may flock together. The first solution, which refers to 'Super SARA', also contains references to 'LOFT' and to 'Super-SARA'— a hyphenated version of the acronym found by our original query. We can design queries using these other acronyms to look for further definitions, and then look through the solutions to these queries for further acronyms to use in further queries, in an ever-widening cycle. In each case, however, it is important to select the type of query which will best maximise recall and precision.

(33) **Design a POS QUERY for 'loft' as a proper noun (**NN1-NP0 **or** NP0**).** There are 15 solutions, three of them involving acronyms rather than attics. One of these follows the acronym with an explanation in parentheses ('Line Oriented Flight Training'). It also contains a reference to something called 'OATS'.

(34) **Thin the solutions to remove the attics, and bookmark the solution containing an explanation as** ACR (DEF).

(35) **Save the query with a suitable mnemonic, then design a further query to find occurrences of 'OATS'.** If you use POS Query, you will find that 'oats' is not tagged as a proper noun in the corpus.   To avoid references to porridge or horse-breeding, you might either use the Query Builder to restrict a Word Query to the text which contained the acronym, as in 10.2.3 on page 182, or else design a case-sensitive Phrase Query. *The fact that 'Oats' is not tagged as a proper noun here is a reminder that the automatic POS annotation applied to the BNC is not one hundred percent reliable (see 7.3.1 on page 140).*

(36) **Click on the PHRASE QUERY button on the toolbar.** The Phrase Query dialogue box will be displayed.

(37) **Uncheck the IGNORE CASE box and type in the string** OATS **(in upper case). Then click on OK to send the query to the server.**

(38) **Page through the 10 solutions to see if any provides a definition.** You will discover that 'OATS' stands for 'Oxford Air Training School' and for 'Office Automation Technology and Services'.

(39) **Bookmark these definitions and save the query with suitable mnemonics.**

(40) **Page through the solutions to look for any further acronyms.** You will find, *inter alia*, a reference to 'CPL/IR'.

Now design a query to find occurrences of 'CPL' and its compounds, such as 'CPL/IR'.

Invoke the QUERY BUILDER, click in the content node, and select EDIT then WORD. The Word Query dialogue box will be displayed.

Type in the string cpl and click on LOOKUP to display the forms in the index beginning with this string. You will see that as well as 'cpl', the list contains a number of compound forms.

Select all the forms in the list to see their total frequency in the corpus. There are 63 occurrences of forms beginning 'cpl'.

'Cpl' is of course not merely an acronym in English, but also an abbreviation for 'Corporal'. In this latter sense, it is likely to be written with its first letter in upper case. Acronyms, on the other hand, are likely to be completely in upper case. One way to exclude occurrences of the military sense is therefore to make the query case-sensitive, specifying that the string 'CPL' must be in upper case throughout. To make a query case-sensitive, however, you must use Phrase Query, which, unlike Word Query, does not allow you to specify a list of alternative forms. Here we shall use the Query Builder in order to combine both query types to maximise the advantages of each.

In the Word Query dialogue box, select all the forms in the list other than 'cpl', then click on OK to insert this query into the Query Builder. This part of the query does not need to be case-sensitive, since there is little risk of confusion with abbreviations except for 'Cpl', which we have excluded.

Click on the right-hand branch of the content node to create an alternative content node.

Click in the new node and select EDIT then PHRASE. The Phrase Query dialogue box will be displayed.

Uncheck the IGNORE CASE box and type in the string CPL (in upper case). Then click on OK to insert this component in the Query Builder.

Check that the 'Query is OK' message is displayed, and click on OK to send the query to the server. The Too many solutions dialogue box will be displayed, stating that there are 35 solutions in 12 texts.

Download all the solutions, then select QUERY TEXT under QUERY OPTIONS to display the query text. You will see that the text of the query is: ("cpl/ir"|"cpl/irs"|"cpls"|$('CPL')) The dollar sign indicates that the final component of the query is case-sensitive. *You can also use the $ symbol to make all or part of a CQL QUERY case-sensitive (see 7.2.3 on page 137).*

(50)   **Turn off the Query Text display, then page through the solutions looking for acronym definitions.** You will discover that 'CPL' has a variety of meanings, including 'Command Processing Language', 'Communist Party of Lithuania', and 'Cats' Protection League'.

(51)   **Create bookmarks for those solutions which provide definitions, using appropriate mnemonics. If the same pattern occurs more than once, add a number to the bookmark name.** The bookmarks you create should include a number of versions of ACR (DEF) and of DEF (ACR). *Within any single query, each bookmark must have a different name, providing an unambiguous indication of the solution it refers to. If, as in this task, you are using bookmarks to categorize solutions, this means that you must give solutions in the same category slightly different names, for instance by adding a different number in each case.*

(52)   **Save the query as** cpl.sqy.

We could go on with the process of browsing through solutions for acronyms, and then designing appropriate queries to find their definitions, more or less ad infinitum. Such lateral movement through the corpus can be extremely productive: here we have in a matter of minutes come up with a fair number of definitions. As we have categorized them using bookmark names, we can now retrieve and compare the solutions in particular categories. Before doing so, however, let us return briefly to one of the acronyms in the original query, 'Super SARA'.

10.2.5   *Finding compound forms: combining Phrase and Word Queries*

The spelling of compound forms in English is notoriously varied. We have found, for instance, both 'Super SARA' and 'Super-SARA' in one text, as well as 'Super- SARA' in another, and it would not be surprising to also find 'Supersara' as a single unhyphenated form, nor other combinations of upper and lower case. One-word forms, whether unhyphenated or hyphenated, are listed in the SARA word index, and can therefore both be included in a Word (or Pattern) Query by specifying a pattern such as super-?sara: the pattern will also match any case variants (see 8.3.2 on page 159). Two-word realisations, on the other hand, can only be found by a Phrase Query (the Ignore case box must be checked to match case variants). To include all these possibilities in a single query, we must therefore use the Query Builder, specifying the Word or Pattern Query super-?sara and the Phrase Queries super sara and super- sara in alternative nodes.

(53)   **Invoke the QUERY BUILDER and insert a Pattern Query to find occurrences of the pattern** super-?sara **in the content node.**

Add an alternative content node containing a Phrase Query to find occurrences of the two-word form super sara. IGNORE CASE should be checked.

Add a further alternative node containing a Phrase Query for the two-word form super- sara.

Check that the 'Query is OK' message is displayed, and click on OK to send the query to the server. There are 48 solutions in 9 texts.

Download all the solutions, then page through them to look for any definitions.

These solutions illustrate further ways in which acronyms may be defined. For instance, the acronym may pre-modify a *general noun* such as 'project' or 'experiment' ('Europe's Super-SARA experiment into nuclear safety', 'the Super-sara nuclear safety experiment', 'Europe's super-SARA project'). Or it may post-modify a general noun followed by 'known as' ("the project, known as Super-SARA [...]").

Bookmark these solutions with suitable names, such as ACR GN **and** GN, KA ACR, **adding numbers if the same pattern occurs more than once. Then save the query with a suitable mnemonic.**

10.2.6   *Viewing bookmarked solutions*

We have now identified several categories of acronym definitions. Let us try and summarise the results of the investigation so far by examining the bookmarked solutions in the various queries.

Check that all the queries you have designed in this task are still open; re-open any that have been closed. You can only work with bookmarks in queries that are currently open.

Under the EDIT menu, select GOTO. The GOTO dialogue box will be displayed. The list should include all the bookmarks you have assigned in alphabetical order: each bookmark name is followed by the name of the query in which it is found.

Scroll through the bookmarks and make a list of the various categories to which you have given different names. These categories should include ones where:

- the acronym is followed by a definition between commas or parentheses: ACR, DEF and ACR (DEF);

- a definition is followed by the acronym between commas or parentheses: DEF (ACR) and DEF, ACR;

- the acronym pre-modifies a general noun which partly explains it, such as 'project' or 'experiment': ACR GN;
- a definition using a general noun is followed by a comma and 'known as', plus the acronym: DEF, KA ACR;
- the acronym refers anaphorically to a definition earlier in the text: ACR ANA.

Commas vs parentheses in definitions   Using the Windows TILE or CASCADE commands in order to show multiple windows, we can now select and simultaneously display all the solutions from a particular category or categories. Let us start by examining all the examples of the following:

- ACR, DEF
- ACR (DEF)

This will enable us to see whether there are differences between the use of commas and parentheses to introduce definitions of acronyms.

(62) **Scroll through the bookmarks and make a list of the names of all the queries which contain solutions in these categories.**

(63) **Click on CANCEL to close the Goto dialogue box, then close any queries which are not included in the list.**

(64) **Select GOTO from the EDIT menu once more, and scroll through the bookmarks to find the first from the category ACR, DEF.**

(65) **Click on OK to display the solution corresponding to the bookmark.** The window containing this solution will become the active window.

(66) **Click on the CONCORDANCE button to display the solution in Page mode.**

(67) **Select GOTO from the EDIT menu once more, and find the next bookmark in this category. If this bookmark indicates a solution in a different query to the previous one, select and click on OK to display it.**

(68) **If this bookmark indicates a solution in the same query as the previous one, click on CANCEL to close the Goto dialogue box, and select the NEW WINDOW command from the Window menu. Then return to the Goto dialogue box and select this bookmark. Click on OK to display it.** The corresponding solution will be displayed in the new (duplicate) window. *You must create additional windows in order to simultaneously display more than one bookmarked solution from a given query.*

(69) **Return to the GOTO dialogue box and repeat the procedure for each bookmark from the same category.**

Select TILE from the WINDOW menu to view all the bookmarked solutions.

Repeat the procedure with the bookmarks ACR (DEF).There appears to be little difference between the examples with parentheses and commas.

Now do the same for the bookmarks where these components are in the reverse order:

- DEF, ACR

- DEF (ACR)

Use the CLOSE ALL option from the WINDOW menu to close the current array of windows.

Re-open all the original queries and select GOTO to display the full list of saved bookmarks.

Repeat the procedure described in this section for these new categories.

10.2.7   Including punctuation in a query

Clearly, we have not found anything like all the ways acronyms are defined in the corpus. We have however identified some patterns such definitions take, and may now be able to design queries to find all the occurrences of particular patterns in order to see how widely they are used, and whether they have other functions. There are limits to this procedure, since it is only feasible to look for patterns containing specific words. It would, for example, be absurd to attempt a query looking for the pattern ACR, DEF, as this would involve finding all the commas in the corpus. We could at most download a sample of the solutions, sort them using POS CODE collating to group those where the comma was preceded by a proper noun (see 7.2.4 on page 137), and then look to see how many of this group involved acronyms — probably a miniscule proportion. Similarly, were we to try to investigate acronyms which pre-modify a general noun, we could at most look for specific general nouns, such as 'project' and 'scheme', and sort the solutions to group the relatively few cases where the general noun was preceded by a proper noun.

Where, on the other hand, the acronym and its definition are linked by a recurrent lexical form, we can design a query which has much greater precision. The pattern DEF, known as ACR contains a fixed lexical sequence which we can incorporate in a Phrase Query. To increase precision, this query can include not only the words 'known as', but also the comma which precedes them in the pattern.

(75) **Click on the PHRASE QUERY button on the toolbar to display the Phrase Query dialogue box. Then type in the string** , known as **and click on OK to send the query to the server.** The Too many solutions dialogue box will be displayed, stating that there are 767 solutions in 487 texts.

(76) **Check the ONE PER TEXT box and download the first 250 solutions.** We are once more assuming that the first occurrence in any text is as likely as any to involve a definition.

(77) **Sort the solutions using the first three words to the right as Primary key, with ASCII collating.** This will group the solutions where 'known as' is followed by a word beginning with an upper case letter, such as an acronym, at the top of the display.

You will see that many of the solutions at the beginning of the list have the next word in inverted commas — generally a nickname. Following these, however, you should find some acronyms in upper case.

(78) **Save the query as** known_as.sqy.

(79) **Scroll through the solutions and mark those which correspond to acronym definitions.** While the majority of acronyms are in upper case, there may be some in which only the first letter is capitalised.

(80) **Delete the unmarked solutions using the THIN option.** You should be left with 5-10% of the original solution set.

Results: the Collocation option as a query heuristic   While ', known as' clearly has a wide range of other uses (particularly in introducing nicknames), one of its regular functions would appear to be that of defining or explaining acronyms.   There appear to be two main patterns in the data: in the first, the full name is spelt out, followed by ', known as [acronym]'; in the second, an expression including a general noun such as 'project', 'method', or 'scheme' is used to describe the referent, followed by ', known as [acronym]'.

As we have not downloaded all the solutions (or even a random set), we do not know exactly how frequent these two patterns are. There is no way to design a query to investigate the first pattern, but we can do so for the latter, for instance in the form:

```
("project"|"scheme"|"method")(', known as)
```

To decide whether it is worthwhile doing so (i.e. whether recall will be enhanced, with many more solutions than those already noted being found), you can use the COLLOCATION option in the current query in order to find how frequently these three words occur close to ', known as'. Not all these occurrences will necessarily be definitions, but their number may indicate whether this idea is worth following up. When calculating collocations, remember to use all the available solutions, not just the ones downloaded in the current query results.

10.3 Discussion and suggestions for further work

10.3.1 Using Bookmarks

While the limited investigation in this task does not allow any generalised conclusions as to ways in which definitions are provided in the corpus, we have seen how SARA allows you to accumulate instances of particular features which have been located, memorising them under the form of bookmarks, so as to return to them when the range of instances is sufficient to warrant tentative conclusions, or to formulate testable hypotheses. Bookmarks allow you to

- record particular solutions so you can return to them easily;
- annotate particular solutions by assigning them distinctive names;
- record and annotate solutions from several queries, so that similarly classified solutions can be retrieved and displayed simultaneously in different windows.

These features are particularly useful when you are

- working simultaneously on various features of a solution set, since different types of bookmark names can be assigned to solutions displaying different features, and more than one bookmark can be assigned to a particular solution;
- working with provisional categories of solutions, since bookmarks do not affect the composition of the solution set and can be deleted, relocated or renamed as required (unlike the THIN option, which deletes marked or unmarked solutions irrevocably: see 2.2.4 on page 68).

10.3.2 Punctuation in different query types

SARA only allows you to search for sentence punctuation using PHRASE QUERY. In a WORD QUERY, you can only use punctuation where this forms part of an L-word, typically in abbreviations such as 'Dr.' or 'M.P.' You cannot include such forms in a PHRASE QUERY, as the punctuation will not be interpreted as being part of the word. PATTERN QUERY functions in the same way as Word Query, always providing that dots, parentheses, inverted commas or question marks are preceded by a backslash to indicate that the character is to be interpreted literally, not as a variable or special character. In a CQL QUERY the interpretation of any punctuation will depend on whether it is included within a word — i.e. whether it is included in the double inverted commas surrounding the word — or within a phrase, i.e. within single inverted commas.

10.3.3 Some similar problems

More serendipity   The solutions to the final query in the last section (see 10.2.7 on page 189) included some very strange nicknames. How not to be intrigued by 'Bridget Bostock, known as the Cheshire Pythoness' or 'Zen Sharpik, known as Nostrils'? Reopen the unthinned version of the query (KNOWN_AS.SQY) and allow yourself a few minutes to browse through the solutions, switching to Page display mode, checking sources and browsing in the original text as and when your curiosity is aroused.

If nothing else takes your fancy, find out what else comes from Cheshire in the corpus, or whether any other people called Zen are mentioned. *Download a random 30 occurrences of 'Cheshire' to see what collocates appear to recur with Cheshire in the solutions. Then use the* COLLOCATION *option to investigate their frequency in the entire set of solutions on the server. Use* POS QUERY *to find occurrences of the name 'Zen', downloading one per text.*

There are many more Cheshire cats in the BNC than there is cheese. As well as Zen philosophy, you will find a number of restaurants, a 5-year-old twin, an Italian detective, and an elkhound.

Looking for misunderstandings   Not all pragmatic phenomena are so easily identified as definitions. How might you attempt to find instances of misunderstandings in spoken dialogue in the BNC? *As, presumably, anything can be misunderstood in talk, we can hardly predict particular features which are likely to give rise to misunderstandings in the way we could predict that acronyms might be defined. But we can think of expressions which are likely to be used when a misunderstanding is suspected or discovered: 'What I meant was'; 'I thought you said'; 'I didn't mean'; 'Ah, I see' and the like. Use the Query Builder to design queries to find these and similar phrases in spoken dialogue, and browse the preceding context of their solutions to see if they index misunderstandings. Bookmark those which appear to do so, and see which queries appear most effective as a means of locating misunderstandings.*

Several of these phrases appear to regularly occur in contexts of misunderstanding, including 'what I meant was' (all 4 occurrences), and 'I didn't mean' (about half the 46 occurrences). Many of the solutions to the latter query occur in apologies — another pragmatic function which it might be interesting to investigate using the BNC.

Not Ms(.) Thatcher   What proportion of the uses of 'Mrs' or 'Mrs.' in the BNC are in reference to Margaret Thatcher? Is she ever referred to as 'Ms Thatcher' or 'Ms. Thatcher'? *Use* WORD QUERY *to look up the joint frequency of 'Mrs' and 'Mrs.' in the word index, then use the* QUERY BUILDER *to find all the occurrences of either form together with 'Thatcher' as a proper noun, in a span of 3. Read off the number of solutions from the Too many solutions dialogue box, then edit the query to find the frequency of 'Ms Thatcher' or 'Ms. Thatcher'.*

Mrs Thatcher is referred to 1759 times in 336 texts, out of a total of 22,150 occurrences of 'Mrs' or 'Mrs.'. She is never referred to as 'Ms' or 'Ms.'. Interestingly, the opposite is true of Ms. Bhutto.

Other SARA acronyms   The acronym 'SARA' has a variety of meanings in the BNC. What about some of the other acronyms used in this handbook, such as 'POS' or 'CQL'? *A search for 'pos' as a proper noun yields 7 solutions, mainly referring to postal orders and point-of-sale debiting equipment. There are no solutions for 'cql', which is absent from the word index.*

The British National Pumpkin   Acronyms are often defined by spelling out the corresponding name immediately before or afterwards, as in the various 'CPL' examples (see 10.2.4 on page 184). This suggests that a further strategy we might use to find acronyms is to look for common name components and see if they have acronyms associated with them. For instance, this handbook regularly uses the acronym 'BNC' to refer to the British National Corpus. Design a query to find out if the words 'British National' form part of other names, and whether any of these define acronyms. *To look for occurrences of 'British' and 'National' you cannot productively use POS queries, since both these forms are tagged as adjectives, regardless of whether they form part of a name. Instead you should use the* IGNORE CASE *option in Phrase Query to restrict the query to cases where 'British' and 'National' are both capitalised. Sort the solutions by the right with a span of 1, using* ASCII *collating, so as to group at the head of the display those solutions where the word following 'British National' begins with a capital letter.*

As well as the BNC, you will encounter the BNB ('British National Bibliography') and the BNP ('British National Party') — a rather different organization from the 'British National Pumpkin society', which, alas, has no acronym cited.

III: Reference Guide

1 Quick reference guide to the SARA client

This section summarizes the facilities provided by the SARA client program. In the previous part of the *BNC Handbook*, these facilities were introduced in the context of specific tasks, and as a means of exploring the BNC. In this section, for ease of reference we review them in the same order as they are presented on the initial menu bar. In a number of cases, references are also provided to the tasks in which particular functions listed here are used. You will also find extensive cross references between the descriptions, and in the on–line help system.

We begin by describing the process of *logging on* to the server. Once logged on you will see a *menu bar* across the top of the screen, from which all the functions of the client program are accessible. The remainder of this section of the *BNC Handbook* describes these functions.

1.1 Logging on to the SARA system

Once the SARA client program has been correctly installed on your system, you launch it in the same way as any other Windows application, for example by double-clicking on an icon. A box will appear, displaying version information for the release of SARA you are using. Click on OK or press ENTER and the LOGON dialogue box will appear. You must have a username and a password before you can access a networked SARA server, for licensing reasons. These will normally be allocated by the person responsible for managing the BNC server to which you are connecting. Note that the username may be quite different from that you use for other network services such as e-mail. SARA can also be run in local mode (i.e. with both the server and the client running on the same machine). In this case, you may not need to log on.

When you have typed in your username, press the TAB key to move to the password box, and type in your password. It will not appear on the screen, but will be validated by the server when you press the ENTER key or click on the OK button. If you have typed a valid password and username, the box will be replaced by the message of the day, identifying the server to which you are connected. Press ENTER again, or click on OK, and you will see the main SARA screen. If you make a mistake entering your password, the system will let you try again. If you want to give up, click on the CANCEL button. You can change your password — but only once you have successfully logged on! (see further section 1.7.5 on page 227).

If your system is not configured correctly, or if the server which you are trying to reach is not available, you will be offered the chance to select a different server address, or to run SARA in local mode, as further discussed in section 1.7.5 on page 227. Do not change the server address unless you need to: any changes made here will apply to all subsequent use of SARA on your machine. Press on the CANCEL button to close the Communications dialogue box if you simply want to try the same server again later.

See section 1.2.1 on page 49 for a more detailed description of the log on procedure.

1.2   The main SARA window

All use of SARA is done within the main SARA window. There is a menu bar across the top of this window, which can be used to select the various SARA commands available to you, and a tool bar which can be used to select particular commands rapidly. The buttons on this bar are reproduced on the inside cover of this book: see section 1.7.1 on page 225 for a summary of the commands accessible from the tool bar. At the bottom of the screen, there is an iconified representation of the corpus which you are currently searching (in the current release, this is always the whole of the BNC).

The SARA client can operate in either of two modes. In *query mode* (the default, and usual mode of operation) the client accepts queries, acts on them, and displays their solutions in one or more query windows. In *browse mode*, the client opens a browse window showing the whole of a particular text, which you can then read. In browse mode, the Query menu is replaced by a Browser menu.

We use the terms *query* and *solution* throughout this handbook to refer to two distinct aspects of your interaction with the system. When you use SARA, you will usually be asking it to find examples of the occurrences of particular words, phrases, patterns, etc. within the BNC. We refer to the request you make of the system as a query; the set of examples or other response which this request produces we refer to as the solutions. For example the query dog _ cat will find occurrences of phrases such as 'dog and cat', 'dog or cat', etc., which may be sorted or thinned in a variety of ways; these are called solutions to the query. The distinction is important, because SARA allows you to save and manipulate queries and their solutions independently.

To use SARA you give various commands, selected from the menu bar or the tool bar. Some commands affect the behaviour of the client or the server, for example by setting limits for the amount of text to be downloaded in response to a query, or to change the format of text being displayed by the client. Other commands create new queries and open new windows in which to display their solutions.

The commands available are logically grouped together according to Microsoft interface guidelines. The order in which they are discussed follows their order on the menu bar.

To select an item from the menu bar, click on the appropriate word with the mouse, or type the appropriate keyboard shortcut. A menu will open up, from which further options can be selected with the mouse, possibly with further sub-menus in some cases.

The following options are available from the top level menu structure.

FILE Most choices on this menu manipulate SARA query files. Select it to create, re-use, or save a query, as well as to print the solutions to a query, or to exit from the program, as further described in section 1.3 on the next page.

EDIT Choices on this menu manipulate the current SARA query. Use it to copy selected solutions to the Windows clipboard, or to attach named bookmarks to particular solutions, for later recovery, as further described in section 1.4 on page 213.

BROWSER This menu option appears instead of the QUERY menu option if no query is currently open, or when SARA is in browse mode; choices on this menu control how texts are displayed when you are browsing through them. Use it to turn on or off the display of low level SGML tags in browse mode, as further described in section 1.5 on page 215.

QUERY This menu option appears only when you have sent a query to the server to be processed, when it replaces the BROWSER menu option. Most choices on this menu modify the solutions to the current SARA query. Use it to re-submit a modified version of the current query, to thin, save, or sort the solutions to the current query, or change the way they are displayed. It can also be used to calculate collocations and to view the source of a particular solution, as further described in section 1.6 on page 216.

VIEW Choices on this menu determine how solutions are displayed by SARA. Use it to limit the length of downloaded solutions, and their number, to choose a default format for displaying them, to set the colours and format of the display, and to configure various options for this and subsequent SARA sessions, as further described in section 1.7 on page 225.

WINDOW Choices on this menu allow you to manipulate the windows on the screen. Use it to open a new main SARA window, to tidy the way that existing windows are displayed, etc., as further described in section 1.8 on page 228.

HELP   Choices on this menu allow you to read the built-in SARA help file. Use it to browse the on-line SARA documentation, as further described in section 1.9 on page 229.

1.3   The File menu

Most of the commands on this menu manipulate queries, as opposed to the solutions which they return from the corpus: the exceptions are PRINT and PRINT PREVIEW, both of which relate to the solutions returned by the current query.

The following commands are provided on the File menu.

NEW QUERY   Open a submenu, from which you can select the kind of query you wish to define. A new query window is then opened for you to define that kind of query. See 1.3.1 on the following page for information about the types of query that may be defined.

OPEN   Open a previously defined query.

CLOSE   Close the current query and its associated window.

SAVE   Save the current query as a file, using the name specified in the title bar of the query window.

SAVE AS   Save the current query as a file, giving an option to change its name from that specified in the title bar of the query window.

PRINT   Print the solutions to the current query.

PRINT PREVIEW   Display on the screen the format in which the current solutions will be printed.

RECENT FILE   Open a recently accessed query (a list of filenames is displayed in the menu at this point).

EXIT   Exit from the Client program.

By default, the first query defined during your SARA session is named *Query1*, the second *Query2*, and so on. The name of a query appears in the title bar of the window containing its solutions, and is also used to identify the file in which the query is saved. This implies that a query name must also be a valid MS-DOS filename. You can rename a query by means of the SAVE AS command, provided that the name you supply contains only characters which are legal in filenames under MS-DOS, and does not exceed eight characters in length. The file extension .sqy is assigned by default.

Queries are opened or saved using the normal Windows dialogue boxes for file manipulation, which allow you to change drives, specify filenames, etc. If you do not know how to use these, consult any introductory text on using Microsoft Windows.

1.3.1   Defining a query

The NEW QUERY option on the File menu opens a submenu from which you can select which type of query you want to perform. SARA allows you to define the following different kinds of query:

WORD searches the SARA word index, and then optionally also searches the BNC for a word or words selected from those found (see section 1.3.2);

PHRASE searches the BNC for a phrase (see section 1.3.3 on page 202);

POS searches the BNC for a word with a specific part of speech (POS) code or codes (see section 1.3.4 on page 203);

PATTERN searches the BNC for words matching a pattern or regular expression (see section 1.3.5 on page 204);

SGML searches the BNC for SGML tags (see section 1.3.6 on page 206);

QUERY BUILDER combines queries of different or the same kinds into a single complex query using a visual interface (see section 1.3.7 on page 207);

CQL searches the BNC using a query defined in the Corpus Query Language (CQL), SARA's own internal command language (see section 1.3.8 on page 210).

More detail about each kind of query is given in the appropriate section. There is a button on the tool bar for each kind of query: it is generally quicker to press the button than to select it from the menu. All the buttons on the toolbar are reproduced on the inside of the cover of this book, along with the names used to refer to them.

1.3.2   Defining a Word Query

Example Word Queries are discussed in sections 2.2.1 on page 64 and 2.3.1 on page 72. A Word Query may be defined in any of the following ways:

- select WORD from the submenu of the NEW QUERY option on the FILE menu;
- press the WORD QUERY button on the tool bar;
- within Query Builder, select WORD from the EDIT submenu..

Any of the above will cause the Word Query dialogue box to be displayed, containing a window into which you can type a word, or part of a word, to be searched for in the SARA index. If the PATTERN checkbox to the right of the window is checked, whatever you type will be interpreted as a *pattern*. If it is not checked, whatever you type will be interpreted as a word stem. (Strictly speaking, a word stem is also a kind of pattern: the word stem XXX is exactly equivalent to the pattern XXX.*)

The LOOKUP button carries out a search of the SARA index. Every form found in the index which starts with the same letters as the word or part of a word you typed in will be displayed in the lower window. If the PATTERN checkbox was checked, every word matching the pattern you typed in will be displayed.

For example, typing in colour with the PATTERN checkbox unchecked will produce a list of words beginning with the letters 'colour', ('colour', 'colours', 'colouring', etc.) If the box is checked, only the word 'colour' will be produced, since this is the only word which matches that pattern. (Patterns are described in section 1.3.5 on page 204.) Typing in colou?r.* with the pattern box checked will produce a list of all words beginning with the letters 'color' and 'colour'. Note that, in this case, if the box is not checked, no words will be returned, since there is no word beginning 'colou?r.*' in the BNC.

A pattern expression which begins with anything other than a literal will usually involve a search through the whole BNC index, which will take a very long time indeed, and should be avoided. This implies that searches for word-endings are not easily done.

Hyphenated words and words followed by some punctuation characters may not always be indexed in the way you expect. Note that not every item in the index is a conventional orthographic word: as further discussed in section 2.1.2 on page 34, the index uses *L-words* which may be parts of conventional orthographic words, such as 'n't', or orthographic phrases, such as 'in spite of'.

The lower window will not display more than 200 items: a warning message will appear if the word or word part you typed was not specific enough, perhaps because it was too short. If the word you wish to look up is also a very common prefix, check the PATTERN box to select only the word, rather than all words beginning with that string of characters.

You can click on one or more of the word forms displayed in the lower window to select them. As is usual with Windows application, clicking on one or more items with the CTRL key depressed will select each of them; clicking one and then another with the SHIFT key depressed will select both those two and all the other items between them in the list.

When an item is selected in this way it is highlighted on the screen, and a count is displayed in the box indicating the frequency and z-score for the selected word forms within the texts (but not the headers) making up the BNC. (For fiurther discussion of these statistics, see section 2.2.1 on page 64.)

When items are selected, the QUERY button can be pressed to carry out a search for these word forms within the BNC. Section 1.3.9 on page 212 gives further details of the process of downloading the solutions found.

The other buttons in the Word Query dialogue box have the following effects:

COPY copies the input string to the Windows clipboard;

CLEAR deletes any previous input and selections from the dialogue box;

CANCEL leaves the dialogue box without starting a query.

When a Word Query is carried out as a part of a Query Builder query (see 1.3.7 on page 207 below), the QUERY button is labelled OK and clicking on it simply adds the selected word or words into the query being constructed.

1.3.3   Defining a Phrase Query

Example Phrase Queries are discussed in sections 1.2.5 on page 51 and 4.2.1 on page 87. A Phrase Query may be defined in any of the following ways:

- select PHRASE from the submenu of the NEW QUERY option on the FILE menu;
- press the PHRASE QUERY button on the tool bar;
- within Query Builder, select PHRASE from the EDIT submenu.

Any of the above will cause the Phrase Query dialogue box to be displayed. This dialogue box contains a window into which you can type a word or phrase, a checkbox labelled IGNORE CASE, and a checkbox labelled SEARCH HEADERS.

You can type any sequence of words, or a single word, into the window. Press the OK button (or the ENTER key) and a search is carried out for the specified phrase within the BNC.

If the SEARCH HEADERS checkbox is checked, then the search is carried out within the text headers as well as the texts. Otherwise, only the texts are searched.

If the IGNORE CASE checkbox is checked, the search treats upper and lower case forms of a letter as identical. For example, with the box checked, a search for SARA will recover occurrences of 'SARA', 'Sara', or 'sara'; otherwise, only the first of these will be found.

These two check boxes are the only ways SARA provides for searching in a case sensitive way, or for searching within the headers, other than by using a CQL query (on which, see section 1.3.8 on page 210).

A Phrase Query can contain punctuation characters as well as words. For example, the query , whereas will find occurrences of 'whereas' only where they are preceded by a comma. When searching for a match, new lines between components of a Phrase Query are not significant: for example, it makes no difference if the comma is at the end of one line and the 'whereas' at the start of the next.

A special punctuation character known as the *Anyword* character _ can be used within a Phrase Query (but not at the start or end of one). It will match any L-word, that is, any item in the index. For example, the Phrase Query home _ centre will recover phrases such as 'home loan centre', 'home improvement centre', 'home planning centre', etc. As noted above, an L-word may be a clitic (such as 'n't') or a phrase (such as 'matter of fact'): this should be borne in mind when defining queries containing the Anyword character.

Each part of a Phrase Query is searched for separately, and the results are then combined. Consequently, if a Phrase Query contains any very common words (for example, 'to', 'the', etc.) it may take a very long time to execute: in such cases it is usually better to replace the very high frequency word with an Anyword character. For example, to find the phrase 'die the death', type die _ death and discard the (fairly small) number of false positives such as 'die a death', using the THIN command described in section 1.6.3 on page 218.

There is no limit on the number of words a Phrase Query may contain, but the total length of the string may not exceed 200 characters.

Click on the OK button to send the query to the server, or click on the CANCEL button to cancel it; see further 1.3.9 on page 212.

1.3.4 *Defining a POS Query*

An example POS Query is discussed in section 7.2.1 on page 131. A POS, or part of speech query behaves in the same way as a Word Query, except that it can only search for a single word, which can be further restricted according to its part of speech (POS) code. It may be defined in any of the following ways:

- select POS from the submenu of the NEW QUERY option on the FILE menu;
- press the POS QUERY button on the tool bar;
- within Query Builder, select POS from the EDIT submenu.

All of the above will cause the POS Query dialogue box to be displayed, containing two display windows. When the word to be searched for is typed into the upper window, and the mouse is clicked in the lower window, the lower window is filled with a list of the different parts of speech that the word in question has been assigned within the corpus. The same effect can be obtained by typing in a word and pressing the TAB key.

For example, the word 'snore' appears in the corpus as the base form of a verb (VVB), as a singular common noun (NN1), and as a portmanteau (NN1-VVB), as well as with various other less frequent codes. All these possibilities appear in the lower box. (The POS codes used in the BNC are further discussed in section 2.1.2 on page 34.)

To search for the nominal senses only, highlight the NN1 in the lower window, and press OK. To search for both nominal and portmanteau cases, hold down the control key while highlighting the NN1 and NN1-VVB entries, and then press OK.

Note that it is not possible to search for a particular part of speech without specifying the word to which it is attached. This implies that you cannot use SARA to search for such things as sequences of three or more adjectives, nor for occurrences of a specific word preceded by any word with a particular part of speech. You can however group together solutions which have particular POS codes on either side of a given word form by using the SORT option (see further section 1.6.2 on page 217).

The Help system contains an annotated list of POS codes used in the current version of the corpus: this list also appears in appendix 2.1 on page 230. A brief explanation of each POS code is also displayed when you select it from the upper box in the POS Query dialogue box.

Click on the OK button to send the query to the server, or click on the CANCEL button to cancel it; see further 1.3.9 on page 212.

1.3.5   Defining a Pattern Query

An example Pattern Query is discussed in section 8.2.2 on page 150. A Pattern Query may be defined in any of the following ways:

- select PATTERN from the submenu of the NEW QUERY option on the FILE menu;
- press the PATTERN QUERY button on the tool bar;
- within Query Builder, select PATTERN from the EDIT submenu.

All of the above will cause the Pattern Query dialogue box to be displayed. This dialogue box contains a window into which you can type a pattern. The pattern is validated, and a search is carried out for all the words which match it. See further 1.3.9 on page 212.

As noted above in section 1.3.2 on page 200, a pattern can also be typed as part of a Word Query in order to produce a list of matching words. This is a very useful way of checking the result of a Pattern Query without actually carrying it out by searching the BNC: for an example, see 8.2.1 on page 147.

A *pattern* is a string of characters which is used as a template to match words in the SARA index. The characters making up a pattern can be:

- *literal characters*, such as A, B or C, which simply match occurrences of the same character; pattern–matching is never case-sensitive, so a and A are equivalent;

- *special characters* which behave in a special way within patterns; if a special character is to be used within a pattern but interpreted as if it were a literal, it must be preceded by the backslash character.

The special characters recognized by SARA are:

```
. - [ ] ( ) ^ ? * + | \
```

The *dot* special character matches any single character. For example the pattern f... matches any four letter word beginning with F.

A *bracketed sequence* matches any one of the characters contained within it. For example, the pattern [aeiou] matches any vowel.

A sequence can contain a *hyphen* to express a range. For example, the patterns [0-9] and [0123456789] are equivalent: either one will match any digit.

The *caret* special character can appear at the start of a sequence, to indicate that any character *not* in the sequence should be matched. For example, the pattern [^aeiou] will match any which is not a vowel; the pattern [^0-9] will match anything which is not a digit.

Single characters or bracketed sequences can be repeated as often as necessary to make up a complete pattern. For example, the pattern [0-9][0-9][0-9] will match all three-digit numbers; the pattern m[0-9][0-9] will match an M followed by two digits.

The *question mark* special character can follow either a single character or a bracketed sequence of characters, to indicate that the character is optional. For example, the pattern colou?r will match either 'colour' or 'color'; the pattern [0-9][0-9][0-9]? will match all two- or three- digit numbers, e.g. 99 or 42 or 123 or 912.

The *star* special character can follow either a single character or a bracketed sequence of characters, to indicate that the character is optional and may be repeated. For example, the pattern hm[hm]* will match words beginning with HM and containing only those two letters, no matter how long they are, for example 'hm' or 'hmmmm' or 'hmmhmhmmmm'; the pattern sorrow.* will match any word beginning with the letters 'sorrow', including 'sorrow' itself.

The *plus* special character can follow either a single character or a bracketed sequence, to indicate that the character appears at least once. For example, the pattern sorrow.+ will match any word beginning with the letters 'sorrow', except for 'sorrow' itself; the pattern m[0-9]+ will match all words composed of the letters M followed by at least one digit, and nothing but digits, e.g. 'M1', 'M2345'; similarly, the pattern e+k will find 'ek', 'eek', 'eeeeek', etc.

The plus or star characters can be used to indicate repetition at any point in a pattern. However, matching of patterns *beginning* with such sequences (for example, .*ing to recover all words ending with 'ing') is likely to be unacceptably slow, since it requires a scan through the entire word index. In general, it is best to make the first component of any pattern a literal. Repetition can however be effectively used in the middle of a pattern: for example effec.*ly will match 'effectively' or 'effectually'.

Two or more patterns can be combined as alternatives using the *disjunction* special character. For example, the pattern seek|sought will match either the word 'seek' or the word 'sought'. *Parentheses* can be used to group parts of a pattern together: for example, the same effect could be obtained by the pattern s(eek|ought).

Any character preceded by the *backslash* special character will be treated as a literal even if it is a special character. For example, the pattern Mr?s?\. will match any of 'M.', 'Mr.', 'Mrs.' or 'Ms.'. Without the backslash, the final dot would be interpreted as a special character, matching any character at all. A backslash is unnecessary within square brackets: the pattern M[rs.]* would have a similar effect to the above, except that it would also match forms lacking a final dot (plus a number of probably unintended matches, such as 'mss.').

1.3.6   *Defining an SGML Query*

Example SGML Queries are discussed in sections 5.2.2 on page 100 and 6.2.1 on page 115. An SGML Query searches for an SGML start- or end-tag, optionally further qualified by attribute values. (SGML — the ISO Standard Generalized Markup Language — is briefly described above at section 2.1.2 on page 33; see also chapter 5 of the *BNC Users' Reference Guide*.) An SGML Query may be defined in any of the following ways:

- select SGML from the submenu of the NEW QUERY option on the FILE menu;
- press the SGML QUERY button on the tool bar;
- within Query Builder, select SGML from the EDIT submenu.

All of the above will cause the SGML dialogue box to be displayed.

As well as information about words and their parts of speech, the BNC index searched by SARA contains details of where the *SGML elements* of which the corpus is composed begin and end. The start of an SGML element is indicated by a *start-tag*; its end is indicated by an *end-tag*. Start-tags may additionally carry named *attributes*, with particular *values*, to convey additional information about the element occurrences they delimit.

You can use this information to restrict searches to particular types of text (the categorization of a text is indicated by attributes of a <CATREF> element within its header), or to find particular types of text component — for example newspaper headlines, which are mostly tagged <HEAD TYPE=MAIN> in the BNC, or pauses (<PAUSE>) in spoken texts.

The SGML dialogue box contains a scrollable list of the element names defined for the corpus. For an explanation of the way these elements are used in the corpus, refer to the *BNC Users' Reference Guide*. If the SHOW HEADER TAGS checkbox is checked, the names of all elements used in the corpus will appear; if it is not, then those which are used only in the headers will be excluded. To search the corpus for an SGML start- or end-tag, you select the name of the element concerned from this list by clicking on it. A brief description of the way this element is used is then displayed.

Provided that the START radio button is selected, a list of any attributes defined for this element will be displayed in the lower left hand window. You can restrict the search to occurrences of this element having particular values for some combination of these attributes by selecting attribute names from the list, one at a time, and adding them into the query. Alternatively, if you do not select any attribute name fom the list, the query will select occurrences of this SGML element whatever attribute values it may have.

When you select an attribute name from the list, clicking on the ADD button will open a further dialogue box in which you can specify the desired value for the attribute you have selected. For some attributes, the range of possible values is defined in advance, and SARA will therefore present you with a list from which you can select one or more particular values; for other attributes, the range of possible values is not defined, and SARA will therefore present you with a window into which you must type the required value explicitly. In either case, when you have specified the value, press OK to close this dialogue box. Several attribute value constraints may be added in this way. You can also remove a particular constraint by selecting it from the right hand window in the SGML dialogue box, and then clicking on the REMOVE button, or remove all of them by clicking on the REMOVE ALL button.

Click on the OK button to send the query to the server, or click on the CANCEL button to cancel it; see further 1.3.9 on page 212.

1.3.7   Defining a query with Query Builder

Query Builder is a special purpose tool which allows you to create complex queries using a visual interface. Some sample uses of Query Builder are described in sections 4.2.2 on page 91, 4.3.2 on page 95, and 5.2.4 on page 105. The Query Builder command can be used in either of the following ways:

- select QUERY BUILDER from the submenu of the NEW QUERY option on the FILE menu;
- press the QUERY BUILDER button on the tool bar.

Either of these will cause the Query Builder dialogue box to be displayed. This dialogue box is used to define a Query Builder query as further described in this section.

Parts of a complex query are represented in the Query Builder dialogue box by *nodes* of various types. A Query Builder query always has at least two nodes: one, the *scope node*, defines the *scope* (that is, context) within which a complex query is to be evaluated. The other nodes, which may be linked in various ways, are known as *content nodes*. These define the various things which are to be found within this scope. Any form of query can be used in a content node (except for a CQL or Query Builder query).

For example, you might use the Query Builder to search for the word 'fork' followed or preceded by the word 'knife' within the scope of a single <s> (sentence) element. Alternatively, you might specify the same search but define its scope as a number of L-words. The default scope for all Query Builder queries is a <BNCDOC> element, i.e. any one of the 4124 distinct text samples making up the BNC.

The scope of a query is represented in the scope node which appears on the left of the dialogue box. To the right of this is a single empty content node. Clicking with the mouse inside a content node opens a submenu, from which you can select either EDIT, CLEAR, or (for nodes other than the first one) DELETE. Selecting EDIT opens a further submenu, from which you select the type of query you wish to define for that node, or, if you have already defined a query for the node, to edit it. Selecting CLEAR cancels any previous choice, allowing you to select a new query type for the node. DELETE removes the content node, but leaves the rest of the query unchanged. When a node has been defined, its content can be copied to the clipboard by selecting COPY from the submenu; this content can then be retrieved into another node by selecting PASTE.

Further content nodes can be added to the right of, above, or below the initial node, simply by clicking the mouse on the branch in that direction. Nodes added to the right of a node represent alternatives to it. For example, the Query Builder representation of a query to find either the word 'fork' or the word 'knife' within the scope of a single <s> element would have two content nodes linked horizontally, one searching for 'knife' and the other for 'fork'. (An alternation of this kind could also be represented within a single content node by using a Pattern Query, or a Word Query with alternatives.) The scope node for this query would indicate the SGML element <s>.

Nodes added above or a content node represent additional constraints. If a content node searching for 'fork' is placed below one searching for 'knife', then both terms must be found within the scope defined by the scope node, rather than just one of them. The vertical line linking the two content nodes indicates the order and proximity required. Clicking on the line opens a submenu from which you can select one of the following possibilities:

NEXT (represented by a thick line): no words or punctuation can appear between the query term indicated above the line and the term below the line;

ONE-WAY (represented by a downwards pointing arrow): the query term indicated above the line must precede the term below the line within the scope indicated by the scope node. This is the default link type;

TWO-WAY (represented by a double-headed arrow): the query terms above and below the line may appear in any order within the scope indicated by the scope node.

In the current version of SARA, you must use the same kind of link (Next, One-way, or Two-way) between all the content nodes of a single query. If the content nodes in a query are joined by different kinds of link, no solutions are found.

To change the scope, click on the scope node. A submenu opens, from which you can choose either SGML or SPAN. Choosing SGML opens the SGML dialogue box, from which you can select an SGML element, possibly modified by attribute values, as in an SGML Query (see further section 1.3.6 on page 206). Choosing SPAN opens a dialogue box in which you can enter the number of L-words within which the whole query must be satisfied. With a span of n words, the total number of L-words matched (including both content nodes and any intervening words) may not exceed n. For example, searching for 'knife' and 'fork' within a span of 4 will find 'knife and sharp fork' as well as 'knife and fork' but not 'knife and very sharp fork'. The maximum span is 99 L-words.

All the content nodes making up a Query Builder query must be satisfied one way or another. Where several content nodes are specified as alternatives, at least one of them must be satisfied in addition to any constraints expressed by content nodes specified or above the set of alternatives, and vice versa. Thus, a query in which 'fork' or 'spoon' are specified as alternatives, with an additional node below specifying 'knife' with a one-way link, will find 'fork and knife' and 'spoon and knife' but will not find either 'spoon' on its own or 'fork and spoon'.

A content node can contain *any* kind of query (other than a CQL or a Query Builder query) — one or more alternatives chosen from the Word Query dialogue box; a Phrase Query; a POS Query; a Pattern Query; or an SGML Query. The Anyword character can also be entered as a content node in its own right.

Once you have completed defining the query, press the OK button to carry out a search, or press CANCEL to cancel it; see further 1.3.9 on page 212.

1.3.8 Defining a CQL Query

CQL is short for the *Corpus Query Language*. It is the command language which the SARA client program uses to communicate with the SARA server. Usually expressions in CQL are generated for you by the client program, but there is no reason why you should not type them in directly as well. There are also a few features of the command language which cannot be easily (or at all) expressed by the current client except in this way.

Some example CQL Queries are discussed in sections 7.2.3 on page 135 and 9.3.1 on page 176. A CQL Query may be defined in either of the following ways:

- select CQL from the submenu of the NEW QUERY option on the FILE menu;
- press the CQL QUERY button on the tool bar.

Either of the above causes the CQL dialogue box to be displayed. This dialogue box contains a window into which you can type a CQL Query. The query is then validated, and a search is carried out (see further 1.3.9 on page 212).

The syntax of CQL is defined informally here. More detailed information about the language is provided with the SARA server documentation. The CQL form of any query can always be viewed by switching on the QUERY TEXT option on the QUERY menu (see 1.6.4 on page 218).

Atomic queries A CQL Query is made up of one or more *atomic queries*. An atomic query may be one of the following:

- a word, punctuation mark, or delimited string, e.g. jam, ?, "Mrs.";
- a word-and-POS pair, e.g. "can"=NN1;
- a phrase, e.g. 'not on your life';

- a pattern, e.g. {reali?e};
- an SGML query, that is, a search for a start- or end-tag: attribute values may also be searched for, e.g. <head type="main">;
- the ANYWORD character _, which will match any single L-word.

Unary operators The following unary operators are defined in CQL:

CASE The $ operator makes the query which is its operand case-sensitive.

HEADER The @ operator makes the query which is its operand search within headers as well as in the bodies of texts.

Binary operators A CQL expression containing more than one atomic query may use the following binary operators:

SEQUENCE One or more blanks between two queries matches cases where solutions to the first immediately precede solutions to the second.

DISJUNCTION The | operator between two queries matches cases where either query is satisfied.

JOIN The * operator between two queries matches cases where both queries are satisfied in the order specified; the # operator between two queries matches cases where both queries are satisfied in either order.

Query scope When queries are joined, the scope of the expression may be defined in one of the following ways:

SGML A joined query followed by a / operator and an SGML start-tag query matches cases where the joined query is satisfied within the scope of the specified SGML element.

NUMBER A joined query followed by a / operator and a number matches cases where the joined query is satisfied within the number of L-words specified.

Some simple examples follow:

cat _ dog finds three-word phrases of which the first word is 'cat' and the last is 'dog'

cat*dog finds occurrences of 'dog' preceded anywhere within the same document by 'cat'

cat#dog finds occurrences of 'dog' preceded or followed by 'cat' anywhere within the same document

cat*dog/10 finds occurrences of 'dog' preceded by 'cat' within a span of 10, i.e. with fewer than eight L-words intervening

cat*dog/<head> finds occurrences of 'dog' preceded by 'cat' within a single <HEAD> element

1.3.9   Execution of SARA queries

Whichever type of SARA query you define, the process of executing it is the same, and proceeds as follows:

- press the OK button to send the query to the server;
- the red BUSY light on the status bar at the bottom of the main window will be lit, indicating that the server is processing your query;
- the server returns a count of the number of hits found to the client;
- if this number is less than the Max Downloads figure set in the User Preferences dialogue box (see 1.7.5 on page 227), solutions will start to appear in a new window, named *Query* N (where N is the number of this query in the session);
- if the number of hits is greater than the Max Downloads figure, the TOO MANY SOLUTIONS dialogue box will appear.

The Too many solutions dialogue box allows you to reset the download limit temporarily, and also to specify which of the available solutions should be displayed. For an example of its use, see 2.2.3 on page 66. The number of solutions to be downloaded can be re-set manually, by typing a new number into the box at the bottom, or automatically, by clicking on either or both of the DOWNLOAD ALL and ONE PER TEXT buttons.

In either case, when solutions are downloaded, they appear in order, starting from the beginning of the corpus. If the RANDOM checkbox is selected, solutions are chosen at random until the specified number has been reached; if it is not, then either all solutions are chosen, or (if ONE PER TEXT is chosen) the first in each text, until the limit has been reached.

When downloading is complete, the red BUSY light will go out.

You can scroll, sort, thin, save, see the sources of, or otherwise manipulate the solutions using options from the Query menu, as described in section 1.6 on page 216.

You can interrupt execution of a query at any time before downloading of solutions begins by pressing the ESC key. This will abort processing of the query as soon as possible.

1.3.10 Printing solutions to a query

You can print the solutions to a query in three different ways:

- using the PRINT command on the FILE menu (or the PRINT button on the toolbar), you can print the currently displayed set of solutions one-per-line;

- using the COPY command on the EDIT menu (or the COPY button on the toolbar), you can save a single solution on the Windows clipboard, and then import it to a word processor for later printing;

- using the LISTING command on the QUERY menu, you can save the whole of a set of solutions to a file in SGML format, and then import it to a word processor for later printing.

Only the first of these is discussed in this section; for an example of its use, see section 3.2.3 on page 81. The other two are discussed in sections 1.4 and 1.6.6 on page 222 respectively.

Choosing the PRINT command will open a standard Windows Print dialogue box. You can select whether printing should be done in landscape or portrait mode, the printer to be used, and configure the printer in the normal Windows manner, either from the PRINT dialogue box or directly from the PRINT SETUP command on the FILE menu.

The current version of SARA does not allow you to change the page layout of the report printed: it contains a running title, derived from the query, and page numbering. References for each solution are printed down the left margin, indicating the text and the sentence number from which it comes. As much of each solution as will fit on a single line is included.

You can use the PRINT PREVIEW command on the FILE menu to see a rough indication on the screen of how the solutions will look when printed.

For more flexible formatting of query solutions, use the LISTING command on the QUERY menu to save the solutions in SGML format, as described in section 1.6.6 on page 222. This file can then be formatted in any way appropriate using the word processor of your choice.

1.4 The Edit menu

The Edit menu allows you to save or manipulate one of the solutions to a query, known as the *current solution*. The menu has three commands:

COPY copies the current solution to the Windows clipboard;

BOOKMARK creates a *bookmark*, that is, a named pointer to the current solution;

GOTO moves to a previously defined bookmark, and makes the solution to which it points the current solution.

At any time one of the set of solutions being displayed is known as the *current solution*: in Page display mode, this is the solution which is visible on the screen; in Line display mode, it is the solution which has a broken line above and below it (see 1.6.4 on page 218). In Line mode you make a solution current by scrolling to it, and clicking on it with the mouse. In either mode, you can move forward or backward through the solutions by using the arrow keys on the tool bar or the cursor keys on the keyboard. For examples of their use, see 1.2.6 on page 51.

Choosing the COPY command from the Edit menu copies the current solution to the Windows clipboard, in whatever format it has on the screen. For an example of its use, see 7.2.1 on page 131. If you now open a Windows application such as *Notepad* or some other word processor, and select the PASTE command from its Edit menu, the current solution will be available to that application. This is a simple way of copying information from SARA to other programs.

A *bookmark* is a name which you can attach to the current solution so that you can refer to it again, after it has ceased to be current. Bookmarks are specific to particular queries, and are saved and retrieved along with queries. For an example of their use, see 10.2.2 on page 181.

To create a bookmark for the current solution, select the BOOKMARK command from the Edit menu. The BOOKMARK NAME dialogue box will appear, into which you can type any short name for the bookmark. If the name is already in use, you will be offered the choice of overwriting the current bookmark of that name. A list of the names you are currently using appears in the lower part of the window.

To make a different solution current, you can choose one of your named bookmarks by means of the GOTO command on the Edit menu. Choosing this command opens the GOTO dialogue box.

Clicking on a bookmark in this window will make the solution to which it points the current one, assuming that the solutions concerned are still available. If you delete a solution, for example by thinning, any associated bookmark will also be deleted. Sets of solutions remain available for as long as they are either visible in an open window or present as minimized icons on the desk top. If you save a query (using the SAVE or SAVE AS command on the FILE menu), its associated bookmarks are saved along with it. If you subsequently close the query (using the CLOSE command on the FILE menu, or the window controls), its associated bookmarks disappear from the Goto dialogue box, but will re-appear if you re-open the query.

1.5   The Browser menu

The Browser menu is available only when SARA is in *browse mode*. In this mode, you are able to browse through the whole text of any part of the corpus in a special purpose window. For an example of its use, see 1.2.7 on page 52.

When SARA starts, it is initially in browse mode. As soon as you open a query, or create a new one, SARA switches out of browse mode, and the Browser menu is replaced by the Query menu, discussed in section 1.6 on the following page. To open the browse window, click on the BNC icon at the bottom left of the SARA main screen, or click on the BROWSE button which appears on the bottom right of the SOURCE window described in section 1.6.7 on page 223.

In browse mode, you can move from one text in the corpus to the next, simply by using the arrow keys on the button bar, or their equivalent keyboard shortcuts. The texts appear in alphabetical order, according to their three character identifiers.

Each text sample of the BNC has a similar structure, represented by SGML elements. Each text is represented by a <BNCDOC> element, which is composed of a <HEADER> element and either a <TEXT> or an <STEXT> element, depending on whether the text is written or spoken. These elements are all further subdivided into elements of other named kinds. <HEADER> elements have a rather complex substructure, following international standards for bibliographic description. Both <TEXT> and <STEXT> elements are composed fundamentally of <S> (sentence) elements, which contain a mixture of <W> (word) elements and <C> (punctuation) elements. In written texts, these are grouped into elements such as <P> (paragraph) or <HEAD> (heading); in spoken texts, they are grouped into <U> (utterance) elements. (For a more detailed description, see the *BNC Users' Reference Guide*.)

In browse mode, this structure is presented visually in the form of a list of container elements, each of which can be selectively expanded. When a text is first displayed, only the outermost <BNCDOC> element containing it is visible. It appears in the Browse window, with a plus sign to the left of the SGML start-tag, which indicates that this element is not yet fully expanded. Click on the plus sign to see the SGML elements of which it is composed: a <HEADER> element, and a <TEXT> or <STEXT> element. Click on the plus sign before one of these elements to expand this in its turn.

When an element is expanded, the plus sign in front of its start-tag turns into a minus sign, indicating that that element has been expanded. You can continue in this way, expanding elements down to the lowest level <w> and <c> elements for any text. If you click on a minus sign, the expansion of the element will be removed.

If you entered browse mode by clicking on the BROWSE button during display of the solutions to a SARA query, a red horizontal line will also appear in the Browse window. This line marks the place in the text where the current solution was found; you can move directly to this point by clicking on the box at the left end of the red line. Since this requires that the whole of the text must be downloaded from the server to the client, there may be some delay between your clicking on the box, and the display of the element containing the solution. Once the text is available, the display will automatically scroll to it.

You can now inspect the content of any elements before or after the hit by clicking on the plus signs, as before.

You use the TAGS command on the BROWSER menu to determine which of the SGML tags around parts of the text are to be displayed. By default, all tags are displayed in the Browse window (the TAGS command on the BROWSER menu is checked); click on this command to switch off display of the low-level tags <w>, <c> and <s>.

1.6   The Query menu

The Query menu allows you to manipulate the solutions to a query in various ways. You can edit a query using the EDIT command; sort the solutions in various ways using the SORT command; thin the solutions using the THIN command; set various options about the appearance of the solutions using the CONCORDANCE, OPTIONS, QUERY TEXT or ANNOTATION commands; save the solutions to a file in SGML format using the LISTING command; or display bibliographic information about a particular solution using the SOURCE command. You can also calculate collocational information for the solutions to a query using the COLLOCATION command.

1.6.1   Editing a query

For an example of the use of the EDIT command, see section 4.2.1 on page 88. Selecting the EDIT command from the Query menu will re-display whichever dialogue box it was that launched the query whose solutions are currently displayed. The command is grayed out and unavailable if no solutions are being displayed.

The query dialogue box will be displayed as it was when the query was sent to the server by pressing the OK button. You can change any part of the dialogue box, and resubmit it by pressing the OK button again, or press CANCEL to close the dialogue box and return to the previous display of solutions.

1.6.2 Sorting solutions

By default, the solutions to a query are displayed in their order of appearance within the corpus, alphabetically ordered by its three character filenames. This is rarely of any particular significance, except to group solutions from the same text, and so it is generally desirable to re-order a line mode (concordance) display. This is done by selecting the SORT command from the Query menu, which displays the SORT dialogue box. For an example of its use, see section 3.2.2 on page 78.

You can use the radio buttons in this dialogue box to specify either one or two *keys* for the sort, and a single *collating* sequence, applicable to both keys. The keys determine which part of each hit is to be used to sort the solutions; the collating sequence determines how these keys are to be compared when deciding on their relative order.

The PRIMARY keys for all the context lines are compared first, according to the collating sequence indicated. If any duplicates are found, the SECONDARY keys are used to order them. Note that the same collating method must be used for both keys.

The SPAN box indicates how many words make up the key in each case. The LEFT, CENTRE or RIGHT radio buttons indicate the position of the key relative to the *query focus* (i.e. the hit word, phrase, or SGML element in the context). If the LEFT radio button is selected, and the SPAN is 1, the key will be the word to the left of each query focus. If the CENTRE radio button is selected, and the SPAN is 1, the key will be the first word of the query focus itself. If the RIGHT radio button is selected and the SPAN is 1, the key will be the first word following the query focus.

The ASCENDING and DESCENDING radio buttons indicate whether the keys are to be sorted into ascending or descending alphabetical order.

The collating method used for both keys is indicated by the radio buttons to the right of the dialogue box. With the ASCII radio button selected, keys are compared according to the ASCII character sequence, in which all uppercase letters precede all lower case ones: 'Zebra' precedes 'antelope'. With the IGNORE CASE button selected, case distinctions are ignored, so that 'Zebra' and 'zebra' are regarded as the same key. With the IGNORE ACCENTS button selected, accented letters are treated as if they were unaccented, so that 'élève' and 'élevé' are regarded as the same key.

In Plain and Custom format displays, span is calculated and sorting carried out by orthographic (i.e. blank-delimited) words, as displayed on the screen. If the solutions being sorted are being displayed in either POS or SGML format (see further section 1.6.4 on the following page), then span is calculated and sorting carried out by L-words; additionally, the POS CODE button is available for selection. Selecting it causes keys to be sorted not by their orthographic form but the alphabetical order of their part of speech code. This has the effect of grouping together keys with the same POS code. You can use it, for example, to sort a set of solutions by the POS code of the word following the query focus.

1.6.3   Thinning solutions

Selecting the THIN command from the QUERY menu opens up a sub-menu from which four selections are available, each of which allows you to reduce the number of solutions for the current query. For an example of its use, see section 2.2.4 on page 68. The commands available are:

SELECTION   discards from the solutions all those which have *not* previously been selected (i.e. all those solutions which do not appear on the screen in reverse video are discarded);

REVERSE SELECTION   discards from the solutions all those which have previously been selected (i.e. all those solutions which appear on the screen in reverse video are discarded);

RANDOM   solutions are discarded at random until the number of solutions matches the number you specify in a sub-window;

ONE PER TEXT   discards all but the first solution from any one text.

The current item in a displayed list can be selected either by double-clicking on it, or by pressing the space bar.

Each time you request a random selection from a given set of solutions, you will get a different random sequence. The only way to get the same random selection more than once is to save the query after thinning it. When a thinned query is saved, any thinning is saved at the same time.

1.6.4   Options for displaying solutions

The solutions to a query can be displayed in one of two modes and in one of four different formats. You can also vary the amount of context or scope displayed for each solution. Which options are in effect for a particular query will depend on the initial settings specified by the USER PREFERENCES dialogue box (see 1.7.5 on page 227).

Display mode   In *Line* mode, each occurrence of the item searched for is displayed as a single line on the screen; in *Page* mode, each occurrence is displayed in full on the screen, taking as many lines as necessary. For a detailed discussion, see section 1.2.6 on page 51.

The CONCORDANCE button is used to switch between one mode and the other. The initial mode is set by the CONCORDANCE checkbox in the USER

PREFERENCES dialogue box (see 1.7.5 on page 227): if this is checked, Line mode
is used; otherwise Page mode is used. Clicking on the CONCORDANCE button
or selecting the CONCORDANCE command from the QUERY menu enables you
to switch modes for a particular set of solutions.

The usual Windows controls are available to enable you to display different
parts of a large set of solutions. In Line mode, you can use the vertical scroll bar
to the right of the window to scroll up and down the solutions; in either mode,
you can use the arrow buttons in the tool bar to step through the solutions one
at a time. You can also use the cursor keys, PGUP and PGDN, HOME and END,
to move through the solution set in the usual way.

Display format   For further discussion of the four display formats, see section 1.2.8 on page 55. Select the OPTIONS command from the QUERY menu
to display the QUERY OPTIONS dialogue box. The radio buttons selected here
determine the format used to display the current solutions and the amount of
context (or *scope*) visible to either side of the *query focus*, as further discussed in
section 1.6.4.

The following four display formats are available:

PLAIN only the words and punctuation of each hit are displayed, optionally
    with the query focus in a different colour or typeface (as determined by
    the fonts and colour selected: see 1.7.4 on page 227);

POS part of speech information for any word on the screen can be displayed
    by clicking on it with the right mouse button; in addition, words may
    be displayed in different colours depending on their part of speech, as
    determined by the colour scheme in use (see 1.7.4 on page 227); selecting
    this format also makes it possible to sort the solutions by their part of
    speech code (see 1.6.2 on page 217);

SGML each hit is displayed with its full SGML markup;

CUSTOM each hit is displayed according to a user-defined format, as further
    discussed in section 1.6.4 on the following page; the CONFIGURE button
    can be used to change this format if the default is inappropriate.

Changing any of these options will affect the display of the current query
only. To change the display of all subsequent queries, changes must be made
in the USER PREFERENCES dialogue box (see 1.7.5 on page 227). Note also
that changing the format of the display will usually require that the solutions be
downloaded again.

Display scope   The maximum amount of context which can be displayed
for each hit is set by the MAX DOWNLOAD LENGTH specified in the USER
PREFERENCES dialogue box (see 1.7.5 on page 227). This sets an upper limit, as

a number of characters. Setting it very high will result in long download times; setting it too low will limit the usefulness of what can be displayed on the screen.

Within this overall limit, there are four options for determining the amount of context displayed on the screen by default:

AUTOMATIC the whole of the smallest unit (larger than a <w>) within which the query focus appears;

SENTENCE the whole of the <s> element within which the query focus appears;

PARAGRAPH the whole of the <p> or <u> element within which the query focus appears;

MAXIMUM as many <s> elements as possible on either side of the query focus, up to the limit imposed by the Max download length.

If the scope setting results in less than the Max download length being displayed, you can always expand what is displayed up to that maximum by double-clicking on the display with the right mouse button. This will expand the context up to what would have been obtained if the Maximum scope setting were in force, for the current hit only.

The *query focus* is that part of a downloaded hit which is normally highlighted within the display. In a simple Word, Pattern, or Phrase Query, it is the whole of the word or phrase found which matched the query. In an SGML Query, it is the SGML start- or end-tag which matched the query. In a Query Builder query, it is either the part of the text which was matched by the last content node, i.e. that nearest the bottom of the screen, or the part matched by a group of content nodes joined by NEXT links.

Custom display format In CUSTOM format, hits are displayed according to a format which you can tailor to your own liking. You can specify whether or not particular SGML elements should be displayed starting on a new line, whether or not their associated attributes should be displayed, and also specify additional characters to be displayed in association with them.

Two such specifications can be supplied; one, held in the file `linefmt.txt` determines how hits should be displayed in Line mode displays; the other, held in a file called `pagefmt.txt`, determines how hits should be displayed in Page mode displays. These are ordinary ASCII files which can be edited and displayed by any editor (such as *Notepad*), or by pressing the CONFIGURE button in the QUERY OPTIONS dialogue box. The files must be held in the working directory used by the SARA client on your system, and must be writable. (See further section 1.10 on page 229.)

The syntax of these files is fairly self explanatory. Each line specifies how a particular element type is to be displayed: if no line is supplied for any element, no special action is taken for it. A line begins with the name of an element (optionally followed by one or more attribute names) or an entity. This is followed by a quoted string, which gives the replacement value for the named entity or for the element's start-tag. A second quoted string can also be supplied to provide a replacement for an element's end-tag. Within replacement strings, the string %s is used to represent the value of the attribute whose name was specified. Formats intended for use in Page mode displays can also use the string \n to indicate a new line and \t to indicate a tab indent.

For example, the default page format file contains the following lines:

```
div1 "\n"
pause "..."
event desc "[%s]"
u who "\n{%s}: "
```

The first line indicates that the display should start a new line at the start of each new <DIV1> element. The second line indicates that any <PAUSE> element should be displayed as three dots. The third line indicates that any <EVENT> element should be displayed as whatever value has been supplied for its DESC attribute, enclosed in square brackets. Finally, the last line indicates that the content of every <U> element should be prefixed by the start of a new line, the value of its WHO attribute within curly brackets, followed by a colon and a space.

For a more detailed example, see section 9.2.2 on page 165. Care should be taken in preparing custom format files, as no syntax checking is currently performed; if you plan to modify them extensively, you are recommended to make back-up copies of the files linefmt.txt and pagefmt.txt before you begin.

1.6.5   Additional components of the Query window

In addition to the display of solutions, the query window can contain two other components, each in a separate pane.

QUERY TEXT   The QUERY TEXT command from the QUERY menu opens or closes a pane in which the CQL text of the current query appears. This cannot be changed, but is useful for documentary purposes. For the syntax of CQL, see section 1.3.8 on page 210. Any thinning options applied to the query are also displayed.

ANNOTATION The ANNOTATION command from the QUERY menu opens
or closes a pane in which you can write any comment or annotation you
wish. Such documentation may be useful for future reference when re-
running a query.

Both query text and annotation are saved together with the query, along
with any valid bookmarks you defined for it.

1.6.6 Saving solutions to a file

Selecting the LISTING command from the QUERY menu opens a standard file
dialogue box in which you can specify a name for the file in which the current
solutions are to be saved. For an example of its use, see section 8.2.5 on page 154.
The solutions are saved in SGML format in a file with the same name as the
query itself and with the suffix .sgm.

Here is the start of a sample listing file, showing the results of a search for
the word 'corpuses'.

```
<!DOCTYPE bncXtract
    PUBLIC "-//BNC//DTD BNC extract 1.0//EN">
<bncXtract>
<hdr date='10-Nov-1996 00:03:29' user=lou
server='163.1.32.247' format=untagged>
<source>This data is extracted from the
British National Corpus. All rights in the
texts cited are reserved. This data may not
be reproduced or redistributed in any form,
other than as provided for by the Fair Use
provisions of the Copyright Act</source>
<query><![CDATA["corpuses"] ]></query>
</hdr>
<hit text=EWA n=531><left> Where an absolute norm
for English cannot be relied on, the next best
thing is to compare the corpus whose style is
under scrutiny with one or more comparable
<focus>corpuses<right>, thus establishing a
relative norm. </hit>
<hit text=FRG n=1222><left> These methodological
difficulties are associated with a more general
problem of deriving generalizations
```

```
from <focus>corpuses<right>. </hit>
</bncXtract>
```

Housekeeping information about the query itself is saved in a <HDR> element at the start of the file, giving the date the query was solved, the name of the user, and the server machine, as well as the actual text of the query. Each solution to the query is saved as a separate <HIT> element. The TEXT attribute gives the three character identifier of the text in which the hit was found; the N attribute gives its sentence number. The query focus of the hit is represented as a <FOCUS> element; its left context is represented as a <LEFT> element, and its right context as a <RIGHT> element.

Solutions are saved in a listing file in the format in which they are displayed. Thus, if the solutions include SGML tags (i.e. solutions are being displayed in POS or SGML format), these tags will also appear in the listing file, which may make it difficult to process by other SGML-aware software. To make this less problematic, any angle brackets appearing as content of a <HIT> element are converted to square brackets before the listing file is produced. For example, the second <HIT> element above would appear as follows if the same query were saved in SGML mode:

```
<hit text=FRG n=1222><left>[s n=1222] [w DT0]These
[w AJ0]methodological [w NN2]difficulties [w VBB]are
[w VVN]associated [w PRP]with [w AT0]a [w AV0]more
[w AJ0]general [w NN1]problem [w PRF]of
[w AJ0-VVG]deriving [w NN2]generalizations
[w PRP]from [w NN2]<focus>corpuses<right>[c PUN].
</hit>
```

Note that both the above examples have been reformatted to fit on the printed page: in an actual listing file, no extra line breaks are introduced within the body of a <HIT> element. A full specification of the listing file format is included in 3 on page 240.

1.6.7 *Displaying bibliographic information and browsing*

Selecting the SOURCE command from the QUERY menu or clicking on the SOURCE button on the tool bar will display a BIBLIOGRAPHIC DATA window containing information about the text in which the currently selected solution appears. It also gives an indication of the size of the text in words and s-units. The information presented is the same as that available from the reference list included in the *BNC Users' Reference Guide.* Further information about a text, for example its classification, is available only by inspecting elements in its header.

The Bibliographic data for a written text will generally specify its author, title, date, and publisher. The Bibliographic data for a spoken text will identify the situation in which it was recorded, and will also supply demographic or descriptive details for each person speaking in a lower window. This window can be scrolled left to right or up and down as needed.

Click on the OK button to close the Bibliographic data window. Click on the BROWSE button to switch to browse mode, enabling you to inspect the whole of this text, as discussed above in section 1.5 on page 215.

1.6.8   *The Collocation command*

The COLLOCATION command allows you to calculate how frequently words *collocate*, i.e. appear together within the current results. For an example of its use, see section 3.2.1 on page 76. For example, if your current query solutions show occurrences of the word 'death', you might wish to see how often the word 'die' appears within a certain number of words of the query focus.

Selecting the COLLOCATION command from the QUERY menu opens the COLLOCATION dialogue box. The name of the current query is displayed, together with the number of hits. Enter the L-word, punctuation mark, or SGML start-tag for which a collocation score is required (the *collocate*) in the box labelled COLLOCATE and press the CALCULATE button. Two counts appear in the box, indicating how often this collocate appears within a specified span, and what proportion of the hits this represents. You can repeat this process as often as you like, with each new collocate appearing in the same results box. If the collocate appears more frequently than the query focus itself, it is displayed in the highlight colour.

Collocation scores are calculated within the SPAN (i.e. number of L-words) indicated in the box at the bottom left of the dialogue box, by default one word to either side of the first word in the query focus. The span is always counted from the leftmost end of the query focus. Changing the span causes the scores for all words to be recalculated. The maximum span is 9 L-words to either side of the first word in the query focus.

You can calculate collocation scores either with respect to the number of hits actually downloaded, or with respect to the number of hits present in the corpus, depending on the setting of the USE DOWNLOADED HITS ONLY checkbox in the top left corner of the dialogue box.

Note that it is not possible to find out which words collocate strongly with a given word other than by trial and error: you must specify the words for which a collocation score is required. It is also impossible to specify a pattern or phrase as a collocate.

You can print the contents of the Collocation dialogue box at any time, by clicking on the PRINT button. This is the only way of saving the results of a Collocation analysis in the current release of the software.

1.7   The View menu

This menu contains commands which allow you to customize the appearance of the main SARA window.

1.7.1   Tool bar command

Choose this command to display or hide the tool bar at the top of the window. A check mark appears next to this menu item when the tool bar is displayed.

The tool bar contains a row of buttons, each of which provides rapid access to one of the following commonly used SARA functions. The buttons on the tool bar are reproduced inside the cover of this handbook. Here they are listed in left to right order, together with a brief description of what each one does.

OPEN Opens an existing query. Equivalent to selecting OPEN from the FILE menu (see 1.3 on page 199).

SAVE Saves the current query. Equivalent to selecting SAVE from the FILE menu (see 1.3 on page 199).

COPY Copies the current solution to the clipboard. Equivalent to selecting COPY from the EDIT menu (see 1.4 on page 213).

PRINT Prints the solutions to the current query. Equivalent to selecting PRINT from the FILE menu (see 1.3 on page 199).

WORD QUERY Opens the Word Query dialogue box (see 1.3.2 on page 200).

PHRASE QUERY Opens the Phrase Query dialogue box (see 1.3.3 on page 202).

POS QUERY Opens the POS Query dialogue box (see 1.3.4 on page 203).

PATTERN QUERY Opens the Pattern Query dialogue box (see 1.3.5 on page 204).

SGML QUERY Opens the SGML dialogue box (see 1.3.6 on page 206).

QUERY BUILDER Opens the Query Builder dialogue box (see 1.3.7 on page 207).

CQL QUERY Opens the CQL dialogue box (see 1.3.8 on page 210).

CONCORDANCE Toggles between Line and Page mode for display of solutions. Equivalent to selecting CONCORDANCE from the QUERY menu (see 1.6.4 on page 218).

ALIGN Toggles between left, centre, and right alignment of the highlighted query focus in a Line mode display (no menu equivalent).

FIRST SOLUTION Selects the first of a set of solutions (no menu equivalent).

PREVIOUS SOLUTION Selects the solution preceding the current one (no menu equivalent).

NEXT SOLUTION Selects the solution following the current one (no menu equivalent).

LAST SOLUTION Selects the last of a set of solutions (no menu equivalent).

SOURCE Opens a Bibliographic data window for the currently selected solution. Equivalent to selecting SOURCE from the QUERY menu (see 1.6.7 on page 223).

HELP Opens the on-line Windows help file. Equivalent to pressing F1 (see 1.9 on page 229).

CONTEXT HELP Switches to Context Help mode (no menu equivalent). In this mode, the cursor changes to a large question mark. Move the cursor to any button or box and click on it to display a brief explanation of its function.

1.7.2 Status bar command

Choose this command to display or hide the *status bar* at the bottom of the main SARA window. A check mark appears next to the menu item when the status bar is displayed.

The status bar has three areas: the leftmost part is used to display messages describing the action to be executed by the currently selected menu item or tool bar button; the central part provides information about the currently selected solution; the rightmost part displays information about the current state of the keyboard.

The left area of the status bar describes actions of menu items as you use the arrow keys to navigate through menus. This area similarly shows messages that describe the actions of tool bar buttons as you depress them, before releasing them. If after viewing the description of the tool bar button command you wish not to execute the command, then release the mouse button while the pointer is off the tool bar button.

The centre area of the status bar identifies the corpus (*BNC*) and then the currently selected solution. The first pane shows the number of this solution, the total number of solutions and the number of texts from which they are taken; the next shows the three letter identifier of the text in which the current solution occurs; and the last gives the number of this <s> element within this text. For example, if the currently selected solution occurs in the 145th s-unit of text ABC, and is the third of 12 solutions taken from 8 texts, the display will read 3:12(8) ABC 145.

The status bar display may not be updated until a set of solutions has been completely downloaded.

The rightmost part of the status bar indicates which if any of the three lockable keys on the keyboard (CAP, NUM, or SCRL) is currently latched down.

1.7.3   Font

Selecting FONT from the VIEW menu causes the standard Windows Font dialogue box to appear. This dialogue box lists the fonts available on your system. You can use it to set the font in which solutions are to be displayed.

1.7.4   Colours

Selecting COLOURS from the VIEW menu causes the COLOURS dialogue box to appear. This is used to specify the colours used to display parts of the solutions. Different colours may be specified for each part of speech code, for the query focus (i.e. the actual hit word) and for the default. You can also specify that any of these items is to be displayed in a bold face, in italic, or both.

To change the colour used for words of a particular type, first highlight the relevant item or items from the list at the left of the dialogue box by clicking on them with the mouse, in the same way as words are selected from the Word Query box. Next press the COLOUR button, which causes the Windows Color dialogue box to open. Click on the desired colour. The dialogue box disappears, and the SAMPLE window in the COLOURS dialogue box changes to show the effect of the choice just made. If this is unsatisfactory, click the RESET button to revert to the original colour. The BOLD and ITALIC check boxes can be selected to change the weight and slant of the selected items independently of their colour.

A set of such specifications is known as a *colour scheme*. Each colour scheme is saved in a file with extension .col. The name of the colour scheme currently in force is displayed at the top right of the Colours dialogue box: to select a new scheme, press the OPEN SCHEME button. This opens a file dialogue box, in which the scheme may be named. The SAVE SCHEME button saves the set of colours currently defined. The MERGE SCHEME button opens an existing colour scheme and allows you to modify it further.

Click the OK button to close the dialogue box and save all changes. Click the CANCEL button to leave without changing the colour scheme.

1.7.5   User preferences

Selecting PREFERENCES from the VIEW menu causes the USER PREFERENCES dialogue box to be displayed.

This dialogue box is used to set the default behaviour of the SARA client. Changes made here affect all subsequent queries in this and following sessions, but not any currently displayed solutions. In addition to changing the defaults for the way that results are displayed (as discussed above in section 1.6.4 on page 219) you can reset

- the maximum download length;
- the maximum number of hits to be downloaded;
- the address of the server to which the client will attempt to connect;
- your personal password.

Pressing the COMMS button displays the COMMUNICATIONS dialogue box. To connect to a different server, you will need to know two numbers: the host name or IP address of the computer concerned, and the *port* on which it listens for calls from a SARA client. Consult your local administrator for more information on these.

Pressing the PASSWORD button displays the PASSWORD dialogue box. To change your password, you must supply your current password, and type the new password twice. The new password will take effect from the next time you try to log in.

1.8   The Window menu

The commands on this menu allow you to move and manipulate the windows on the screen, in the same way as most other Microsoft Windows applications. The following commands are available:

NEW WINDOW Opens a new window with the same contents as the currently active window. You can open multiple query windows to display different parts or views of a query at the same time. If you edit the query or thin the set of solutions, all other windows containing the same query reflect those changes. When you open a new window, it becomes the active window and is displayed on top of all other open windows.

CASCADE This command arranges the open windows so that they overlap each other, with the title bar of each window staying visible.

TILE This command re-arranges the open windows so that none of the windows overlaps any other.

ARRANGE ICONS Choose this command to arrange the icons for minimized windows at the bottom of the main window. If there is an open query window at the bottom of the main window, then some or all of the icons may not be visible because they will be underneath this query window.

WINDOW 1, 2, ... At the bottom of the Window menu SARA displays a list of all currently open query windows, with a check mark in front of the one which is currently active. You can choose a different query name from this list to change the currently active window.

1.9 The Help menu

The commands on this menu allow you to consult SARA's built-in help system, in the same way as most other Microsoft Windows applications. The following commands are available:

INDEX Displays the opening screen of the built-in help file, which contains an index of its contents.

USING HELP Displays general instructions on using the Windows help system.

ABOUT SARA Displays the copyright notice and version number of your copy of SARA.

1.10 Installing and configuring the SARA client

Before trying to install the SARA client, you should find out the following information:

- the host name or IP address of the computer system on which the server you plan to use is running;
- the port on this computer system where the server you plan to use listens for incoming calls.

You should also check that the computer on which you plan to install the client has the following characteristics:

- direct connection to a TCP/IP network from which the server you plan to use is accessible;
- about 1 Mb free disk space;
- runs either Microsoft Windows 3.1 or above, or Windows95.

The installation process creates a SARA directory to hold client executables and a number of parameter files. If you are installing the software on a local network, you should take care that these parameter files are installed in a writable directory, though the executable itself need not be.

Please read the README file supplied with the software for details of any changes and for specific details of the installation process. Up to date information about the current state of the SARA software is also regularly announced on the *Bnc-discuss* mailing list, and on the BNC's own web site. For further details, see http://info.ox.ac.uk/bnc/sara.html

2 Code tables

2.1 POS codes in the CLAWS5 tagset

The following tables list the codes used for part of speech. These codes appear as attribute values within <w> or <c> elements as appropriate. Note that some punctuation marks (notably long dashes and ellipses) are not tagged as such in the corpus, but appear simply as entity references.

Code	Usage
AJ0	adjective (general or positive), e.g. 'good', 'old'.
AJC	comparative adjective, e.g. 'better', 'older'.
AJS	superlative adjective, e.g. 'best', 'oldest'.
AT0	article, e.g. 'the', 'a', 'an', 'no'. Note the inclusion of 'no': articles are defined as determiners which typically begin a noun phrase but cannot appear as its head.
AV0	adverb (general, not sub-classified as AVP or AVQ), e.g. 'often', 'well', 'longer', 'furthest'. Note that adverbs, unlike adjectives, are not tagged as positive, comparative, or superlative. This is because of the relative rarity of comparative or superlative forms.
AVP	adverb particle, e.g. 'up', 'off', 'out'. This tag is used for all 'prepositional adverbs', whether or not they are used idiomatically in phrasal verbs such as "Come *out* here", or "I can't hold *out* any longer".
AVQ	*wh*-adverb, e.g. 'when', 'how', 'why'. The same tag is used whether the word is used interrogatively or to introduce a relative clause.
CJC	coordinating conjunction, e.g. 'and', 'or', 'but'.
CJS	subordinating conjunction, e.g. 'although', 'when'.
CJT	the subordinating conjunction 'that', when introducing a relative clause, as in "the day *that* follows Christmas". Note that this is treated as a conjunction rather than as a relative pronoun.
CRD	cardinal numeral, e.g. 'one', '3', 'fifty-five', '6609'.
DPS	possessive determiner form, e.g. 'your', 'their', 'his'.
DT0	general determiner: a determiner which is not a DTQ, e.g. 'this' both in "This is my house" and "This house is mine". A 'determiner' is defined as a word which typically occurs either as the first word in a noun phrase, or as the head of a noun phrase.

continued on next page

Code	Usage
DTQ	*wh*-determiner, e.g. 'which', 'what', 'whose', 'which'. The same tag is used whether the word is used interrogatively or to introduce a relative clause.
EX0	existential 'there', the word 'there' appearing in the constructions "there is...", "there are ...".
ITJ	interjection or other isolate, e.g. 'oh', 'yes', 'mhm', 'wow'.
NN0	common noun, neutral for number, e.g. 'aircraft', 'data', 'committee'. Singular collective nouns such as 'committee' take this tag on the grounds that they can be followed by either a singular or a plural verb.
NN1	singular common noun, e.g. 'pencil', 'goose', 'time', 'revelation'.
NN2	plural common noun, e.g. 'pencils', 'geese', 'times', 'revelations'.
NP0	proper noun, e.g. 'London', 'Michael', 'Mars', 'IBM'. Note that no distinction is made for number in the case of proper nouns, since plural proper names are a comparative rarity.
ORD	ordinal numeral, e.g. 'first', 'sixth', '77th', 'next', 'last'. No distinction is made between ordinals used in nominal and adverbial roles. 'next' and 'last' are included in this category, as 'general ordinals'.
PNI	indefinite pronoun, e.g. 'none', 'everything', 'one' (pronoun), 'nobody'. This tag is applied to words which always function as heads of noun phrases. Words like 'some' and 'these', which can also occur before a noun head in an article-like function, are tagged as determiners, DT0 or AT0.
PNP	personal pronoun, e.g. 'I', 'you', 'them', 'ours'. Note that possessive pronouns such as 'ours' and 'theirs' are included in this category.
PNQ	*wh*-pronoun, e.g. 'who', 'whoever', 'whom'. The same tag is used whether the word is used interrogatively or to introduce a relative clause.
PNX	reflexive pronoun, e.g. 'myself', 'yourself', 'itself', 'ourselves'.

continued on next page

Code	Usage
POS	the possessive or genitive marker "'s' or ' ' '. Note that this marker is tagged as a distinct L-word. For example, "Kids' work or someone else's" is tagged <w NP0>Kids<w POS>' <w NN1>work <w CJC>or <w PNI>someone <w AV0>else<w POS>'s
PRF	the preposition 'of'. This word has a special tag of its own, because of its high frequency and its almost exclusively postnominal function.
PRP	preposition other than 'of', e.g. 'about', 'at', 'in', 'on behalf of', 'with'. Note that prepositional phrases like 'on behalf of' or 'in spite of' are treated as single words.
PUL	left bracket (i.e. (or [ )
PUN	any mark of separation (. ! , : ; - ?)
PUQ	quotation mark (' ' " ")
PUR	right bracket (i.e.) or])
TO0	the infinitive marker 'to'.
UNC	unclassified items which are not appropriately classified as items of the English lexicon. Examples include foreign (non-English) words; special typographical symbols; formulae; hesitation fillers such as 'errm' in spoken language.
VBB	the present tense forms of the verb 'be', except for 'is' or ''s', i.e. 'am', ''m', 'are', ''re', 'be' (subjuntive or imperative), 'ai' (as in 'ain't').
VBD	the past tense forms of the verb 'be', i.e. 'was', 'were'.
VBG	the -ing form of the verb 'be', i.e. 'being'.
VBI	the infinitive form of the verb 'be', i.e. 'be'.
VBN	the past participle form of the verb 'be', i.e. 'been'.
VBZ	the -s form of the verb 'be', i.e. 'is', ''s'.
VDB	the finite base form of the verb 'do', i.e. 'do'.
VDD	the past tense form of the verb 'do', i.e. 'did'.
VDG	the -ing form of the verb 'do', i.e. 'doing'.
VDI	the infinitive form of the verb 'do', i.e. 'do'.
VDN	the past participle form of the verb 'do', i.e. 'done'.
VDZ	the -s form of the verb 'do', i.e. 'does'.
VHB	the finite base form of the verb 'have', i.e. 'have', ''ve'.
VHD	the past tense form of the verb 'have', i.e. 'had', ''d'.
VHG	the -ing form of the verb 'have', i.e. 'having'.
VHI	the infinitive form of the verb 'have', i.e. 'have'.

continued on next page

Code	Usage
VHN	the past participle form of the verb 'have', i.e. 'had'.
VHZ	the -s form of the verb 'have', i.e. 'has', ''s'.
VM0	modal auxiliary verb, e.g. 'can', 'could', 'will', ''ll', 'd', 'wo' (as in 'won't').
VVB	the finite base form of lexical verbs, e.g. 'forget', 'send', 'live', 'return'. This tag is used for imperatives and the present subjunctive forms, but not for the infinitive (VVI).
VVD	the past tense form of lexical verbs, e.g. 'forgot', 'sent', 'lived', 'returned'.
VVG	the -ing form of lexical verbs, e.g. 'forgetting', 'sending', 'living', 'returning'.
VVI	the infinitive form of lexical verbs, e.g. 'forget', 'send', 'live', 'return'.
VVN	the past participle form of lexical verbs, e.g. 'forgotten', 'sent', 'lived', 'returned'.
VVZ	the -s form of lexical verbs, e.g. 'forgets', 'sends', 'lives', 'returns'.
XX0	the negative particle 'not' or 'n't'.
ZZ0	alphabetical symbols, e.g. 'A', 'a', 'B', 'b', 'c', 'd'.

The following *portmanteau codes* are used to indicate where the CLAWS system has indicated an uncertainty between two possible analyses:

Code	Usage
AJ0-AV0	adjective or adverb
AJ0-NN1	adjective or singular common noun
AJ0-VVD	adjective or past tense verb
AJ0-VVG	adjective or -ing form of verb
AJ0-VVN	adjective or past participle
AVP-PRP	adverb particle or preposition
AVQ-CJS	wh-adverb or subordinating conjunction
CJS-PRP	subordinating conjunction or preposition
CJT-DT0	'that' as conjunction or determiner
CRD-PNI	'one' as number or pronoun
NN1-NP0	singular common noun or proper noun
NN1-VVB	singular common noun or base verb form
NN1-VVG	singular common noun or -ing form of verb
NN2-VVZ	plural noun or -s form of lexical verb

continued on next page

Code	Usage
VVD–VVN	past tense verb or past participle

2.2   Text classification codes

We list here all classification codes that may appear within the <CATREF> element in the header of each text. Not all of the values defined here are actually used within the BNC. Furthermore, not all of them are searchable using SARA, although they may appear in solutions to SGML queries. A list of the searchable codes is given in section 5.2.3 on page 103.

The following table shows the codes which can be used to classify all kinds of text, according to their availability, or their type.

Code	Usage
allAva	**Text availability**
allAva1	free, world: Freely available worldwide
allAva2	restricted, world: Available worldwide
allAva3	restricted, Not-NA: Not available in North America
allAva4	restricted, Not-US: Not available in U.S.A.
allAva5	restricted, EU: Not available outside the European Union
allAva6	restricted, Not-USP: Not available in U.S.A. & Philippines
allAva7	restricted, Not-NAP: Not available in North America & Philippines
allTyp	**Text type**
allTyp1	Spoken demographic
allTyp2	Spoken context-governed
allTyp3	Written books and periodicals
allTyp4	Written-to-be-spoken
allTyp5	Written miscellaneous

The following table lists the classification codes which can be specified for spoken texts (either demographic or context-governed) only. Note that the classifications for demographically sampled texts apply to the respondent only, not necessarily to all speakers transcribed.

Code	Usage
scgDom	**Domain for context-governed material**
scgDom1	Educational
scgDom2	Business
scgDom3	Institutional

continued on next page

Code	Usage
scgDom4	Leisure
sdeAge	**Age band for demographic respondent**
sdeAge1	0-14
sdeAge2	15-24
sdeAge3	25-34
sdeAge4	35-44
sdeAge5	45-59
sdeAge6	60+
sdeCla	**Social class for demographic repondent**
sdeCla1	AB
sdeCla2	C1
sdeCla3	C2
sdeCla4	DE
sdeSex	**Sex of demographic respondent**
sdeSex1	Male
sdeSex2	Female
spoLog	**Interaction type**
spoLog1	Monologue
spoLog2	Dialogue
spoReg	**Region where text captured**
spoReg1	South
spoReg2	Midlands
spoReg3	North

The following table lists all classification codes which may be specified for any written text.

Code	Usage
wbpSel	**Books & periodicals: selection method**
wbpSel1	Selective
wbpSel2	Random
wmiPub	**Miscellaneous materials: publication status**
wmiPub1	Published
wmiPub2	Unpublished
wriAAg	**Author age band**
wriAAg1	0-14
wriAAg2	15-24
wriAAg3	25-34

continued on next page

Code	Usage
wriAAg4	35–44
wriAAg5	45–59
wriAAg6	60+
wriADo	**Author domicile**
wriAD036	Australia
wriAD124	Canada
wriAD250	France
wriAD276	Germany
wriAD372	Ireland
wriAD380	Italy
wriAD422	Lebanon
wriAD492	Monaco
wriAD554	New Zealand
wriAD620	Portugal
wriAD702	Singapore
wriAD756	Switzerland
wriAD826	United Kingdom
wriAD840	United States
wriAD920	UK North (north of Mersey-Humber line)
wriAD921	UK Midlands (north of Bristol Channel-Wash line)
wriAD922	UK South (south of Bristol Channel-Wash line)
wriASe	**Sex of author**
wriASe1	Male
wriASe2	Female
wriASe3	Mixed
wriASe4	Unknown
wriATy	**Type of author**
wriATy1	Corporate
wriATy2	Multiple
wriATy3	Sole
wriATy4	Unknown
wriAud	**Intended age of audience**
wriAud1	Child
wriAud2	Teenager
wriAud3	Adult
wriAud4	Any
wriDom	**Domain**
wriDom1	Imaginative

continued on next page

Code	Usage
wriDom2	Informative: natural & pure science
wriDom3	Informative: applied science
wriDom4	Informative: social science
wriDom5	Informative: world affairs
wriDom6	Informative: commerce & finance
wriDom7	Informative: arts
wriDom8	Informative: belief & thought
wriDom9	Informative: leisure
wriLev	**Circulation level**
wriLev1	Low
wriLev2	Medium
wriLev3	High
wriMed	**Medium**
wriMed1	Book
wriMed2	Periodical
wriMed3	Miscellaneous published
wriMed4	Miscellaneous unpublished
wriMed5	To-be-spoken
wriPP1	**Place of publication**
wriPP372	Ireland
wriPP826	United Kingdom
wriPP840	United States
wriPP920	UK North (north of Mersey-Humber line)
wriPP921	UK Midlands (north of Bristol Channel-Wash line)
wriPP922	UK South (south of Bristol Channel-Wash line)
wriSam	**Type of sample**
wriSam1	Whole text
wriSam2	Beginning sample
wriSam3	Middle sample
wriSam4	End sample
wriSam5	Composite
wriSta	**Reception status**
wriSta1	Low
wriSta2	Medium
wriSta3	High
wriTas	**Target audience sex**
wriTas1	Male
wriTas2	Female

continued on next page

Code	Usage
wriTas3	Mixed
wriTas4	Unknown
wriTim	**Time period**
wriTim1	1960-1974
wriTim2	1975-1993

For all the classifications listed above, the absence of of information may be indicated either by the absence of any code, or by the presence of a code ending with a zero instead of a number. For example, written texts for which type of author is unknown may be indicated either by the absence of any value beginning wriAty or by the presence of the specific value wriAty0.

2.3   Dialect codes

A single set of codes, derived from the International Standard for language and country identification, is used to identify regional origins, first language, and dialects spoken by participants, as specified in the <PERSON> element in the text header. Speakers for whom such information was recorded will use one or more of the following codes as values for the WHO.FLANG or WHO.DIALECT attributes.

Code	Usage
CAN	Canada
CHN	China
DEU	Germany
FRA	France
GBR	United Kingdom
IND	India
IRL	Ireland
USA	United States
XXX	Unknown
ZZG	Europe
XDE	accent: German
XEA	accent: East Anglia
XFR	accent: French
XHC	accent: Home Counties
XHM	accent: Humberside
XIR	accent: Irish
XIS	accent: Indian subcontinent
XLC	accent: Lancashire

continued on next page

Code	Usage
XLO	accent: London
XMC	accent: central Midlands
XMD	accent: Merseyside
XME	accent: north-east Midlands
XMI	accent: Midlands
XMS	accent: south Midlands
XMW	accent: north-west Midlands
XNC	accent: central northern England
XNE	accent: north-east England
XNO	accent: northern England
XOT	accent: unidentifiable
XSD	accent: Scottish
XSL	accent: lower south-west England
XSS	accent: central south-west England
XSU	accent: upper south-west England
XUR	accent: European
XUS	accent: U.S.A.
XWA	accent: Welsh
XWE	accent: West Indian

2.4 Other codes used

Chapter nine of the *BNC Users' Reference Guide* includes exhaustive tables for the following:

- all SGML elements used in the corpus, with a brief description of each;
- all SGML entity references used in the corpus, with a brief description of each;
- all values used in the corpus for the TYPE attribute on division elements (<DIV1>, <DIV2> etc.);
- all values used in the corpus for the R (rendition) attribute, chiefly on <HI> elements, to indicate typographic rendering of the source;
- all values used in the corpus for the NEW attribute on the <SHIFT> element, to indicate changes in voice quality for spoken texts;
- codes used to identify relationships documented between participants, as specified in the <RELATION> element in the text header;
- all non-orthographic words ('L-words') recognized by the CLAWS system in the current version of the corpus.

3 SGML Listing format

This section defines the format in which the LISTING command on the QUERY menu saves its results. The files produced are valid SGML documents, conforming to a simple document type description specified, and distributed with the SARA client. The purpose of this format is to preserve contextual information about the source of each solution in the Listing file, and to make possible subsequent re-processing of the results file by software which may or may not be SGML-aware.

- Each file begins with the following DOCTYPE statement:

```
<!DOCTYPE bncXtract PUBLIC
        "-//BNC//DTD BNC extract 1.0//EN">
```

- Any SGML tags present in the solutions are retained but made invisible by changing their delimiters from < and > to [and]
- Each file contains a single <BNCXTRACT> element, conforming to the following document type definition:

```
<!ELEMENT bncXtract - - (hdr,hit+)>
<!ATTLIST hdr date CDATA #required
             user CDATA #REQUIRED
             server CDATA #REQUIRED
             format (plain|tagged) plain>
<!ELEMENT hdr - - (source,query,note?)>
<!ELEMENT (source|note) - o (#PCDATA)>
<!ELEMENT query - - (CDATA)>
<!ELEMENT hit - - (left, focus, right)>
<!ATTLIST hit text CDATA #REQUIRED
             n   NUMBER #REQUIRED>
<!ELEMENT (left|focus|right) - o (#PCDATA)>
```

A more detailed description of the elements used by this DTD, specifying their possible contents and attributes follows. Elements are described in the order in which they appear within a <BNCXTRACT>.

<HDR> contains only <SOURCE>, <QUERY>, and <NOTE> elements, which must be supplied in that order. The first two are mandatory; the last can be omitted if no comment is attached to the query. The following attributes must be supplied:

DATE date the file was saved, in form DD-MMM-YYYY HH:MM:SS;

4 Bibliography

Aarts, J. 1991. 'Intuition-based and observation-based grammars' in Aijmer and Altenberg 1991. 44-62.

Aarts, J., de Haan, P. and Oostdijk, N. (eds.) 1993. *English language corpora: design, analysis and exploitation.* Amsterdam: Rodopi. 57-71.

Aijmer, K. and Altenberg, B. (eds.) 1991. *English corpus linguistics.* Harlow: Longman.

Aijmer, K., Altenberg, B. and Johansson, M. (eds.) 1996. *Languages in contrast.* Lund: Lund University Press.

Alatis, J. (ed.) 1991. *Georgetown round table on language and linguistics. Lingustics and language pedagogy: the state of the art.* Washington DC: Georgetown University Press.

Altenberg, B. 1991. 'A bibliography of publications relating to English computer corpora' in Johansson and Stenström 1991. 355-396.

Altenberg, B. 1990-1994. *ICAME Bibliography, parts 1 to 3.* Bergen: Computing Centre for the Humanities (files available from `ftp://nora.hd.uib.no/ICAME`).

Anderson, A.H., Badger, M., Bard, E.G., Boyle, E., Doherty, G., Garrod, S., Isard, S., Kowtko, J., McAllister, J., Miller, J., Sotillo, C., Thompson, H.S. and Weinert, R. 1991. 'The HCRC map task corpus' *Language and speech* 34: 351-366.

Armstrong, S. (ed.) 1994. *Using large corpora.* Cambridge MA: MIT Press.

Armstrong-Warwick, S., Thompson, S., McKelvie, D. and Petitpierre, D. 1994. 'Data in your language: the ECI multilingual corpus 1' in Matsumoto 1994.

Aston, G. 1995. 'Corpora in language pedagogy: matching theory and practice' in Cook and Seidlhofer 1995. 257-270.

Aston, G. in press. 'Enriching the learning environment: corpora as resources for ELT' in Wichmann *et al* in press.

Atkins, S., Clear, J. and Ostler, N. 1992. 'Corpus design criteria' *Literary and linguistic computing* 7: 1-16.

Atwell, E. 1996. 'Machine learning from corpus resources for speech and handwriting recognition' in Thomas and Short 1996. 151-166.

Baker, M., Francis, G. and Tognini-Bonelli, E. (eds.) 1993. *Text and technology: in honour of John Sinclair.* Amsterdam: Benjamins.

Bauer, L. 1993. 'Progress with a corpus of New Zealand English and some early results' in Souter and Atwell 1993. 1-10.

Bell, R. 1991. *The language of news media.* Oxford: Blackwell.

USER SARA user name under which the query was performed;

SERVER IP address (name or number) of the server from which the client obtained this set of solutions;

FORMAT value either `tagged` (solutions were displayed in POS, Custom, or SGML format) or `plain` (solutions were displayed in Plain format).

<SOURCE> contains the following (fixed) text:
```
This data is extracted from the British National
Corpus. All rights in the texts cited are reserved.
This data may not be reproduced or redistributed
in any form, other than as provided for by the Fair
Use provisions of the Copyright Act.
```

<QUERY> text of the CQL query as displayed by SARA (including any thinning information). Enclosed within a CDATA marked section.

<NOTE> any user-supplied annotation may appear here. The element may be omitted if no annotation was supplied.

<HIT> a single solution from the solution set. It always contains three elements <LEFT>, <FOCUS> and <RIGHT>, described below, and always bears the following attributes:

TEXT three-character identifier of the text in which this solution appears;

N sequence number of the <s> element within which the query focus of this solution begins, taken from its N attribute.

<LEFT> the left context for the solution, i.e. everything preceding the query focus.

<FOCUS> the focus of the solution, i.e. the part which is highlighted in Line display mode.

<RIGHT> the right context for the solution, i.e. everything following the query focus.

For an example Listing file, see 1.6.6 on page 222.

Biber, D. 1988. *Variation across speech and writing.* Cambridge: Cambridge University Press.

Biber, D. 1993. 'Using register-diversified corpora for general language studies' in Armstrong 1994. 219-241.

Biber, D. and Finegan, E. 1989. 'Styles of stance in English: lexical and grammatical marking of evidentiality and affect' *Text* 9: 93-124.

Biber, D. and Finegan, E. 1991. 'On the exploration of computerized corpora in variation studies' in Aijmer and Altenberg 1991. 204-220.

Biber, D. and Finegan, E. 1994. 'Intratextual variation within medical research articles' in Oostdijk and De Haan 1994. 201-221.

Biber, D., Conrad, S. and Reppen, R. 1994. 'Corpus-based approaches to issues in applied linguistics' *Applied linguistics* 15: 169-189.

Biber, D., Conrad, S. and Reppen, R. 1996. 'Corpus-based investigations of language use' *Annual review of applied linguistics* 16: 115-136.

Biber, D., Finegan, E. and Atkinson, D. 1993. 'ARCHER and its challenges: compiling and exploring a representative corpus of historical English registers' in Fries *et al.* 1993. 1-13.

Blount, B. and Sanches, M. (eds.) 1975. *Sociocultural dimensions of language use.* New York: Academic Press.

Bolinger, D. 1976. 'Meaning and memory' *Forum linguisticum* 1: 1-14.

Burnard, L. (ed.) 1995. *Users' reference guide to the British National Corpus.* Oxford: Oxford University Computing Services.

Butler, C. (ed.) 1992. *Computers and written texts.* Oxford: Blackwell.

Chafe, W., Du Bois, J.W. and Thompson, S.A. 1991. 'Towards a new corpus of spoken American English' in Aijmer and Altenberg 1991. 64-82.

Chomsky, N. 1965. *Aspects of the theory of syntax.* Cambridge MA: MIT Press.

Church, K.W. and Hanks, P. 1990. 'Word collocation norms, mutual information, and lexicography' *Computational linguistics* 16: 22-29.

Church, K.W. and Mercier, R.L. 1993. 'Introduction to the special issue on computational linguistics using large corpora' in Armstrong 1994. 1-22.

Cobuild 1995. *COBUILD collocations on CD-ROM.* London: HarperCollins.

Collins, P.C. and Peters, P. 1988. 'The Australian corpus project' in Kytö *et al* 1988. 103-121.

Cook, G. 1995. 'Theoretical issues: transcribing the untranscribable' in Leech *et al.* 1995. 35-53.

Cook, G. and Seidlhofer, B. (eds.) 1995. *Principle and practice in applied linguistics.* Oxford: Oxford University Press.

Coulthard, M. 1993. 'On beginning the study of forensic texts: corpus concordance collocation' in Hoey 1993. 86-97.

Coulthard, M. (ed.) 1994. *Advances in written text analysis.* London: Routledge.

Crowdy, S. 1995. 'The BNC spoken corpus' in Leech *et al.* 1995. 224-235.

Davison, R. 1992. 'Building a million-word computer science corpus in Hong Kong' *ICAME journal* 16: 123-124.

Dunning, T. 1993. 'Accurate methods for the statistics of surprise and coincidence' in Armstrong 1994. 61-74.

Edwards, J. 1993. 'Survey of electronic corpora and related resources for language researchers' in Edwards and Lampert 1993. 263-310.

Edwards, J. 1995. 'Principles and alternative systems in the transcription, coding and mark-up of spoken discourse' in Leech *et al.* 1995. 19-34.

Edwards, J. and Lampert, M.D. (eds.) 1993. *Talking data: transcription and coding in discourse research.* Hillsdale NJ: Erlbaum.

Ellegård, A. 1978. *The syntactic structure of English texts: a computer-based study of four kinds of text in the Brown University Corpus. Gothenberg Studies in English* 43. Gothenberg: Acta Universitatis Gothoburgensis.

Fillmore, C.J. 1992. 'Corpus linguistics or computer-aided armchair linguistics' in Svartvik 1992. 35-60.

Firth, J.R. 1957. *Papers in linguistics 1934-1951.* London: Oxford University Press.

Fligelstone, S. 1993. 'Some reflections on the question of teaching, from a corpus linguistic perspective' *ICAME journal* 17: 97-109.

Fligelstone, S. 1992. 'Developing a scheme for annotating text to show anaphoric relations' in Leitner 1992. 153-170.

Francis, G. 1993. 'A corpus-driven approach to grammar. Principles, methods and examples' in Baker *et al.* 1993. 137-156.

French, J.P. 1992. 'Transcription proposals: multi-level system' NERC-WP4-50. Working paper for NERC.

Fries, U., Tottie, G. and Schneider, P. (eds.) 1993. *Creating and using English language corpora.* Amsterdam: Rodopi.

Garside, R. 1987. 'The CLAWS word-tagging system' in Garside *et al.* 1987. 30-41.

Garside, R, 1993. 'The marking of cohesive relationships: tools for the construction of a large bank of anaphoric data' *ICAME journal* 17: 5-27.

Garside, R. 1996. 'The robust tagging of unrestricted text: the BNC experience' in Thomas and Short 1996. 167-180.

Garside, R., Leech, G. and Sampson, G. (eds.) 1987. *The computational analysis of English: a corpus-based approach*. Harlow: Longman.

Goldfarb, C. 1990. *The SGML handbook*. Oxford: Clarendon Press.

Goffman, E. 1979. 'Footing' in Goffman 1981. 124-159.

Goffman, E. 1981. *Forms of talk*. Oxford: Blackwell.

Granger, S. 1993. 'International corpus of learner English' in Aarts *et al.* 1993. 57-71.

Grabowski, E. and Mindt, D. 1995. 'A corpus-based learning list of irregular verbs in English' *ICAME journal* 19: 5-22.

Greenbaum, S. 1991. 'The development of the International Corpus of English' in Aijmer and Altenberg 1991. 83-91.

Greenbaum, S. 1992. 'A new corpus of English: ICE' in Svartvik 1992. 171-179.

Guthrie, L., Guthrie, J. and Cowie, J. 1994. 'Resolving lexical ambiguity' in Oostdijk and De Haan 1994. 79-93.

Halliday, M.A.K. 1992. 'Language as system and language as instance: the corpus as a theoretical construct' in Svartvik 1992. 61-77.

Hoey, M. (ed.) 1993. *Data, description, discourse: papers on the English language in honour of John McH. Sinclair*. London: HarperCollins.

Hofland, K. and Johansson, S. 1982. *Word frequencies in British and American English*. Bergen: Norwegian Computing Centre for the Humanities/London: Longman.

Holmes, J. 1994. 'Inferring language change from computer corpora: some methodological problems' *ICAME journal* 18: 27-40.

Johansson, S. 1980. 'The LOB corpus of British English texts: presentation and comments' *ALLC journal* 1: 25-36.

Johansson, S., Atwell, E., Garside, R. and Leech, G. 1986. *The tagged LOB corpus: user's manual*. Bergen: Norwegian Computing Centre for the Humanities.

Johansson, S. and Ebeling, J. 1996. 'Exploring the English-Norwegian parallel corpus' to appear in the Proceedings of the Sixteenth ICAME Conference, Toronto, May 1995.

Johansson, S and Hofland, K. 1989. *Frequency analysis of English vocabulary and grammar based on the LOB corpus*. Oxford: Clarendon Press.

Johansson, S. and Hofland, K. 1993. 'Towards an English-Norwegian parallel corpus' in Fries *et al.* 1993. 25-37.

Johansson, S. and Stenström, A.-B. (eds.) 1991. *English computer corpora: selected papers and research guide.* Berlin: Mouton de Gruyter.

Jones, S. and Sinclair, J.McH. 1974. 'English lexical collocations' *Cahiers de lexicologie* 24: 15-61.

Karlsson, F. 1994. 'Robust parsing of unconstrained text' in Oostdijk and De Haan 1994. 122-142.

Kennedy, G. 1992. 'Preferred ways of putting things with implications for language teaching' in Svartvik 1992. 335-373.

Kjellmer, G. 1991. 'A mint of phrases' in Aijmer and Altenberg 1991. 111-127.

Knowles, G. 1996. 'Corpora, databases and the organization of linguistic data' in Thomas and Short 1996. 36-53.

Kucera, H. and Francis, W.N. 1967. *Computational analysis of present-day American English.* Providence RI: Brown University Press.

Kytö, M. 1993. *Manual to the diachronic part of the Helsinki corpus of English texts.* Helsinki: University of Helsinki, Department of English.

Kytö, M., Ihalainen, O. and Rissanen, M. (eds.) 1988. *Corpus linguistics hard and soft.* Amsterdam: Rodopi.

Kytö, M. and Rissanen, M. 1996. 'English historical corpora: report on developments in 1995' *ICAME journal* 20: 117-32.

Lakoff, R. 1975. *Language and woman's place.* New York: Harper and Row.

Leech, G. in press. 'Teaching and language corpora: a convergence' in Wichmann *et al.* in press

Leech, G. and Falton, R. 1992. 'Computer corpora — what do they tell us about culture?' *ICAME journal* 16: 29-50.

Leech, G. and Fligelstone, S. 1992.'Computers and corpus analysis' in Butler 1992. 115-41.

Leech, G. and Garside, R. 1991. 'Running a grammar factory: the production of syntactically analysed corpora or treebanks' in Johansson and Stenström 1991. 15-32.

Leech, G., Garside, R. and Bryant, M. 1994. 'The large-scale grammatical tagging of text: experience with the British National Corpus' in Oostdijk and De Haan 1994. 47-63.

Leech, G., Myers, G. and Thomas, J. (eds.) 1995. *Spoken English on computer: transcription, mark-up and application.* Harlow: Longman.

Leitner, G. (ed) 1992. *New directions in English language corpora.* Berlin: Mouton de Gruyter.

Ljung, H. 1991. 'Swedish TEFL meets reality' in Johansson and Stenström 1991. 245-256.

Louw, B. 1993. 'Irony in the text or insincerity in the writer? The diagnostic potential of semantic prosodies' in Baker *et al.* 1993. 157-176.

Mair, C. 1993. 'Is see becoming a conjunction? The study of grammaticalisation as a meeting ground for corpus linguistics and grammatical theory' in Fries *et al.* 1993. 127-137.

McEnery, A. and Wilson, A. 1996. *Corpus linguistics.* Edinburgh: Edinburgh University Press.

Matsumoto, Y. (ed). 1994. *International workshop on shareable natural language resources. (Proceedings of the 15th International Conference on Computational Linguistics.)* Nara: Institute of Science of Technology.

Miller, G. 1990. 'Wordnet: an on-line lexical database' *International journal of lexicography* 3: 235-312.

Mindt, D. 1996. 'English corpus linguistics and the foreign language teaching syllabus' in Thomas and Short 1996. 232-247.

Murison-Bowie, S. 1996. 'Linguistic corpora and language teaching' *Annual review of applied linguistics* 16: 182-199.

O'Donoghue, T. 1991. 'Taking a parsed corpus to the cleaners: the EPOW corpus' *ICAME journal* 15: 55-62.

Oostdijk, N. and De Haan, P. (eds.) 1994. *Corpus-based research into language.* Amsterdam: Rodopi.

Quirk, R. 1974. *The linguist and the English language.* London: Arnold.

Quirk, R., Greenbaum, S., Leech, G. and Svartvik, J. 1985. *A comprehensive grammar of the English language.* Harlow: Longman.

Rundell, M. 1995. 'The word on the street' *English today* 43: 29-35.

Sacks, H. 1975. 'Everyone has to lie' in Blount and Sanches 1975. 57-80.

Sacks, H. 1992. *Lectures on conversation.* Oxford: Blackwell.

Sampson, G. 1994. *English for the computer.* Oxford: Oxford University Press.

Sampson, G. 1996. 'From central embedding to corpus linguistics' in Thomas and Short 1996. 14-26.

Shastri, S.V. 1988. 'The Kolhapur corpus of Indian English and work done on its basis so far' *ICAME journal* 12: 15-26.

Sinclair, J.McH. (ed.) 1987. *Looking up.* London: Collins.

Sinclair, J.McH. 1991. *Corpus, concordance, collocation.* Oxford: Oxford University Press.

Sinclair, J.McH. 1992. 'The automatic analysis of corpora' in Svartvik 1992. 379-397.

Sinclair, J.McH. 1996. 'Preliminary recommendations on corpus typology' EAGLES Document TCWG-CTYP/P (available from http://www.ilc.pi.cnr.it/ EAGLES /corpustyp /corpustyp.html).

Souter, C. and Atwell, E. (eds.) 1993. *Corpus-based computational linguistics.* Amsterdam: Rodopi.

Sperberg-McQueen, C.M. and Burnard, L. 1994. *Guidelines for electronic text encoding and interchange (TEI P3).* Chicago and Oxford: Text Encoding Initiative.

Stenström, A.-B. 1991. 'Expletives in the London-Lund corpus' in Aijmer and Altenberg 1991. 230-253.

Stenström, A.-B. and Breivik, L.E. 1993. 'The Bergen corpus of London teenager language (COLT)' *ICAME journal* 17: 128.

Stubbs, M. 1995. 'Collocations and semantic profiles: on the cause of the trouble with quantitative studies' *Functions of language* 2: 23-55.

Stubbs, M. 1996. *Text and corpus analysis.* Oxford: Blackwell.

Svartvik, J. (ed.) 1990. *The London-Lund corpus of spoken English.* Lund: Lund University Press.

Svartvik, J. (ed.) 1992. *Directions in corpus linguistics.* Berlin: Mouton de Gruyter.

Svartvik, J. and Quirk, R. 1980. *A corpus of English conversation.* Lund: Gleerup.

Thomas, J. and Short, M. (eds.) 1996. *Using corpora for language research: studies in the honour of Geoffrey Leech.* Harlow: Longman.

van Halteren, H. and Oostdijk, N. 1993. 'Towards a syntactic database: the TOSCA analysis system' in Aarts *et al.* 1993. 145-61.

Wichmann, A., Fligelstone, S., McEnery, A. and Knowles, G. (eds.) in press. *Teaching and language corpora.* Harlow: Addison-Wesley-Longman.

Widdowson, H.G. 1991. 'The description and prescription of language' in Alatis 1991. 11-24.

Willis, D. 1990. *The lexical syllabus.* Glasgow: Collins.

Zipf, G. 1935. *The psychobiology of language.* Boston: Houghton-Mifflin.

Index